SOMALIA
A Government at War
With Its Own People

**Testimonies About the Killings and
the Conflict in the North**

AN AFRICA WATCH REPORT

January 1990

485 Fifth Avenue
New York, NY 10017
(212) 972-8400

1522 K Street, N.W.
Washington, DC 20005
(202) 371-6592

90 Borough High Street
London SE1 1LL
England
378-8008

D1248464

THE AFRICA WATCH COMMITTEE

The Africa Watch Committee was established in May 1988 to monitor and promote observance of internationally recognized human rights in Africa. The Executive Director is Rakiya Omaar, the Research Director is Richard Carver, Joyce Mends-Cole is the Washington Representative and Karen Sorensen is Research Associate.

HUMAN RIGHTS WATCH

Human Rights Watch comprises Africa Watch, Americas Watch, Asia Watch, Helsinki Watch and Middle East Watch. The Chairman is Robert L. Bernstein, the Vice Chairman is Adrian W. DeWind. The Executive Director is Aryeh Neier and Kenneth Roth is Deputy Director. For further information, including a full publications list with subscription forms or an annual report, please write to:

Human Rights Watch
485 Fifth Avenue
New York, NY 10017
FAX (212) 972-0905
Attn: Publications Coordinator

Human Rights Watch
1522 K Street, N.W.
Washington, DC 20005
FAX (202) 371-0124
Attn: Publications Coordinator

Before people talk about the future, it is necessary to under-stand what brought this situation about. It is not only a question of what the solution is, but firstly undertanding how and why all this happened. A part of the solution must lie in the answer to that question. We all have homes, cities to which we are deeply attached. Today, the lucky ones are refugees in Britain, Canada and Holland and the majority are in camps in Ethiopia, or waiting in Dire Dawa and Djibouti to get out or are trapped inside Somalia. Prosperous city-dwellers, civil servants, businessmen, the experienced, the educated and our youth, all those who should be at home building our futures are all refugees. The world must understand that we are not here because we wanted to live elsewhere. We have been driven out.

> Khadra Muhumed Abdi,
> Interview with Africa Watch,
> London, June 2, 1989

We couldn't believe that taxes paid by the Somali people, the weapons bought to defend the people and the army, created and trained to defend the nation, were now all being used against the people. Who could believe that planes belonging to the Somali army would take off from Hargeisa airport to bomb Hargeisa itself and its population? From dawn to dusk, day in and day out, and intermittently during the night, there was shelling, bombing, people being slaughtered by soldiers on the streets, in their homes and in all the places they sought refuge. It makes you wonder if the people who did this believe in God. How can they? There is no place like home and we want to go home. But first, the system has to go and we must get new leaders.

> Hassan Ismail,
> Interview with Africa Watch,
> Cardiff, July 8, 1989

Table of Contents

GLOSSARY

DFSS — Democratic Front for the Salvation of Somalia — an armed opposition group based in Ethiopia which has been fighting the Somali government since 1978.

Gulwadayaal (Victory Pioneers) — a large paramilitary force established in 1972, operating under direct supervision of the President. Its powers of arrest are independent of the regular police.

HANGASH (*Hayada Nabadgelyada Gaashaandhiga*) — a Somali acronym for military intelligence, created in 1978.

Mobile Military Court (*Maxkamada Wareegta*), originally created as a military tribunal for the army , its jurisdiction was extended to civilians in the early eighties.

NSC — National Security Court, a special court created in 1970 to deal with all political cases, matters pertaining to public order and murder.

NSS — National Security Service, the country's principal secret service organization.

RSC — Regional Security Court, a special committee that has the power to order arrests and to draw up and implement political measures, such as the curfew system.

SNM — Somali National Movement, an opposition movement fighting the government in northern Somalia.

SPM — Somali Patriotic Movement, an opposition group fighting the government in southern Somalia.

SRSP — Somali Revolutionary Socialist Party — the ruling party in the country created in 1976.

SRC — Supreme Revolutionary Council — 25 member military council which ruled the country immediately after the coup of October 21, 1969, which brought Mohamed Siad Barre to power.

WSLF — Western Somali Liberation Front — the principal group fighting

iii

Ethiopia for the Ogaden.

USC — United Somali Congress, an opposition group fighting the government in southern Somalia.

An explanatory note about Somali names

Somalis use three names — their own name, followed by their father's first name and then their grandfather's first name. Whenever possible, we have referred to all three names. Many Somalis are known by their nicknames, both formally and informally. The use of nicknames is so common that even colleagues and neighbors may not be aware of someone's real name. In some instances, we have had to use only the nickname. Nicknames appear throughout the text in quotation marks.

An explanatory note about Somalia's clan system

While ethnically homogenous, Somalis have traditionally been divided into groups who are linked to each other by having a common ancestor, traced through the male line. These groups are known as clans. Groups of clans form a clan-family, based on having one ultimate ancestor from which the sub-groups descend.

PREFACE

This report is based on research and extensive interviews conducted by Africa Watch with newly arrived refugees in Djibouti in August 1989, and from June-October in England and Wales, where there is now a sizable refugee community, following the outbreak of war in Somalia.

This is not a comprehensive study of civil and political rights in Somalia. It is a detailed analysis of the conflict in the north, providing information and eye-witness accounts concerning the human rights abuses that preceded the outbreak of way in May 1988, and examines in depth the government's conduct of the war, relying principally on the direct testimony of eye-witnesses. Wars have broken out more recently in the central and southern regions of the country. Most of those uprooted from their homes as a result of these conflicts are displaced within Somalia, although several thousand people have crossed the border and sought refuge in Kenya and tens of thousands have joined the refugees in Ethiopia. For lack of access to those displaced and refugees, Africa Watch has not been able to gather sufficient information about the wars in the central and southern regions to include relevant material in this report. Consequently, the focus of this report is exclusively the conflict in the northern region, which is the oldest and the most bloody of the wars in Somalia.

We sought permission from the Ethiopian government to visit the refugee camps. We regret that the Ethiopian government did not comply with our request. However, given the number of refugees, all recent arrivals in Djibouti and in Europe, we believe that the information we have been able to collect and the testimonies we have gathered are sufficient to enable us to present a comprehensive report about the war in the north. We sought interviews only with civilian victims of war. None of those we interviewed was a combatant. Interviews were conducted privately, for the most part in people's homes.

To the extent possible, we have included information about abuses by the Somali National Movement (SNM), the guerrilla movement fighting the government in the north, principally against Ethiopian refugees living in northern Somalia. The Somali government's unwillingness to allow Africa Watch to visit northern Somalia — despite a promise to us by Prime Minister Ali Samatar that we would be allowed to visit — has hampered our ability to gather additional information by interviewing Ethiopian refugees and civilians.

We would like to express our appreciation to the many Somalis who have been generous with their time, and who have provided us with invaluable information and background material. We are particularly grateful to the Somali Advice and Information Office in Cardiff, Wales, which facilitated our interviews with the large Somali community in Cardiff and Newport.

Above all, we wish to thank the many refugees who shared with us their painful memories. In spite of their harrowing experiences, the loss of so many loved ones, the destruction of their homes and their towns, the economic and psychological dislocation of their lives and the constant anxiety about the future, we are impressed by the courage and humor that has helped them to survive this nightmare. We hope that our next report on Somalia will not have to focus so much on the war and related issues. Rather, we hope that it will prove possible for the refugees to return home and that we will be able to monitor their efforts to piece together the lives shattered by war.

An indication of the gravity of the current situation in Somalia is that, unlike most human rights reporting where victims and their families request strict confidentiality, with a few exceptions, every refugee we interviewed stated that we could use their name and affiliation where relevant. Brushing aside the prospect of additional government retaliation against relatives living at home, the spontaneous and unanimous response was "what more could they do to us?"

INTRODUCTION

There is a painful irony in Somalia's predicament. Internal conflict is tearing apart the one nation in Africa that is truly homogeneous — ethnically, culturally, and linguistically, a unity that has been strengthened by a common Islamic heritage. Somalia had other advantages. Independence was celebrated in 1960 amidst genuine enthusiasm at the opportunity to unite the southern and northern regions, which had been colonized by Italy and Britain respectively. History bequeathed Somalia a unique opportunity to forge a united nation. Today, after twenty years of rule by the regime of President Mohamed Siad Barre, all that seems a distant memory. Massive human rights abuses, resulting in war, disintegration and mistrust, have made it impossible to keep alive the dream of unity. The flight of hundreds of thousands of refugees to Ethiopia, Djibouti, Kenya, the United Kingdom, Holland and Canada, and the additional hundreds of thousands displaced within the country are a sad testimony to the colossal failure of the dream of unity. The loss of their homes is also a powerful indictment of the repressive policies and practices of the regime in power.

It is difficult to overstate the Somali government's brutality towards its own people, or to measure the impact of its murderous policies. Two decades of the presidency of President Siad Barre have resulted in human rights violations on an unprecedented scale which have devastated the country. Even before the current wars the human rights of Somali citizens were violated systematically, violently and with absolute impunity.

The cost is staggeringly high in any terms, with people dead, wounded, displaced and impoverished and cities demolished. The most bloody conflict, and the longest lasting, has been the war in the north against the Isaak clan, the largest in the region. The government has been actively at war with the Isaaks throughout the 1980s, and particularly since 1981, after the creation of an Isaak-based anti-government guerrilla organization, the Somali National Movement (SNM). Suspecting every Isaak of supporting the SNM, the government unleashed a reign of terror and lawlessness in northern Somalia. The authorities exploited the emergence of the SNM to justify the savagery against

1

individuals and groups that criticized government policies and leadership, or merely because of their clan affiliation.

The abuses we describe in this report are not only a concern of the past. Abuses that have become well-established in the north have become common elsewhere. Similar policies are now also being pursued in southern and central Somalia against the Ogaden and Hawiye clans in reprisal for their support of two rebel movements, respectively the Somali Patriotic Movement (SPM) and the United Somali Congress (USC).

The Somali government's campaigns against the SNM, the SPM and the USC have been waged as if such wars were subject to no rules. The Geneva Conventions, which the Somali government has ratified, and other rules of war, have been disregarded. It is enough that someone belongs to the clan behind the insurgency group to be regarded as "anti-government," a label that justifies any abuse, including murder. Increasingly harsh counter-insurgency measures have resulted in wholesale slaughter of non-combatants, aerial bombardment of civilian targets, secret detentions in squalid conditions, the burning of villages, the indiscriminate use of landmines, the deliberate destruction of reservoirs and the killing of livestock, the lifeline of the rural population. For many years, there has been no respite from the cruelty of the army and security agencies. Entire regions have been devastated by a military engaged in combat against its own people, resembling a foreign occupation force that recognizes no constraints on its power to kill, rape, or loot. Somalia is torn by violence and anger that express deep-seated grievances. Nothing in recent memory prepared the victims for the sheer scale of the atrocities.

The survivors have not escaped either. The violence has taken its toll in ways that reach beyond physical survival. What of the minds gone mad with grief? The minds of mothers mourning the baby boys seized from their backs and bayonetted because "the little bastard will grow up to be an SNM supporter"? The minds deranged by the death of so many loved ones? The anger that festers in so many fathers and husbands held at gunpoint outside their houses while soldiers raped their daughters, their wives and their sisters?

Among many of those interviewed by Africa Watch, the effort to find words to describe their experiences invoked a bewildering range of emotions:

2

anger, bitterness, anxiety and determination that the world should know the truth. The savagery of the government's policies far exceeds the capacity of language to capture the horrors of state-sponsored terrorism. The look of anguish, the pain and suppressed fury that crept into their voices and the intensity of the emotions that accompanied their words made it easier to imagine the unimaginable and made the unthinkable mundane. The psychological price of their trauma is suggested by the number of people who complained of depression, insomnia, nightmares, loss of appetite and fatigue. Many refugees spoke of being "psychologically overwhelmed". Coping with lives imbued with so much fear and insecurity makes the prospect of "normality" beyond the grasp of most of the survivors.

War broke out on May 27, 1988, when the SNM attacked Burao, one of the main towns in the north. On May 31, they attacked Hargeisa, the provincial capital of the region and the second city in the country. Refugees told Africa Watch repeatedly that, frustrated by their efforts to defeat in direct combat the small and poorly armed SNM guerrilla force, the army turned its firepower, including its air force and artillery, against them, the civilian population, causing predictably high casualties. Our estimate of the number killed during the past nineteen months, shot point blank range, or as a result of aerial bombardment and artillery shelling is in the vicinity of 50,000 to 60,000. In that period, nearly half a million have fled the country, the majority for the inhospitable refuge of the desert in neighboring Ethiopia. The figures are so high because the army sought both to punish civilians for their presumed support for the SNM attacks and to discourage them from further assistance to the guerrillas.

We are publishing this report at a time when the pattern of abuses that characterized northern Somalia is becoming "normal" in the central and southern regions. The indiscriminate use of deadly force, massacres, the looting of private homes and the rape of women by soldiers that accompany arrests and house-to-house searches are, once again in Hiran, Gallkayo and Kismayo the government's response to any hint of resistance.

The government has consistently denied that civilians have been killed or that civilian targets have been destroyed deliberately. It has dismissed criticism

3

of its conduct as "propaganda." Cultivating the fiction that the damage has been the work of "bandits," it has sought to legitimize its practices by describing civilian casualties as "exceptional episodes," "unfortunate" but "inevitable" consequences of counter-insurgency operations. We disagree. The military exigencies that justify the shelling of residential districts without any effort to evacuate or warn civilians, the aerial bombardment of non-combatants fleeing the war, and massacres of civilians who had set-up temporary shelters in the countryside are not apparent to us. The frequency with which such practices have been employed belie the effort to label them as "exceptional."

The first-hand testimonies Africa Watch has gathered from many witnesses make it clear that the slaughter of defenseless civilians was not an "aberration." Rather, it was the result of calculation, the outcome of a specific conception of how the war against the insurgents should be fought. This strategy has no regard for the civilians living in the zones of conflict. Such methods were first employed in central Somalia in 1978-1981 against Majerteen civilians, to deprive the Somali Democratic Salvation Front, formed by members of the Majerteen clan, of a social and political base.

The Somali government has denied journalists, representatives of human rights groups and representatives of humanitarian organizations access to the war-affected regions. Though the obvious consequence is to cast doubts on the government's denials of brutality, the exclusion of independent observers has also limited pressure against abuses. Also, the decision by an increasing number of aid agencies to withdraw because of the lack of security places civilians beyond the protective reach of international observation.

In the long-term, some of the most troubling consequences are the destruction of social values that underpinned a whole way of life. Particularly damaging is the demise of Somalia's delicate clan structure. As one refugee told Africa Watch, "one's clan used to be essentially an address. Under Siad Barre, it has become literally a matter of life and death, both for the individual and the group."* After years of manipulation, this has been turned into a

---

*   Mohamed Ali Abdillahi, interview with Africa Watch, Djibouti, August 3, 1989.

4

mechanism for political domination, a tool for the exploitation of targeted clans and a means for those in power to sustain a life of spectacular profit and plunder.

With the exception of South Africa, the world has been slow to condemn the cruelties of despotic regimes in Africa, in spite of abundant evidence that violations are widespread and serious. The reasons are varied, but underlying this neglect is the attitude that little can be done for people living under such regimes nor may anything better be expected of these governments. These are not reasons the world can be proud of. Whatever the reasons for failing to exert pressure on the responsible governments, the effect is to facilitate massive abuses. Speaking out about human rights abuses is the responsibility of all those whose circumstances give them a free voice to defend the rights of those whose rights have been denied to them.

For too long, many Africans, foreign governments and observers have welcomed the intervention of military regimes in the political affairs of African nations, as a means of providing the "stability" Africa needs, the bulwark against chaos and weak government. The regime of Mohamed Siad Barre highlights the fact that in Somalia, as elsewhere in Africa and Latin America, military control of the political process has not in fact been a guarantor of stability. On the contrary, military supremacy has emasculated political development, left a society that is deeply divided, retarded economic progress, failed to legitimize the rule of those in power, created turmoil in neighboring countries and has contributed significantly to instability in a volatile region.

Rebuilding a society that has been utterly devastated politically, economically and socially will be a daunting task. It will be even more difficult unless the international community is ready to act in a decisive manner to stem the violence and to halt the fragmentation of the country. Africa Watch calls in particular on the governments of the United States, the European Community, Saudi Arabia, Egypt and the United Arab Emirates to exert pressure on the government to end its violent policies. By recording in detail the experiences of the victims, we hope to make international opinion aware of the tragedy in Somalia and to make it impossible to ignore the anguish of its people. Above all, we hope the result will be a concerted effort to alleviate the human misery that Somalia has come to represent.

5

SUMMARY OF FINDINGS

Immediately after the government of President Mohamed Siad Barre seized power in a coup on October 21, 1969, it adopted far-reaching legislative and administrative reforms that infringe internationally protected civil and political rights. These legislative reforms were based on "national security," enforced by a broad and vaguely worded anti-subversion law that enabled the state to remove real or potential opponents. Twenty "offenses" which constitute, for the most part, internationally protected political activites are punishable by a mandatory death sentence. Lesser crimes are subject to lengthy sentences. This system remains intact.

Strict controls prohibit independent political activity and ensure that there are no legal avenues for the expression of dissent. These laws have been supplemented by a broad range of extra-legal forms of repression, implemented by such groups as the "Victory Pioneers," a uniformed para-military organization that act as the regime's watchdog at the neighborhood level and has extensive powers of arrest and detention for which there is no legal basis. A powerful secret police organization was established, the National Security Service (NSS). The NSS has a network of informers at the workplace, in mosques, in schools and in other public bodies and even encourages spying among family members. A special judicial system handles all "political" and public order cases, and has consistently subordinated justice to the government's political interest.

- For nearly a decade before there was any armed insurgency, the army and various security forces, protected by blanket immunity from prosecution, sought to stamp out dissent and to prohibit criticism of government policies and leadership by extreme and systematic repression. The pervasive and general control of political activity and freedom of expression, association and movement effectively discouraged opposition. Those who defied the system were arrested and

7

subject to indefinite detention. The government's response to any political opposition was excessively and indiscriminately violent.

- Until the war with Ethiopia over the Ogaden in 1977, there was no organized opposition. Somalia's defeat in the war in March 1978 had profound economic, political and social consequences.

- One of the most serious consequences was the influx of hundreds of thousands of Ogadeni refugees into Somalia. A substantial percentage of the refugees were settled in the north-west region, close to main towns. Their presence created severe political and social tensions, taxing further the already inadequate public facilities. The government created paramilitary groups among the refugees, as well as hiring and conscripting them into the national army, contrary to Somalia's obligations under a number of international conventions to which it is a party. In addition, the government encouraged armed militias among other civilian groups. These militias committed atrocities against the Isaak civilian population living along the Somali/Ethiopian border. Killings, rape and looting became common. The government failed to take action to halt the abuses. In addition, the perception that the refugees had access to far better facilities than the local population, bred resentment, fueled by a struggle over land and limited grazing opportunities. This, coupled with anger that the north had been left out of the benefits of independence, in terms of political power and development opportunities in the field of health, education and industry, eventually led to the creation of the Somali National Movement, an Isaak-based anti-government guerrilla organization. The Isaaks are the largest clan in northern Somalia.

- As the government became alarmed at the threat of an armed insurgency, it tightened control. From 1982, special emergency regulations were put into effect and civilians were placed under the jurisdiction of military tribunals and the military police. The extraordinary powers given to the military and security forces under the state of emergency gave them unlimited power over the lives of civilians and led to violent excesses as a matter of policy. As the abuses grew, resistance intensified and the response was increasingly violent.

- The government has been at war with the Isaaks since 1981, after the creation of the SNM. Apparently suspecting every Isaak of supporting the SNM, the government unleashed a reign of terror and lawlessness in northern Somalia. The authorities exploited the emergence of the SNM to justify indiscriminate violence against individuals and groups

8

that criticized government policies and leadership, or merely because of their clan affiliation. The targets of persecution included intermediate and secondary school students who became radically politicized. Challenging the totality of government policies, they articulated the grievances of the wider community and became their spokesmen. * Both the urban population and nomads living in the countryside have been subjected to summary killings, arbitrary arrest, detention in squalid conditions, torture, rape, crippling constraints on freedom of movement and expression and a pattern of psychological intimidation. Nomads, who the government regarded as the manpower and economic base behind the SNM, suffered the worst abuses, especially as the SNM increased its incursions into the towns from late 1984. Whenever the SNM launched an attack or the government learned of their presence in a region, the rural population in that area was subject to harsh reprisals, including summary executions, the burning of villages, the destruction of reservoirs, the indiscriminate planting of landmines and the killing and confiscation of livestock, the lifeline of nomads.

- War broke out on May 27, 1988, when the SNM attacked Burao, one of the main towns in the north. On May 31, they attacked Hargeisa, the provincial capital of the region and the second city in the country. Immediately, in every town, including Berbera, Borama, Sheikh and Erigavo which the SNM did not attack, Isaak men who the government feared would assist an SNM attack, especially members of the armed forces, businessmen, civil servants and elders, were arrested. The army engaged in looting on a massive scale; hundreds of people were shot as their homes and businesses were ransacked.

- Apparently frustrated by their efforts to defeat the SNM in direct combat, the army turned its firepower, including its air force and artillery, against the civilian population, causing predictably high casualties. On the claim of looking for SNM fighters and weapons, systematic house-to-house searches were carried out and thousands were shot in their homes. Residential areas were targets of artillery shelling; a substantial number of people died as their homes collapsed on them.

- Since the war began, the government has intensified its policy of recruiting and forcibly conscripting refugees from the Ogaden. It has financed and armed paramilitary groups among the refugees and pro-government civilians, using these as a fighting force. Refugees and

9

armed civilian groups committed, and continue to commit, gross abuses against unarmed civilians, and have contributed significantly to the casualty rate among civilians.

- As the shelling and the shooting intensified, people began to flee the towns after a few days. The fleeing population was subjected to intense aerial bombardment and strafing, which followed them even after they crossed the border into Ethiopia. Civilians were also attacked by military units patrolling the exits of the towns. A pattern of killings, rape and extortion was characteristic of the troops that intercepted the fleeing civilians.

- Africa Watch's estimate of the number of people killed by government forces, shot point blank, or killed as a result of aerial bombardment and artillery shelling and war-related wounds, is in the vicinity of 50,000-60,000. The figures are so high because the army sought both to punish Isaak civilians for welcoming the SNM attack and to discourage them from further assistance to the guerrillas.

- When it attacked Burao, the SNM shot in their homes and on the streets, a number of senior government officials who were considered particularly cruel to civilians. The SNM sought to have the Ogaden refugees return to Ethiopia, to drive them off Isaak territory. The SNM has attacked a number of refugee camps in which women and children have died, both in retaliation for refugee attacks against Isaak civilians and to force the refugees to leave the camps and return to Ethiopia. There have also been a number of incidents in which young men who joined the SNM after the war began, took matters into their own hands and executed a number of non-Isaak unarmed civilians.

- The war has caused over 400,000 refugees to flee, principally to Ethiopia, where they live in squalid conditions in overcrowded camps. Another 40,000 refugees are in Djibouti, and tens of thousands have gone to stay with relatives in Mogadishu, the capital, or escaped to the United Kingdom, Holland and Canada. In addition, close to 400,000 people, both urban dwellers and nomads, have left their homes because of the insecurity and are displaced within the Somali countryside, living without any international assistance.

- The government has consistently denied that civilians have been killed or that civilian targets have been destroyed deliberately. It has sought to legitimize its practices by describing civilian casualties as "exceptional episodes," "unfortunate" consequences of counter-insurgency operations. The frequency with which such practices have been employed belie the effort to label them as "exceptional."

- The abuses we describe in this report are not only concerned with the past. The war in the north continues. Similar policies are now being pursued in southern and central Somalia against the Ogaden and Hawiye clans in reprisal for their support of two new rebel movements, respectively the Somali Patriotic Movement (SPM) and the United Somali Congress (USC), established in 1989. Increasingly harsh counter-insurgency measures have resulted in the slaughter of non-combatants, aerial bombardment of civilian targets, the burning of villages and the killing of livestock. Given the more recent outbreak of the wars in the central and southern parts of the country, and the lack of access to places where refugees and the displaced congregate, Africa Watch has not been able to gather sufficient information based upon its own independent research to include relevant material in this report.

- The U.S. government has followed an ambiguous course in Somalia since the outbreak of the war. Although the Administration has under-taken thorough investigations of human rights violations and made its findings available to the public, it has refrained from publicly condemn-ing the Siad Barre regime for the abuses it documents. It has continued to request aid for Somalia even while admitting that the government it seeks to assist has murdered and driven out hundreds of thousands of its own citizens and destroyed their homes and cities. Instead of using its influence with the Siad Barre regime to put an end to the violence and persecution that has brought the country to ruin, the effect of this muddled policy has been to help make it possible for the government to hang onto power.

- A positive aspect of U.S. policy towards Somalia has been the high level of interest demonstrated by the U.S. Congress, and its extensive efforts to block aid and to pressure the Administration to change its policy towards the Siad Barre regime.

- In the absence of genuine efforts at reforms that are responsive to the needs of the people affected by the war, the refugees we interviewed were unanimous and adamant in their views that the conditions to enable them to go home do not exist. The government has publicized a number of initiatives that it claims are genuine efforts towards peace and reconciliation in the north. To that end, it has sought international assistance for people displaced in the region. This has been largely an

11

exercise in public relations and apparently an attempt to obtain funds with which to pursue the war. The only concrete measure has been a partial amnesty under which about 300 political prisoners have been released. However, many others have not been released and hundreds, and perhaps thousands, continue to be detained completely outside the framework of the law.

- Africa Watch calls on the international community, in particular the governments of the United States, the European Community, Saudi Arabia, Egypt and the United Arab Emirates, to exert pressure on the Somali government to end its grossly abusive policies, and to alleviate the human misery that Somalia has come to represent.

1. BACKGROUND

Somalia, a country inhabited largely by nomadic or semi-nomadic pastoralists, was proclaimed an independent republic on July 1, 1960, when the United Nations Trust Territory in the south, administered by Italy, and the British Somaliland Protectorate, in the north, merged. Despite very different colonial experiences, and no history of interaction, the two regions were ethnically, culturally and linguistically homogeneous and shared a common religion, Islam, which facilitated the decision to merge. Covering 262,000 square miles, the economy is based principally on the export of livestock, with a small agricultural base in the south.

Italy imposed jurisdiction over the southern region at the beginning of 1889; control was gradually extended and completed in 1927. In the wake of its defeat in the Second World War, Italy lost its colonies. Italian Somaliland became a United Nations Trust Territory in December 1950, which Italy was to administer for a fixed period of ten years prior to independence.

The British Somaliland Protectorate in the northern region was established in 1886. In the late 1950s, as the struggle for independence gathered momentum throughout Africa, the British colonial authorities agreed to grant the Protectorate independence. As a first step towards self-government, general elections were organized in 1959. A new round of elections took place in February 1960, to choose a Legislative Council.

In April 1960, representatives of the two regions held talks and agreed to work towards a merger. The enthusiasm for unity was such that territories with two distinct traditions of colonial administration, historical development, official languages and no commercial ties agreed to unite without any serious negotiations about important political and economic issues, beyond a division of Cabinet seats. The failure to negotiate any preconditions and to foresee potential conflict of interest would in time come to haunt the north.

13

Britain granted the Protectorate independence on June 26, 1960. The Trust Territory attained independence on July 1, 1960 and the merger of the two territories took effect on July 1. On the same day, representatives of the two territories elected Aden Abdullah Osman, hitherto president of the southern Legislative Assembly, as the new republic's first President. Dr. Abdirashid Ali Shermarke was appointed Prime Minister. The legislatures of the two regions merged to form a single National Assembly.

Between 1960-1969, when the current military regime seized power, Somalia's short-lived experience of genuine democracy was notable for its respect for human rights. Democratically elected governments succeeded each other after free elections as scheduled in 1964 and 1969. The country enjoyed a parliamentary system, opposition parties flourished, there was a lively press, no censorship, no political prisoners or exiles and an independent judiciary.

There were, however, constant and serious allegations of corruption, inefficiency and misuse of the political system by politicians for selfish economic ends. Political parties tended to be based on clan lines. A system of proportional representation gave rise to a profusion of small political parties, which by definition were weak and made the system vulnerable to manipulation by the larger parties. The result was increasing instability. There was a perception that the civilian multi-party system was inherently weak, indecisive, open to corruption and had failed to provide effective leadership.

In March 1969, general elections were organized for the second time. There was an explosion of political parties; with a population of only five million, sixty parties participated in a highly politicized and divisive election. The fragmentation facilitated an extraordinary degree of manipulation by civilian politicians. Parties accused each other of fraud and there were widespread charges of election rigging. In an emotionally charged atmosphere, the rumors that some of the parties had weapons made a volatile situation extremely dangerous.

On October 15, 1969, President Shermarke was assassinated by a policeman. Although the killing was not politically motivated, it created a political vacuum and exacerbated an already tense and unstable political atmosphere.

On October 21, there was a bloodless coup; power was assumed by the Commander-in-Chief of the armed forces, Major-General Mohamed Siad Barre, at the head of a 25-member Supreme Revolutionary Council (SRC), consisting of army and police officers. The 1960 Constitution was suspended, the National Assembly was dissolved and political parties and professional associations were abolished. The leading civilian politicians were arrested, most to remain in detention for years. Civic organizations that were not sponsored by the government were prohibited. The new administration nationalized printing presses and the media was owned and operated by the government, subject to strict and pervasive censorship.

The SRC, of which Siad Barre was the chairman, appointed a 15-man Council of Secretaries, civilian technocrats responsible for implementing policy on a day-to-day basis. The regime ruled by decrees approved by the SRC. Executive, judicial and legislative power was concentrated in the hands of the SRC.

The coup was widely welcomed in Somalia, mainly because it relieved the political and social tensions that had built up for over a year, ever since the campaign for the elections had begun. Concern that the civilian administration was unwilling to face the problems in the country, and, in any case, incapable of resolving them, influenced attitudes. There was a widespread view that the coup had saved the country from the mounting crisis, which had it persisted, would have plunged the nation into chaos and violence, releasing all the pent up anger and tensions that had built up over the bitter and divisive elections. This perception enhanced the army's prestige as a powerful political force above the fray of divisive party and clan politics.

It is difficult to exaggerate the instability generated by the 1969 elections. Lack of familiarity with the complexities and compromises inherent in a democratic system led to immediate disappointment and discredited the multiparty system. This set the context for public attitudes towards the coup. Relief that the coup had put an end to the indecisiveness of the civilian rulers, and forced a decision on the country, rather than knowledge of the personalities and program of the coup leaders, was the point of reference for future attitudes towards the army and the new regime.

15

Aware of the relief that greeted the coup, and eager to take advantage of the expectation that the army would be politically more decisive than the civilian governments that preceded it, the government immediately embarked on an ambitious program. In the first year, it adopted a series of sweeping legal reforms and implemented far-reaching political decisions and social programs, which reinforced the impression that the government had clear political objectives, had thought out its strategies and had the confidence to implement its program.

Political and Legal Changes Implemented by the Government

On the first anniversary of the coup, in October 1970, the Second Charter of the Revolution declared Somalia a socialist state; more specifically, "scientific socialism" was to be the ideology of the regime, and the basis for its economic, social and political program.

National Security Service

A top priority was the establishment of a strong intelligence gathering network. The principal secret service was the National Security Service (NSS). One of the first decrees by the Siad Barre government, Law No.1 of January 10, 1970, gave the NSS as well as Regional and District Revolutionary Councils, the right to detain, without any time constraints, anyone "whenever it is proved...to the satisfaction of such organs that such a person (a) is conducting himself so as to endanger peace, order and good government in Somalia; (b) is intriguing against the SRC and by word or by action, acts against the objectives and spirit of the revolution." There is no opportunity to challenge the NSS powers of arrest and detention. Torture and abusive methods of interrogation became the standard operating procedure of the NSS. Eager to ensure close surveillance over the lives of people, more than any other institution, the NSS came to symbolize the government's fierce determination to root out dissent and to discourage criticism of government leadership or policies. In particular, the NSS actively discouraged contact between Somalis and foreigners living in the country. Links with Americans and other Westerners was regarded with extreme sensitivity and treated as evidence of "guilt." Passports and travel abroad

16

were subject to strict controls. Throughout the 1970s, the head of the NSS was Gen. Ahmed S. Abdulle, a son-in-law of president Barre and a member of the SRC.

The Victory Pioneers

Known in Somali as *"Gulwadayaal,"* the Victory Pioneers were a uniformed para-military group, estimated at about 10,000. They report directly to President Barre. From the early seventies, the head of the agency was Abdirahman "Gulwade," another son-in-law of the president. Their task is to encourage a "revolutionary spirit" among the population, by enforcing regular attendance at "orientation" centers for political indoctrination classes, volunteering for government sponsored self-help schemes and participating in political rallies. They kept a close watch on people's activities at the neighborhood level. They had powers of arrest and detention independent of the NSS, though the legal basis for their authority is not clear. There is no legal appeal against a detention ordered by the Gulwadayaal. Their behavior is reminiscent of the Tonton Macoutes in Haiti, and they came to be associated with terror.

The National Committee for the Eradication of Corrupt Practices in the Public

This was an auditing agency to oversee government finances, chaired by the president of the National Security Court. (see below) The Committee had the responsibility to investigate misappropriation of government funds and to recommend penalties. The law provided the death penalty for this offense. (see below, Law No. 54) In practice, the Committee was used as a political tool to punish senior civil servants and businessmen in the private sector. Relatives and cronies of Siad Barre used the Committee to cripple business competitors and to unseat officials in public administration who they regarded as an obstacle to the fulfillment of their economic and political ambitions.

Immediately after the coup, the government dramatically altered the existing legal structure. Far-reaching legislative and administrative "reforms," which constituted substantial infringements of internationally protected civil and political rights, produced sweeping legal and political changes. Strict

17

controls prohibited independent political activity and ensured that there would be no legal avenues for the expression of dissent. These laws were supplemented by a broad range of extra-legal forms of repression. In time, Somali citizens would discover that any expression of independent thought and any effort at political organization provoked the most severe violations of basic civil and political rights. Laws whose apparent justification was national security were used to consolidate the power of the SRC leaders, in particular, the power of the chairman of the SRC, Mohamed Siad Barre.

These legislative reforms were based on "national security." Sweeping and vaguely worded anti-subversion legislation enabled the state to prosecute critics. National security was defined as any act "which may be considered prejudicial to the maintenance of peace, order, and good government." (Law No. 1, January, 1970)*

Power to Detain

The Power to Detain Law (Law No. 1 of January 10, 1970) facilitates long-term detention by allowing arresting agencies to detain people without charge or trial for an unlimited period. There is no possibility for detainees to question the basis of their detention, and there is no opportunity to review administrative detention. Families have no way of knowing where their relatives are held or what the charges are.

By far the most important part of the new body of legislation is Law No.54 passed on September 10, 1970. Entitled *"Law for Safeguarding National Security,"* it spells out in 26 articles a wide range of political activities that constitute "offenses" against "the freedom, unity and security" of the country. Twenty of these "crimes" carry a mandatory death sentence; the law also provides for the expropriation of the victim's wealth and property, a punitive measure against the family. Lesser crimes are punishable by lengthy sentences including life in prison, which in Somalia means imprisonment until death. No court can review the grounds of arrest or order the release of detainees. Law

---

*   See Official Bulletin Supplement No. 4 and No. 9 of September 14, 1970.

No. 54 expressly repeals any other law or provision that is inconsistent with Law No. 54.

Law No. 54 has been the main legislation used by the regime to eliminate real or potential opposition. In every major political trial, the prosecution has relied almost entirely on the provisions of this law to seek the death penalty and to impose lengthy sentences.

Some of the key provisions of the law are:

Grounds For Arrest

- "Any person who commits, takes part or assists the commitment of actions endangering the freedom, unity and security of Somalia will be punished with death and expropriation of his wealth." (Art. 1)

- "Any person who forms an organization whose intentions or activities are against the unity of the people or that is intended to cripple or to weaken the authority of the Government will be punished with death and expropriation of his wealth." (Art. 3)

- "Any person who takes part, assists the formation of the organization mentioned above will be punished with life imprisonment." (Art. 3.b)

- "Any person who causes death or injury, while intending to cause the death, of a member of the Armed Forces or any other person entrusted by the Government and sent on a task of whatever nature, with the intention of stopping that member of the Armed Forces or other person, from doing his duty will be punished with death." (Art. 5)

- "Any person who takes arms, incites or encourages the taking of arms with the intention to cripple or weaken the authority of the Government, or to start an internal war or to stop the National Security Forces designated to enforce the law will be punished with death and expropriation of his wealth." (Art. 6)

- "Any person who manufactures, owns or imports into the country of Somalia weapons, ammunition or explosive materials whose intention is to clandestinely or openly fight the Government with them will be punished with death." (Art. 7)

- "Any person who organizes or takes part in armed banditry with the intention to attack the property of the people or the Government or to cripple or weaken the authority of the Government or obstructs the Forces for the Security of the Nation entrusted to apprend the

19

criminals will be punished with death and expropriation of his wealth."
(Art. 8)

- "Any person who destroys, causes harm by exploding, or by burning or by other methods, to the factories, road, transport, telecommunications or other property owned by the public...will be punished by death." (Art. 9)

- "Occupation or attempted occupation of common public property or any part of the departments of the Government, Municipal Government or Autonomous Agencies with the intention to cripple or to weaken the authority of the Government is prohibited and illegal."

  (a) "Any person who organizes the actions stated in clause 1 above will be punished with death; (b) actively takes part in the instigation of the above-mentioned actions will be punished with life imprisonment; (c) takes part in the above-mentioned actions will be punished with a prison term of one year." (Art. 10)

- "Any person who directly or indirectly takes money from another person, party or foreign Government whose intention is to cripple or to weaken the authority of the leaders will be punished with death and expropriation of his wealth." (Art. 11)

- "Any person who uses religion to create division or to cripple or weaken the authority of the leaders will be punished with death." (Art. 12)

- "Any person who misappropriates for himself or for any other person money or property belonging to the Government will be punished with a prison term of 10 to 20 years, if the value reaches fifty thousand [Somali shillings], punishment will be life imprisonment, for a hundred thousand and above, punishment will be death." (Art. 13)

Lengthy sentences were provided for less "serious" crimes.

- The possession of "seditious" literature, which can be any material written, including fiction, which is written, typed, printed or taped is punishable by five to fifteen years imprisonment.

- Spreading rumors against "the Somali Democratic Republic, the authorities of the State or state policies" is punishable by two to five years in prison.

20

- These provisions were augmented by other decrees in 1970 which placed crippling restrictions on the exercise of internationally recognized civil and political rights.

Power To Search And Confiscate Property

There are no legal restrictions on the right of authorized officials to search homes, arrest, interrogate and detain suspects without a warrant. The Establishment of the National Security Service Law (Law No. 14 of February 15, 1970) empowers security personel to search any person, property or house and confiscate the property belonging to a person suspected of "anti-revolutionary" activities. There are no guidelines that require the arresting officers to have reasonable grounds for suspicion and no judicial review of their actions.

Opportunity To Consult A Lawyer

People arrested under national security legislation do not have a right to be informed of the charges against them. Nor do they have a right to consult a lawyer upon their arrest. Under Law No. 17 of April 7, 1970, a detainee is prohibited access to legal counsel until "all investigations have been terminated." Even when access to counsel is granted, there is no right to a private consultation. By law, the representative of the Attorney General of the National Security Court must be present.

Use of Confessions As Evidence

Decree Law No. 8 of January 26, 1970 amended the Code of Criminal Procedure to exempt, from the prohibition of using confessions as evidence, offenses related to national security. This has contributed to the pervasive use of torture as the principal method of interrogation.

Habeas Corpus

Potentially one of the most effective judicial remedies against arbitrary arrest, *habeas corpus* was abolished by Law No. 64 on October 10, 1970.

National Security Court System

National security legislation was reinforced by the establishment in 1970 of a special judicial system, the National Security Court (NSC). The judges of the NSC are appointed by President Barre. He has been closely involved in all major trials; the NSC President discusses cases with him, both before and during hearings. The NSC has jurisdiction over all security matters, which have included all political cases, as well as cases relevant to public order. The Special Prosecutor of the NSC and his deputies have always been members of the armed forces and are appointed directly by President Barre, in his capacity as Commander-in-Chief of the armed forces. Since 1971, the Special Prosecutor has been Mohamed Ghelle Yusuf, who has become renowned for his cruelty. In general, there is no opportunity for lawyers to cross-examine witnesses at length. On the rare occasions when this has happened, the witnesses were re-called and questioned by the court in the absence of the counsel for the defense. The NSC has District and Regional sections, also presided over by members of the armed forces. No apppeal may be taken against a decision of the NSC though the President has the power to exercise the prerogative of mercy and pardon those convicted.

In spite of the existence of the SRC, Siad Barre immediately emerged as the strongman of the regime. A personality cult was encouraged, and pubic adulation nurtured by constant references to the actions and words of Siad Barre. News of his inauguration of various self-help schemes, his speeches to public rallies and policy pronouncements dominate the radio and the official newspaper.

Inspired by "scientific socialism," the new regime launched radical programs to transform an underdeveloped, conservative, Islamic country, inhabited primarily by nomads and semi-pastoralist nomads overnight into a modern socialist state. To secure the public ownership of the means of production, between 1970 and 1972 the SRC nationalized banking and insurance institutions, as well as most of the country's limited industrial capacity. Wholesale trade was also restricted to the public sector. In 1974, it nationalized shipping lines. Management of the economy was entrusted for the most part to large government agencies.

Armed with this formidable array of powers, President Siad Barre was able to quash any threat to his authority, real or imaginary. Intolerant of dissent, any criticism was interpreted as "subversive." On April 20, 1970, General Jama Ali Korshel, First Vice-President of the SRC was arrested and charged with attempting to launch a coup with the assistance of a foreign power. He was subsequently released. A year later, General Mohamed Ainanshe, Vice-President of the SRC and General Salad Gavere Kedie, a senior SRC member and the Minister of Public Works, were not so lucky. Accused of similar crimes, they were executed by a firing squad on July 23, 1972, together with Major Abdul-Kadir Dhel, a former army officer.

In early January 1975, the SRC decreed an amendment to the Islamic law of inheritance by giving men and women equal rights. In an attempt to forestall public criticism, especially from religious leaders, Siad Barre claimed, in a widely publicized speech, that certain verses of the Koran were obsolete. Many religious leaders disagreed with his interpretation and during sermons at the mosque the following Friday, criticized the initiative as an attack against Islam. Within hours, they were arrested and charged under Law 54. A few days later, ten sheikhs were tried and sentenced to death by the NSC. They were secretly executed by a firing squad on January 23, 1975.

Oblivious of the fact that Somalia had no history of conflict based on class, and none of the economic or political characteristics associated with societies organized on socialist principles, the regime embarked on a drive to create a socialist society. It also implemented a series of programs to educate the people to embrace the doctrines it had enunciated.

In accordance with the SRC's conception of a "modern" country, the regime declared war on tribalism. A common theme at public rallies was the need to "eradicate the scourge of tribalism," which was blamed for the problems under the civilian regimes. To discourage clan affiliations, social gatherings such as engagement and wedding ceremonies, and burials organized privately, were banned in 1973. Such ceremonies were to be arranged at orientation centers. Elders were henceforth to be called "peacekeepers." In spite of the public attacks on tribalism, President Barre from the outset relied on members of his own clan, the Marehan. The Marehan were recruited in large numbers into the army and promoted rapidly. Members of the Marehan clan, and in particular members of Siad Barre's own family quickly rose to the top of the civil service ranks and were given special consideration when it came to government tenders and other business opportunities.

Another important feature of the government's political program were the nationally organized self-help schemes intended to develop the social and economic infrastructure. Initially, self-help activities concentrated on the construction of schools and clinics, regarded as important at the community level; but then, in line with the priorities of the regime, the emphasis shifted to orientation centers and other overtly political goals.

The SRC was disbanded on July 1, 1976. (In October, 1980 the SRC was reinstated, apparently because of the refugee and related problems created by the Ogaden war, and then dissolved again in March 1982.) In its place, the Somali Revolutionary Socialist Party (SRSP) was established as the supreme political authority in the country and the only legal political party. Modeled on the communist parties in Eastern Europe, the SRSP was intended as a mass based party that would draw the citizenry and the government together. President Barre became Secretary-General of the SRSP and head of its politbureau, which consisted of the five leading members of the SRC. All the members of the SRC became members of the party Central Committee. In spite of the appearance that power had been transferred to a civilian administration, power remained where it had always been — in the hands of Siad Barre, with the army and the security forces as his main base of support. The party's main function has always been to support government policies.

Mistrust of intellectuals animated a broad range of government actions and sets the political context for many of its initiatives. From the outset, the regime emphasized the need for the entire population to undergo political indoctrination. The rhetoric stressed the creation of an egalitarian society. Towards this goal, government employees, students, members of womens' organizations, as well as ordinary members of the public were expected to attend, on a regular basis, their local "orientation" center, propaganda centers

24

established at the neighborhood level. The sessions at the center sought to encourage a "revolutionary" and pro-government attitude. One of the principal tasks of the Victory Pioneers was to enforce regular participation at the courses and social activities held at the centers. Neighbors and even family members were encouraged to spy on each other and to report the failure to attend courses. "Orientation" classes at the work place were routine. For those in government service, professional security and mobility depended more on political considerations than upon competence. Those who were regarded as too committed to the "old order" were dismissed.

All public employees, no matter how senior their position in the civil service, except for members of the armed forces, were required to enroll for political indoctrination courses at Halane, a military camp in Mogadishu. This applied to the provinces as well. In the early 1970s, the courses lasted for six months and included three months of stiff military training. From about 1974, the courses were reduced to three months. There were follow-up courses in subsequent years. The objective was to instill "correct" political thinking and to destroy "bourgeois" habits. Soldiers, who for the most part had had no formal educational training, were required to give lessons to senior civil servants and foreign service personnel about the political theory of Marx and Lenin and the economic and social policies necessary to transform Somalia into a socialist state. In reality, the goal was to ensure that public employees understood the supremacy of the armed forces, irrespective of their own qualifications and despite the fact that the army was not qualified to advise on the issues at stake.

Another initiative that had a negative effect on morale in the civil service was that, early on, the SRC appointed military officers at senior levels in the civil service. Inevitably this led to conflict. Frustrated at having to master a task for which they were not trained, military officers frequently did not show up at work. Apart from the fact that it cowed the civil service, the system had another political advantage which many observers regard as the real motive. It provided President Siad Barre with an opportunity to weed out potential threats from the army and deny them daily contact with other soldiers. By placing them in an impossible professional position, it demoralized them, facilitating their departure from their new jobs and relegating them to obscurity.

The government's policies and rhetoric had chilled the development of independent intellecual thought or artistic talent. In an atmosphere reminiscent of the profoundly anti-intellectual era of Pol Pot's Cambodia, initiatives independent of government sponsorship were discouraged and punished. Over the years, this led to a dramatic loss of trained professionals who left the country in despair. The regime's hostility to Western-educated Somalis; shrinking economic opportunities; concern, after the introduction of the Somali script as the principal official language, about the long-term consequences of the government's educational policies;* and the availability of employment in the Middle East, particularly Saudi Arabia and the United Arab Emirates, encouraged mass emigration, particularly from the northern region which had long-standing historical ties to the Middle East, based on trade links.

Between 1971 and 1977, the political structure set up by President Barre and the economic policies he pursued produced mixed results. Many sectors of society were hostile to the rhetoric and the measures, political, economic and social, inspired by "scientific socialism," which they regarded as anathema to Islam. Many educated Somalis were particularly critical of the government's educational and economic policies. The ubiquitous security system, the clampdown on freedom of expression and the lack of any opportunities for political and civic activities were deeply unpopular. On the other hand, the emphasis on self-reliance generated a degree of genuine enthusiam, spurred by mass propaganda techniques and myriad mass civic organizations sponsored and closely controlled by the state. It is important to keep in mind that these policies, in both a positive and negative sense, directly affected, for the most part, urban dwellers. It was not until the late 1970s and particularly, the 1980s, when the government began to implement its counter-insurgency tactics, that the rural population felt the full force of government policies.

---

* For years, one of the most controversial issues had been the question of what script to use to transform Somali into a written language. The choice was between an Arabic script and a Latin script. In October 1972, the government announced the adoption of a Latin script, which became the country's official language. By 1975, Somali was the principal language used in schools and in institutions of higher education.

26

The Ogaden War With Ethiopia

If President Barre had enjoyed even a limited measure of popularity until the mid-1970s, the 1977/78 Ogaden war with Ethiopia would profoundly alter the course of political events in Somalia. The bitter aftermath of defeat led to criticism of the government's handling of the war and created new political tensions. In an effort to deflect criticism of his conduct of the war, and nervous about threats to his position, President Barre sought to reassert control by stifling political activity even further. Every challenge was to be met by fierce retaliation.

"Pan-Somalism," the desire to join under one flag the ethnic Somali populations that live in the Republic of Somalia, in Kenya, Djibouti and the Ogaden, the territory that is in Ethiopia but claimed by Somalia, was even before independence, the single most important foreign policy issue in the country. This led successive Somali governments to lend support to various movements organized by ethnic Somali groups fighting for the right to self-determination in the different disputed territories. Somalia's claims to territory in other countries inevitably brought the country into conflict with its neighbors and periodically led to military skirmishes.

The fall of Emperor Haile Selassie in 1974 and the resulting political turbulence in Ethiopia gave both the Somali government and the Western Somali Liberation Front (WSLF), the main guerrilla group fighting in the Ogaden region for the right to self-determination, an opportunity to take military advantage of the turmoil that engulfed Ethiopia. In 1975, Somalia extended formal recognition to the WSLF. The Somali army was firmly behind the policy of assisting the WSLF, and urged President Barre to strengthen the commitment to the WSLF. By 1976, the WSLF had officers and non-commissioned officers in active military service.

In July 1977, the Somali government openly committed its army to the war in the Ogaden. After it had launched major offensives, the Somali army captured main towns such as Jigjiga and Harar and seemed poised for success. Ethiopia then appealed to the Soviet Union for military assistance. The Soviets changed their allegiance and extended substantial assistance to Ethiopia, in-

27

cluding airlifts of military equipment and Soviet advisors. Cuban combat units were also sent. Stunned by Moscow's decision, on November 13, the Somali government abrogated the Treaty of Friendship and Cooperation signed in 1974, and ordered 6,000 Soviet personnel, advisors and military technicians, to leave the country within seven days. Cuts were imposed on the number of staff working at the embassy. All the facilities which had been granted to the U.S.S.R. were cancelled. Moscow's switch enabled the Ethiopian army to launch two counter-offensives which forced the Somali army to retreat in March 1978.

In addition to its psychological impact, the defeat over the Ogaden war had immediate political and economic consequences. Bitter disappointment created intense dissatisfaction within the army. About eighty officers were executed in Hargeisa for their opposition to the handling of the war. The growing discontent was reflected in a coup attempt on April 9, 1978, led largely by officers from the Majeerten clan. Troops loyal to Barre crushed the effort to seize a military communications center outside Mogadishu and killed and wounded a number of the rebels. Although it had no difficulty in putting down the rebellion, the government's confidence was shaken by so many unexpected developments.

Economically, the effect of the defeat was disastrous. The capture of main towns had created new economic opportunities. Thousands who had left to man the new businesses and government offices in Jigjiga and the other towns captured by the Somali army were now deprived of those opportunities. New government employees had been hired, and the army vastly expanded, but they were now jobless. Development projects had come to a halt as the money had been diverted for the war, and there were no other employment opportunities. Everything suddenly came to a standstill.

Politically, the end of the war created new problems. Thousands of volunteers who had thrown their energies into this new endeavor were now restless. Thousands of new army recruits were jobless and embittered after the defeat. The structure of government and the rigid controls in place until 1977 were shaken. The war was an immensely popular national issue that brought the government and the public together and gave them a common purpose. The government needed the people and people volunteered in great numbers and willingly contributed whatever they could: money, cars and skills. Feeling involved in a "national project," people felt less constrained by the limitations on freedom of expression. They visited government offices and military barracks more openly, seeing their interest in the war effort and their criticism as constructive. As long as the Somali army seemed assured of success, the intense popular involvement was an asset. However, in the aftermath of defeat, feeling both politically and economically weak, the government reacted defensively to criticism. Its response was to lash out at everyone expressing disaffection.

Reprisals against the Majerteen in the Mudug Region

The Majeerten clan, because of their close involvement with the coup attempt, became the first target of repression. In response, they founded an armed opposition movement, the Somali Salvation Democratic Front (SSDF), which later became the Democratic Front for the Salvation of Somalia, (DFSS). The atrocities in the Mudug/Hiran region in 1978-81 have not been documented, partly because international human rights groups had not begun to focus on Somalia, and partly because when the abuses were taking place, there were not as many Somalis living abroad to publicize these developments. The pattern of abuses against Majeerten civilians, concentrated mainly in northeastern and central Somalia, was a bitter foretaste of what was in store for the Isaaks, the Ogaden and the Hawiye — extra-judicial executions, rape, the killing of livestock and the destruction of reservoirs. The government's scorched-earth policy was intended to deprive the SSDF of a civilian base of social and political support.

The 1979 Constitution

In 1979, eager to obtain military and economic support from the West, particularly the United States, after losing the Ogaden war, and the rift with the USSR, President Barre promulgated a new constitution. The new Constitution was approved in a national referendum held on August 29, 1979 and came into effect in September. Elections were held on December 30 for the 171-member parliament created by the Constitution, known as the People's Assembly. The

29

electorate was presented a single list including all 74 members of the SRSP Central Committee and others nominated by the party. The SRSP candidates received 99.99% of the votes cast. At its first session, in January 1980, the new Assembly elected Mohamed Siad Barre as President of the Republic. In December 1986, the second presidential elections were held. Again, Mohamed Siad Barre was the sole candidate and he was re-elected by 99.93% of the votes, for a second seven year term.

The Constitution reconfirmed scientific socialism as the guiding ideology of the regime. It declared the SRSP as the sole legal political party; other political parties and professional associations continued to be banned. It recognized, subject to severe limitations which in effect annulled the main provisions of the Constitution, the Universal Declaration of Human Rights and international convenants on human rights. Many civil and political rights recognized in international instruments, such as freedom of movement, are either not recognized or are subject to qualifications. Most important of all, the exercise of all the rights the Constitution guarantees are subject to the existing national security legislation. In practice, therefore, the adoption of the Constitution did not improve the human rights situation in the country and has had no effect on improving the behavior of the army or the securtiy agencies.

Backgound to the Conflict in the North

Refugees from the Ogaden

One of the most serious consequences of the war was the huge influx of Ogaden refugees into northern Somalia. Hundreds of thousands of refugees arrived and had to be cared for.* Most of the refugees were ethnic Somalis, though there were also Oromos, Gari, Warwaro and other ethnic group that live only in Ethiopia.

---

*   There has been a long standing dispute about the number of Ethiopian refugees in Somalia. The Somali government argues that over 800,000 refugees arrived following the war. International organizations estimate the figure to be half that number.

Militias

Immediately after the war, the government created paramilitary groups among the refugees, as well as hiring and conscripting them into the national army. It also encouraged the creation of armed militia groups among Darood civilians.* Both groups were trained by the Somali army. The expenditure for their arms and equipment, such as radio communications and fuel, came from the army's budget. The militias consisted mainly of untrained, illiterate nomads who were given guns, which they soon learned to use with deadly force. The most significant of these militias was the WSLF. After the war, many Ogadeni refugees were recruited into the WSLF. The WSLF was ostensibly being trained to fight Ethiopia to regain the Ogaden, but, in fact, terrorized the Isaak civilian population living in the border region, which came to fear them more than the Ethiopian army. Killings, rape and looting became common.

As the abuses became widespread and the breadth and depth of the resentment felt by the Isaak civilians intensified, a delegation was sent to see President Siad Barre in September 1979 in an effort to get the government to curb these abuses and to rein in the WSLF. In spite of promises, the abuses continue.

Isaak officers began to desert the army with a view to creating a movement to fight Ethiopia, in the hope that an armed movement would intimidate the WSLF and discourage further atrocities against Isaak civilians. In 1980, a movement called *Afraad* ("fourth unit") was created, and made a sub-unit of the WSLF. The movement was strongly supported by Isaaks who financed it. The WSLF resented this initiative and conflict became inevitable. There were a number of bloody encounters as the new group attempted to push the WSLF out of their strongholds, along the border with Ethiopia. The WSLF, in turn, retaliated further against Isaak civilians living in the border region.

When Mohamed Hashi Gani, a cousin of the President, was appointed military commander of the northern region in 1980, one of his first initiatives

---

*   Darood is the name of a major clan-group that includes the Ogaden, Majerteen, Dulbahante and Marehan clans.

was to deprive *Afraad* of weapons and to transfer the unit to Adaadley, near Berbera, to distance them from the border region. As soon as it became an armed movement, one of the first SNM initiatives was to disband the armed groups which had been operating in the area.

In a memorandum to the President dated March 30, 1982, 21 Isaak elders summarized Isaak grievances, which included the general problems of the region. They made the following comments about the WSLF:

> The Front creates great problems for villagers and inhabitants of rural areas and subjects them to murder and robbery. Responsible officers of the Region turn a blind eye. This breeds in the people animosity towards the Front.

> The inhabitants of the North maintain that they are not allowed to be organized into a Front for their own protection. This is evidenced by the fact that although youth from the Northern Regions are organized (by the authorities) into groups they are not allowed to be armed.*

Political and Social Tensions

Aside from the conflict with Isaak civilians living near the Ethiopian border, government policies towards the refugees who lived in camps near main towns, such as Hargeisa and Berbera, created resentment among the local Isaak population and fed the growing animosity towards the government. The GAO team reported in 1989:

> For more than 10 years, the Issaks and Ogadeni refugees have been competing for the same scarce agricultural and grazing land. During this period, the government has not reached a durable solution to the Ogadeni refugee situation, such as repatriating the refugees to Ethiopia or settling them permanently. The presence of armed Ogadeni refugees on the Issaks' land has added to the tension in the region.**

Ahmed Mohamed Hawsi, "Kirih," a businessman from Hargeisa, told Africa Watch in an interview in London on July 9, 1989:

---

*   Memorandum from a group of 21 Isaak elders to President Barre dated March 30, 1982.

**   GAO report at p. 5.

32

The rights of the people of the region were given to the refugees, and the government was more concerned about their welfare than that of the people who had lived in the area for hundreds of years. Discrimination was obvious. Jobs were given, as a matter of priority, either to refugees or southerners. Northern businessmen were "encouraged" to pay money "to help the refugees." Otherwise, they faced the threat of arrest and having their business crippled. In the countryside, farmers were forced to hire refugees at their own expense. The aim was to drive Isaaks off the land. At Berbera, Isaak men who worked at the port were dismissed so that refugees could be hired in their place.

Safia Ali Mataan, another resident of Hargeisa, interviewed by Africa Watch in London on August 17, 1989 said:

When refugees from Ethiopia flooded the north, they expressed "surprise" to find so many Isaaks living there, as they had been led to believe that the land was more or less empty. They would remark, "But they told us that there were empty houses for us to occupy, when in fact there is nothing." On the other hand, the government would appeal to us to "help our impoverished countrymen" and we gave extravagantly. They brought from Ethiopia both refugees who were ethnic Somalis, as well as many groups who reside only in Ethiopia. They would come to rely on the refugees both as spies and soldiers — at the same time as using them to get massive aid from the world.

Everyone who had a business was ordered to hire refugees or to train them for work in the camps. After six months "training," their minimum wage was 1,300 shillings, going up to 3,000, while the average local citizen earned about 500. Every Isaak in a prominent government job was seconded by a refugee who, after a short while, would take over and be in command. Land in Hargeisa was given to some of them free and we had to buy it back from them. They were given so much land in one area that it was nicknamed "Little Jigjiga."

Siegfried Koch, a Swiss national who worked at *Dhalinta Ka'anka*, an orphange in Hargeisa from 1984-88, interviewed by Africa Watch in London on October 21, 1989, told us:

The refugees in the camps were better off than the local population, which was a great source of tension. The government made a huge profit out of the substantial food and other aid given for the benefit of the refugees. This was resold by the government openly in the markets of Hargeisa, not in the front stalls where foreigners would see too easily the "NOT TO BE SOLD" sign. But if you knew your way around the market, you could see all this for yourself. The fact that the government was using the refugees both to get aid and to weaken the Isaaks politically was a major problem.

Northerners were dismissed from and not allowed to work in government offices dealing with refugee affairs, so that they would not discover the truth about the government's policies. Instead, refugees, registered with the UNHCR were given jobs in the offices dealing with refugee matters.

In their report to the President, the Isaak elders noted:

The number of refugees now in the camps in the North are estimated at 400,000. It is true that the people of the Region received the refugees in a brotherly manner as they valued the objective of the Somali people, namely unity.

The refugees have created new problems for the Region, especially in the fields of health, environment and living conditions and have caused the permanent loss of vegetation and grazing.

It is quite obvious that great emphasis has been placed on the protection of the refugees and that the educational and health plan regarding them is more advanced than that of the entire region. *The circular (and its implementation) providing for the exclusion of the inhabitants of the Region from obtaining jobs in the refugees administration has created resentment.* (emphasis added)*

However, if the refugees were in many ways a priviliged class, they were also vulnerable to political pressures and increasingly forced to take part in a conflict many wanted no part of. As the war against the SNM intensified, Ogadeni refugees were increasingly subject to forced conscription.

---

*   Elders memorandum at pp. 7 and 8.

Economic Grievances

One of the main causes of tension was the government's economic policies. The elders' memorandum provides a full and succinct summary of the relevant concerns.

(A) Commerce

Commercial activity used to be free during the period between 26th, 1960 and 21st, October, 1969 — the date of the Revolution. The Revolution then announced that it was taking the function of importing goods. Afterwards the Government turned out unable to provide for the needs of the people and turned a blind eye to the system of financing external trade which became established in the Northern Regions.* Nevertheless, these regions were susbequently blamed for following the said system and their goods were confiscated.

The goods thus seized were valued at 300 million Somali shillings. Up to now there are no known procedures governing the confiscation. The goods were already on board ship or at sea when the confiscation was announced. What has become of those goods remains a mystery. Moreover, no one can say whether the goods were appropriated by private individuals or actually seized by the Government.

The leadership of the Revolution has recently reintroduced the old system of financing imports through the opening of letters of credit (L/C). This gave rise to the problems set out below:

---

*   From independence to the 1969 coup, commercial activity was on the basis of free enterprise. Subsequently, severe restrictions were imposed and the government took over the function of importing all goods. In practice, the policy was not successful. The restrictions were then lifted and once more, people were allowed to continue importing and exporting goods without hindrance. Then in February 1982, the government reintroduced the Letter of Credit (L/C) system, a system that had previously existed in the south but was unknown in the north. At the same time, the government announced, without any previous warning, that all goods at the port of Berbera (the only port of entry for the north) as well as goods that were due to arrive there would be confiscated. During February, large consignments of goods, including cars, cement, other building materials and tools, furniture, clothes and food, estimated at the time at 300 million Somali shillings (about 50 million U.S. dollars then) were confiscated.

35

(a) Although it was announced that L/Cs could be opened at Hargeisa and Burao, both in the Northern Regions, it turned out that the opening of L/Cs could only be done at Mogadishu and traders in the Northern Regions could obtain trade licenses only in respect of the importation of rice, and even then only 22 persons were granted licenses. Besides, the traders had obviously to wait for their licenses and for the arrival of the goods for a period not less than three months.

(b) Again, when the consignment of rice arrived at Berbera, the traders were not allowed to take it with them, the regional governor having attached it on the grounds that he himself would distribute it.

(c) In order to follow the system of trade licensing, traders in the Northern Regions need to have access to modern communications similar to those established in Mogadishu; this will also ensure equality of opportunity in commercial competition.

(C) Livestock

It is generally believed that although livestock is the backbone of the economy, no plans have been made for the provision of watering and veterinary facilities ... It must be pointed out that there are no plans for the protection of vegetation and grazing so that our country is turning into a desert.

(D) Agriculture

It is a fact that the agricultural authorities have not carried out a single project in the North in the 25 years we have been independent whereas in the South many projects have been completed, some of which are estimated to cost billions.

(E) Public Works

Productivity in the field of public works seems to the people to have been higher during the colonial era than during the period of independence. This is borne out by the following facts:

(i) No new roads have been constructed;

(ii) Government buildings are in a state of disrepair;

(iii) No job-creating projects have been instituted.

It should be pointed out that the above activities are carried out in the South all the time.

(F) The Industrialization of the North

Northerners know that the only factories established in the North are:

(i) The fish factory in Las-Qoray established by the civilian governments;

(ii) The cement factory at Berbera which is not completed yet;

(The memorandum then lists ten factories established in the South since 1969. The report also touches on external communications, health and educational facilities which it describes as wholly inadequate and discriminatory.)

Self-Help Schemes

The levy known as "self-help" is collected only in the Northern Regions. It is administered by the leaders of the Regions. The people believe that if this levy must continue to be imposed, a People's Committee should be established to ensure that the money collected is applied to the development of the Regions. It is an established fact that the central government neglects to supervise the administration of this fund by the regional authorities.*

The Arrest and Trial of the Hargeisa Group

The arrest in December 1981 and the trial in February 1982 of "The Hargeisa Group," thirty doctors, engineers, teachers, government employees and economists who had organized a self-help scheme to improve local facilities, was one of the most important events that triggered the politically explosive situation in the northern region.** The government accused them of belonging to an illegal organization called *"Ragga U Dhashay Magaaladda"* ("Men Born in the City"). The defendants denied the charge.

---

*   Ibid. at pp. 4-8.

**   For a list of the twenty-seven members of the Hargeisa Group who were tried and sentenced, see Appendix Two.

37

Their arrest was interpreted as a signal that the government was unwilling to tolerate criticism and that initiatives by citizens independent of government sponsorship would inevitably be regarded as politically suspect. The trial and the news of the sentences touched off mass protests in Hargeisa and throughout the north, particularly from students.*

A reason for the government's nervous reaction to the activities of the group is that since independence, an overwhelming majority of educated Isaaks, including businessmen and professionals, had migrated to Mogadishu in response to greater professional opportunities in the capital. Anyone who could leave left, either to remain in Mogadishu, to go to the Middle East to seek employment or to the West for advanced education. Now, for the first time, some of Hargeisa's most educated and promising residents had chosen to return, had openly challenged the government's policies with regard to the region and, in an effort to encourage the local population towards self-reliance, had launched new programs, including initiatives to repair public utilities.

In an interview with ten of the political prisoners in Djibouti on August 5, 1989, Africa Watch learned the following details which we present here as a composite testimony.

> As a group, some of us had known each other in the past and had become friends. We all came back to Hargeisa, our home town in 1981, after studying and working in Mogadishu and abroad. We were shocked at the state of Hargeisa. Everything was in such bad shape and dependent on Mogadishu, which had done nothing to maintain standards at public facilities, let alone to improve them. We decided that we had to help our community and to see if the community could become self-reliant, instead of relying on Mogadishu for everything.
>
> We began to have open discussions with government officials, including visiting delegations from Mogadishu, and also to raise money from local businessmen so as to improve local facilities — especially at the General Hospital which lacked everything. [This is the only public hospital in Hargeisa] Dr.

---

* For details about student reactions to the trial and subsequent imprisonment of the Hargeisa Group, see Chapter 8.

Osman Abdi Meygag and Dr. Aden Yusuf Aboker explained that there was no anesthetic, no bandages, and no medicine, not even an aspirin. The generator broke down in the middle of an operation and there would be no light. With the money we raised from the community, we ordered some equipment and, as a priority, decided to build a maternity clinic. We also sought the help of a foreign expatriate group of German doctors who had initially come to assist the Ethiopian refugees. They were impressed by the spirit of self-help which our activities generated in the town and they began to give us material support, as well as participating in the renovation of the hospital.

The government found all this very subversive. Officials resented our criticism of the government's policy of neglect, as well as the independence of our initiative. Everything must depend on the government and this is what we were challenging. That for them was unacceptable and dangerous.

We were arrested at different times in December 1981. We were tortured and forced to confess that we were involved in a subversive organization. [The wives of three of the detainees were arrested and interrogated for a few days.] Two days before the trial, four lawyers were flown in from Mogadishu by the government. They spoke to each of us for 5-10 minutes. They told us that they could do nothing for us. They were just going through the motions.

The trial itself created an atmosphere of intimidation. The tension that was created around the court seemed intended to serve notice on all Isaaks that neither independent initiatives nor political opposition would be tolerated. The trial was scheduled for February 20 but riots led by students broke out when rumors spread in town that three of the defendants were to be sentenced to death. The riots lasted for three days. Soldiers fired on unarmed demonstrators and five people were killed. The trial began on February 28 before the National Security Court.

The trial lasted for two days and then we waited four days for the verdict. At the trial no one asked any questions. Although they accused us of political crimes, we were not asked anything about the political activities they accused us of or about our association. The prosecutor who demanded the death sentence, just stated that we were guilty of many illegal activities. The only "evidence" cited by the prosecution was information provided by an NSS informer who had already fled the country and our "confessions" under torture. All the witnesses were our interrogators. The judge was the man before whom we were forced to sign our "confessions" — confessing, among other things, to having known each other.

Three of the defendants, Mohamed Barud Ali, Ahmed Mohamed Yusuf, "Jabane" and Mohamed Haji Mohamoud Omer Hashi, were sentenced to life imprisonment, on the grounds that they funded the illegal organization. Two were sentenced to thirty years, one to twenty-five years, nine to twenty-years, three to eight years, and three to three years. The other nine defendants were released for lack of evidence. Some were released when they completed their sentences and the remaining fourteen were released in March and April 1989, following an international campaign.

Arrest and Detention of Prominent Isaaks in Mogadishu

The most senior Isaak member of the armed forces was Brigadier General Ismail Ali Aboker, Speaker of the People's Assembly; the most senior civilian member of the government was Omer Arteh Ghaleb, Somalia's Foreign Minister from October 1969 to 1976 and later Minister of Higher Education. By mid-1982, both had become critical of the president's policies. They were arrested on June 9, 1982, together with five southern members of the People's Assembly, accused of conspiracy against the nation. The other detainees were Mohamed Aden Sheikh, former Minister of Higher Education; Mohamed ibrahim Weyrah, former Minister of Commerce and Finance; Mohamed Osman Jelle; former Minister of Animal Husbandry and Warsame Ali, "Juquf". They remained in detention without charge or trial for nearly six years. Other prominent Isaaks were arrested; they included Suleiman Nuh Ali, an architect and civil engineer and Abdi Ismail Yonis, director of Planning of the Somali National University. These arrests were interpreted as a further signal of the government's refusal preference for a policy of confrontation.

In retrospect, the warning spelled out in the report of the elders was to be prophetic. They had written:

[O]n becoming aware of the real threat to the unity of the Somali people, we have undertaken the task of inquiring into the circumstances leading to that threat. We have held regular meetings for two weeks in succession during which we have fully discussed the problems relating to the North. We have now decided to transmit to you this report on public opinion in the firm belief that it is necessary to find solutions.

As to the principles to be adopted to guide the search for solutions we have reached the conclusion:

(1) that collective and peaceful methods must be used;

We hereby transmit to you a short report on the circumstances leading to the grievances, ill-will and the threat of disintegration we want to be removed. We consider the resolution of these matters to be the very basis of the Somali unity and statehood....Today, Comrade President, you are requested to give serious consideration to these matters in order that we may save the unity of the Somali people....This counsel if heeded could contribute to the revival of Somali nationalism and could enable us to stave off the dangers facing us....*

---

*   Elders memorandum at p. 1.

2. THE APPARATUS OF CONTROL

The abuses described in the following chapters set the context in which the massive violations of the war unfolded. The government's practices consisted of a variety of brutal tactics to subdue the local population that bred outrage in those who stood by helpless. Apparently despairing of peaceful political change, an increasing number of Isaaks began to look to armed conflict as the only hope of defeating the government. Many supported the armed opposition, politically or logistically, and a growing number of Isaak men joined the ranks of the SNM as fighters. In turn, the government justified the growing terror by the emergence of the SNM, making a vicious cycle of violence inevitable.

Before the war the government had at its disposal, broad and vaguely-worded laws that enabled it to prosecute its critics. A formidable array of administrative and informal sanctions have been brought to bear against voices of dissent. When the government became alarmed by the emergence of an armed insurgency in 1981, it further tightened the control. From 1982, the Northwest territory was placed under a state of emergency. Special emergency regulations were put into effect and new institutions were created as instruments for political and social control. Civilians were brought under the jurisdiction of military tribunals and the military police. The powers given to the military and security agencies under the state of emergency gave them unlimited authority over political life and led to violent excesses as a matter of policy. Military measures whose apparent aim was to defend the country from its internal enemies made the state itself the enemy many Somalis feared the most. The repression, particularly summary killings, increased dramatically after 1981, resistance intensified and the response became even more violent.

The system of control was reinforced by the fact that all institutions of government — that is, all significant posts in the military, judiciary and security agencies and in such civilian institutions as the regional banks — were placed in

43

the hands of pro-government non-Isaaks. The refugees interviewed by Africa Watch commented that the system created a complete division of "them" and "us." The powers of the arresting officer were reinforced by the fact that the other officials conducting the investigation and the judge were "his cousins."

Throughout the period of the state of emergency, the military commanders were, in effect, also governors. They were, successively, Major General Mohamed Hashi Gani, a cousin of the president, and General Mohamed Saeed Hirsi, "Morgan", a son-in-law of the president. They were apparently following official policies determined by the government and particularly by the president himself. A confidential report from General Morgan to President Barre leaked to the international press in February 1987 detailed the policies that Morgan had been implementing to "liquidate" what he referred to as the "Isaak problem" and which he was recommending to the president. The measures spelled out in the letter included confiscating the property of Isaaks and redistributing their wealth; suspending their business licences; freezing the bank accounts of Isaak businessmen and destroying their businesses by giving opportunities to non-Isaaks; purging Isaaks from all sensitive government positions; accelerating the enrollment of the children of refugees into local schools in order to ensure a "balance"; relocating villages; destroying water reservoirs and resettling Ethiopian refugees on Isaak territory.

The departure from the army of Isaak officers which had begun in 1979 continued throughout the eighties, as they joined the SNM in increasing numbers. As the government felt increasingly vulnerable, Isaak military personnel were removed from positions of power. In 1981-82, about half the army and one third of officers in the north were northerners, which in itself provided a measure of protection against abuses directed against Isaak civilians. After 1982, the percentage of Isaak soldiers was drastically reduced, which was in itself a source of tension.

The Mobile Military Court (MMC)

The Mobile Military Court, is a special court known in Somali as *Maxkamada Wareegta*, literally the mobile court. This figured prominently in the testimonies Africa Watch received about extrajudicial executions. Those we interviewed whose relatives or friends had been killed, frequently attributed their deaths to the MMC.

Although the MMC was created in 1982 after the trial of the Hargeisa group, it established jurisdiction over civilians in 1984, after the SNM launched military attacks in the mountainous region of Sheikh and Buroa. Many victims arrested in the Gebiley region were transfered to Hargeisa and executed there. In most cases, executions takes place the day after sentencing, if not the same day. Executions took place in *Badhka*, an open ground with hills situated in southwest Hargeisa.

Hargeisa served as the headquarters of the court. It was composed only of military officers. It had offices in different sectors of the army which were under different military commands. As soon as "disturbances" were reported, the court would be dispatched to the area. The military were in charge, though they were sometimes accompanied by NSS officers whose task was to conduct investigations.

Initially, it tried businessmen and people with a certain level of education whom the government regarded as potential opponents. But within a short space of time, anyone who was politically active, such as students, or any group that the regime mistrusted and regarded as a social or economic base for the SNM, such as petty traders, nomads and farmers, was also tried.

The military court became synonymous with executions. Colloquially, its name was "Guilty or Innocent, You Will be Found Guilty" (*"Ama Qab, Ama ha Qabin, Ama wa lagu Qabadsiin"*).

The prosecutor of the court, who prepared the charges, Colonel Yusuf Muse, known as "Yusuf Dherre," became notorious for his cruelty and his insistence on the death sentence. Most mass executions took place during 1984-5, and again, from the latter part of 1987 until the outbreak of the war, periods when he was the prosecutor. He had been the prosecutor from 1982-86 during Gani's tenure as military commander. General Morgan transferred him when he took over, as his extreme unpopularity had become a political liability, though that did not signify an end to the policy of executions. He was replaced by Colonel Abdillahi Debob, who refused to carry out some unlawful executions

45

ordered by Morgan. "Yusuf Dherre" was reinstated at the end of 1987, and resumed mass executions.

The Regional Security Council (RSC)

The Regional Security Council, known in Somali as *Gudida Nabadgelyada Gobolka*, consisted of the governor, the military commander, the director of the NSS, a military officer, the police commander, the head of the Party, the commander of the Victory Pioneers and the director of the Somali Custodial Corps, who was a military officer. Theoretically, such committees could be set up in any region; in practice, such a council only was established in the north. After 1982, given the state of emergency that was in effect, the chairman was always the military commander.

The RSC normally met once a week, and more frequently during an emergency. Any quorum of the six, could impose lengthy sentences, up to life imprisonment. The RSC had power over civilians in political cases where there was an element of ambiguity. Superior to all the other branches of the security system, the RSC was, from the very beginning responsible for mass arrests. It had the power to impose a death sentence, but could not order that the execution be carried out. Death sentences passed by the district sections had to be approved at the regional level. The RSC could also confiscate the property and wealth of the victim. There is no appeal system. Only the president may "forgive" and release those sentenced by the RSC, which only happened in rare cases where influential families could intervene. The RSC also had the power to draw up and implement "legal" measures to quell unrest, such as the curfew system imposed in the north. The authority of the RSC derived directly from the president.

In cases where there was suspicion but no hard evidence, the NSS interrogated the suspect and prepared the arrest warrant. The military commander determined the sentence, or in his absence, the governor.

The Party Secretary also prepared a list of people who failed to attend orientation centers on a regular basis and submitted it to the RSC, seeking approval for their arrest and detention.

46

The HANGASH Force

In addition to the existing network of security agencies, new agencies were created. The most important was the *HANGASH*, a Somali acronym for the military police, as distinct from the regular secret service, the NSS. Established in the aftermath of an attempted coup in 1978, the *HANGASH*'s purpose was to keep an eye on the military and the NSS. But as the government's clampdown on political activity became more sweeping, the *HANGASH* acquired formidable powers over civilians and became even more feared than the NSS. There is no legal basis for its authority over civilians.

The military used these new institutions and powers to maintain surveillance over the northern urban population, as well as those living in the countryside. In the process, the military emerged increasingly as a political elite which sustained its privileges by violence.

The blanket indemnity granted to the army and security forces, the absence of human rights orgnizations to monitor and publicize abuses, the lack of an independent media and the denial of visas to foreign jouranlists, removed any constraints on the behavior of government forces.

3. ARREST AND DETENTION

Arbitrary arrests, individual and collective, the vast majority without charges, were the most common form of intimidation and punishment. Especially since 1982, Isaak men of all ages have been liable to arrest. Most arrests were for purposes other than to charge specific crimes: the motive was to threaten those arrested, to incorporate them into an intelligence network, to obtain information, and above all, to facilitate bribes from them. Even when arrests were not politically motivated, all detainees were subject to "persuasion," under abusive interrogation methods, to provide information about SNM sympathizers. The threat of violence was a weapon to ensure the victim's submission. Fear of arrest has been a significant cause of flight from Somalia.

Arrests facilitated ransoms. The armed forces and security personnel were encouraged to regard the local population as a source of plunder. After 1982, military transfers to the north were sought after, as an opportunity for making money. Connections were used to obtain assignments; Hargeisa's central police station became so notorious as a "bargaining" center that it was nicknamed "Saylada Dadka". ("Meat Market") As one refugee put it, "The first person they see will do."*

The existence of the SNM provides a convenient rationale for arrests and detentions. People have been arrested and tortured without evidence to substantiate the accusations, and detained indefinitely without legal process. Indeed, the guilt or innocence of the person has rarely been the issue. In most cases, there has been no arrest warrant, no legal charges have been brought and no judge intervened. Detention in dehumanizing conditions has been part of the process of "breaking down" detainees. Few of the former prisoners interviewed by Africa Watch had been tried; those who had been tried were denied the elements of fair process. Former prisoners' and detainees' testimonies

---

* Jama Osman Sugule, interview with Africa Watch, Djibouti, August 9, 1989.

describe a pattern of harsh conditions and torture. The apparent purpose was to make them confess to involvement with the SNM, to incriminate others as SNM supporters, and to obtain a bribe.

Since there have been no clear guidelines on the information the security and military agencies need for an arrest, and no independent judicial control, many have been arrested on unsubstantiated denunciations of "anti-government" views or activities. This has been facilitated by the Somali government's apparent perception that all Isaaks are an SNM fifth column. Inevitably, many innocent people were swept up.

Soldiers came to people's homes, stores and public tea shops to taunt them. Their response was used as a justification for arresting them. With variations in detail only, grim accounts of arrest, ill treatment and detention were recounted by every refugee interviewed by Africa Watch. If they were not the direct victims, members of their immediate family were.

Mohamed Ismail Kahin, a resident of Hargeisa, interviewed in Cardiff on July 6, 1989, recalled that:

> Mass arrests were routine every February 22, the com-memoration of the demonstrations of 1982. Men who had been arrested would have their heads shaved in a particular way so that they would be labeled and easily recognized as former offenders the next time around.

Mohamed Saban Saeed was interviewed in Cardiff on July 7, 1989, where he had been a seaman for thirty years.

> I had been on holiday in Hargeisa for three months before war broke out. During that time, I was arrested seven times by the NSS and by the *Dhabar Jabinta* [military police]. Each time, I was released only when relatives paid money. Every night during those three months I had a blanket and pillow wrapped up in preparation of arrest. If a car passed by the house at night, I was sure I would be arrested.

Ibrahim Hussein Abdi, a young man in his early twenties, interviewed in Cardiff on July 6, 1989, was a student in Hargeisa:

> In 1986, I was working in my uncle's shop. As October 21 [the anniversary of President Siad Barre's accession to power] approached, NSS officers came into the shop and told us to

50

hang a flag up. I hung up a small flag. They came back and told us to hang a bigger flag up, at least one meter long. I told them we couldn't afford that. I was arrested and detained for five days at the police station. Each person there "belongs" to the policeman who arrests them. He was waiting for me to pay. After five days, my uncle intervened with a higher officer. To be released, either you paid or had connections.

Omer Yusuf Isse, a seaman in his sixties, interviewed in Cardiff on July 6, 1989 where he is a resident. He went to Hargeisa for a holiday in 1985.

On October 20, 1985, I was in a tea shop in the Radio Station Area. A group of NSS officers came in. I recognized one of them. They said today, the eve of the October 21 anniversary, was a great night for Hargeisa, that many senior leaders were in town and that we should all come out and welcome them. I remarked that it might be a great day for them, but we had nothing to celebrate. There were no facilities available. There was not even water to cook with. They wrote my name down, accused me of being counter-revolutionary and told me to present myself at the NSS center the next day. Luckily for me, they were busy the next day with a plane crash. I was warned to leave town. I left through an unusual route and arrived in Djibouti. Although I was innocent, I had to leave in order to avoid arrest.

Ahmed Haji Hussein Omer Hashi, 24, a resident of Hargeisa, interviewed in Djibouti on August 3, 1989, was working with his father, a businessman. Their family suffered particularly from repeated arrests and detentions. He described their ordeals:

Our family had constant problems from 1981 after my cousin, Mohamed Haji Mohamoud Omer Hashi, was arrested for belonging to a self-help group accused of being anti-government. We were being punished for my cousin's "political" involvement. In 1985, my father was arrested briefly for being "qurmis"* and released on bail. In 1986, my cousin, Hassan Abdisalaan Omer Hashi, was arrested and accused of belonging to the Muslim brotherhood. My father went to the NSS

---

*   Qurmis is a derogatory term used by the government for the SNM and their supporters.

center to put up the bail. He himself was arrested on the spot. They took 50,000 shillings from him which he never got back.

Many close relatives were arrested in 1984. In June 1984, my uncle, Ahmed Yassin Omer Hashi, was arrested and became sick while at the station. No-one knew why he had been arrested. My father and I went to the station and pleaded with them to take him to the hospital. They accused us of being anti-government. We saw my sick uncle locked up in a crowded cell. My father couldn't bear it any longer. He exploded and insulted the officers for their cruelty, for treating a sick elderly man who had done nothing in this fashion. They arrested us both. After a few hours, they released me and my father was released later that night. My uncle was detained for three months altogether. He was never taken to hospital.

In July 1984, a group of school students were arrested and accused of anti-government activities, including bombings and distributing anti-government leaflets. My brother, Nur, 21, was one of them. He spent three months at *Qaybta** and was released on October 1. He was tortured very badly. My brother left immediately because once you were arrested, every time something happened you would be the first on the list. Both my brother and another cousin left the country for the same reason.

Even then, the persecution of the family continued.

My mother and other neighbors were asked to become members of the local committees that had been set up to report anti-government activities. My mother refused, using the excuse that she was sick. This was not accepted. Instead, she was arrested, once with six other women. They spent two nights and one day at the police station for "anti-revolutionary" attitudes. We had to arrange bail to get them out. Later in the year, she was arrested again, this time by herself on the same charges, lack of enthusiasm about the revolution.

---

* Qaybta is the Hargeisa headquarters of the military commander of the north-west region. Equipped with underground cells, as well as cells at the back of the compound, it is also used as a center for the interrogation and detention of political suspects. It is notorious for torture and ill-treatment of detainees.

In July 1987, my father was called to the NSS center and detained, without any explanations, from 8:00 a.m. to 11:00 p.m. My father, 67, who is a diabetic and has a heart disease, was kept in a small cell, without any ventilation. He was not given any food. At 11:00 p.m., they announced his release. My father was furious at the arbitrary way they just picked people up and let them go when they decide. He demanded an explanation as to why he had been arrested in the first place. He refused to be released unless he was told why he had been arrested and then released, all without a word of explanation. They forced him out and said he could submit a written complaint if he wanted. He did and of course nothing happened.

In March 1988, my father was arrested again as he came out of the mosque. He was taken to a small police station. The family had a dispute over a piece of land with a C.I.D. officer who was using his position and contacts to win the case. Their plan was to detain my father and, while he was in prison, build on the disputed land and sell the property. As a family, we were a constant target. Our lives and businesses were disrupted by constant imprisonment.

Abdirahman Mohamed Jama of Hargeisa is a businessman in his late thirties. After 12 years in Saudi Arabia, he came back to Hargeisa in April 1986 after his two elder brothers had left the country because of continuous harassment. As he put it when Africa Watch interviewed him in Djibouti on August 3, 1989, he returned to present a "new" face to the authorities. In a voice of angry distress he commented:

I was shocked at what I found. There was so much victimization of innocent people. People were murdered without any proof of wrongdoing and as a result, commercial businesses suffered. One of my brothers had been sentenced to death on the basis that he was assisting the SNM. The business declined and I took over. One of the brothers came back to help me. There was so much fear, which sometimes forced one to become friends with NSS officers as a protection. After the assassination of Ahmed Aden [the local NSS commander] in December 1986, my brother Rashid was arrested and detained for three months at Mandera. He was eventually

53

released because of the NSS people I had come to know. He left the country immediately. After one month, a soldier was killed near Loya'Aade [Somali /Djibouti border]. I was arrested and detained at an NSS center for eight days. They said I was behind the operation. About 15 of us were arrested for this case, including Mohamed Abdi Hawse, "Jowasi." I spent the first nights in solitary confinement and was physically tortured. As they tortured us, they would tell us that we would be released if we paid. Our business ceased eventually.

Yusuf Ahmed Ismail, owned a taxi in Hargeisa and had been in Cardiff for two months at the time of Africa Watch's interview with him in Cardiff on July 8, 1989. He jokingly calls himself a "prison graduate" as he has been detained on many occasions.

On February 20, 1982 [there were serious disturbances at the time in protest against the trials of the Hargeisa group] I was driving my car when a soldier stopped me and held a pistol against my temple. He said that he had seen me throwing stones and chanting the downfall of the government. I was arrested together with 1800 people and held in *Dabada Ada'da* near the airport.*

We were separated into men and women. Every day we were soaked with dirty water. The men were taken to underground cells. We had to sleep on the floor. We were kicked around by the soldiers, who accused us of being "arrogant." I had to pay 25,000 shillings to be released after 23 days. The men who could not pay were used as free laborers to work on houses the military were building.

My car was confiscated by an officer who drove it around. On my release, I asked him to return my car. He replied that he would return it when he was finished with it. When I told him that it was my own money that had paid for the car, not his, he threatened to arrest me if I continued to argue with him.

I was arrested again in January 1983 after the SNM broke into Mandera prison. When the news of the break-in reached Hargeisa, Burao and other towns, I was on my way back from

---

* This is a military compound that is the the headqarters of the 24th sector of the army.

Gebiley. Later that night, the NSS came to my home and accused me of being involved in the prison break-in. I was held at an NSS center for 25 nights. They accused me of collaborating with the SNM. I was beaten with a club that had a big round head nicknamed "The Isaak Head Beater" (*"Madah Garaa'ii Isaakah"*). As they hit you with it, they would say, "This should teach you to be arrogant, you bastards. This will beat it out of you." This time, it was the NSS that took my car. Daud, the head of the NSS, a military officer, drove it around for two months. He said he would keep it while the car he had ordered, (from the extortions he collected) arrived from Berbera port. He said he would arrest me unless I told people that he had rented the car from me. When he returned the car, he said, "I have done you a favor in returning your car after two months. I am warning you that if we have reason to arrest you again, we won't waste our time detaining you — we will simply shoot you."

My next arrest came quite soon after that. On April 12, 1983, Abdillahi Askar, a senior SNM military commander, escaped from prison. A friend of mine, Ibrahim Koodbur, was involved in Askar's escape. They said they had seen Koodbur in my car. At 5:30 on April 12, soldiers, some of them masked, came to my house, and arrested me. They also took my car away. I was taken to a *HANGASH* center. I was interrogated by Dahir Idd, "Af Galoc." He said, "So many of you little Isaak boys are driving cars in Hargeisa that even Ministers in Mogadishu don't drive. Where do you get the money?" I replied that it was God's will. We had a long discussion along these lines. He took my car away and drove it around for a month and 25 days. When he was through with it, another soldier used it for another 28 days. After that, I sold the car.

But his release did not end his ordeal:

On November 24, after a plane was hijacked and the execution of some fighters and others, some of my friends and I were arrested at my house. We were blindfolded and chained together and taken to cells at *Qaybta*. I was beaten savagely. [He had long scars on both arms and on his head which he said had been caused by the beatings.] After one night there, 28 others (including 3 other taxi owners/drivers) and I were taken

55

in a truck to Burao. At Sheikh, some of the soldiers pointed to a spot, looked at us threateningly and said, "At this spot, Colonel Jihad was killed by the SNM; you too will die in a similar way."

We were detained in Burao for 43 days. There were 93 of us altogether including 28 from Hargeisa. Most of the rest were from Burao and a few were brought from Sheikh. On the 43rd day, the Mobile Military Court sentenced 43 men to execution, including 22 of our group. The only reason I wasn't executed is that they couldn't find my name on their list. It was God's will. It just wasn't my day. I was chained to the last person executed, the 43rd victim, Mohamed Abdi Dherre. Many of my friends were killed. They were tied with ropes and then executed by a firing squad near the airport. They were not even given proper graves, just buried in the sand. I was transferred to Mandera prison and detained there together with some of the other detainees. Some of the older men remained in prison longer.

I was arrested again in May 1985, accused of helping SNM sympathizers leave the country. They said that I had such a long record of "offenses" that they should just kill me. I was taken to Hargeisa Central Prison where I remained, without being charged with anything, for six months. I spent the whole six months in a special punishment cell with three other Isaak men also accused of involvement with the SNM. They had all been sentenced to death. At one stage, they even brought a mentally disturbed man who had committed murder, to share our cell. The conditions in these special cells were disgusting. To humiliate us, we were not allowed to use toilets, so we had to relieve ourselves in our cells. They also confiscated another car I had bought. I never saw that car again.

I was eventually released when the president amnestied some of the prisoners who had not been charged or tried. I left the country, to escape this situation. I went to Djibouti where I stayed throughout 1986. I returned to Hargeisa at the end of December 1986. Then the head of the NSS, Ahmed Aden, was assassinated. I fled again for fear that I would become a victim in their revenge killings and arrests. I went to Mogadishu and then to Abu Dhabi and did not return to Hargeisa till the end of 1987. I left Burao for Mogadishu the night before the war broke out.

The following account of the arrest and detention of Khadra Muhumed Abdi, mother of two young boys and former manager of Oriental Hotel in Hargeisa, illustrates the authorities' unlimited powers over the lives of civilians. She was interviewed by Africa Watch in London on June 2, 1989.

My father, who managed the hotel, died in 1981 and my eldest brother, who just returned from studying abroad, was expected to assume responsibility for the hotel. He became involved in the activities of the Hargeisa group. He fled the country after their arrest, and after learning that he was on a list of people to be arrested. Soon afterwards, masked men wearing black and carrying bazookas came to the house at 2:30 a.m. They interrogated us about his whereabouts, his connections to the SNM and how much money we gave to encourage people to leave the country and join the SNM.

In February 1982, Elizabeth Blunt, an English journalist working for the BBC, visited Hargeisa and stayed at our hotel. It was the day they brought the Hargeisa group to trial. There were demonstrations and soldiers fired at the protesters. She saw everything for herself and reported it back to the BBC. Her report was broadcast [on the BBC Somali Service] that same afternoon in Hargeisa. Immediately, the NSS came to the hotel. They questioned her and she left Hargeisa. They blamed everything on me. They said I had advised her to come because of my anti-government attitude. I told them that it was not I, but the government, that gave her the visa and which controls the country's borders and airports. We were business people and had to act according to our business interests. Nothing more, nothing less. I was locked up for a day and a night at the NSS headquarters and questioned constantly, to say who else was involved in this "plot."

I was released after a bail of two million shillings was put up by seven prominent Isaak elders of Hargeisa. They had to agree that if I escaped, all seven of them would be arrested and detained for a long time. They also decided that from then on, no foreigners would be allowed to stay at the Oriental Hotel or the Union Hotel, the two main hotels in Hargeisa.

After her release, Khadra was subjected to constant pressure:

Ahmed Aden, the head of the NSS and his deputy, Daud, used to harass me constantly. They offered to drop my case if I paid them 270,000 shillings each, which I said my family could not spare. They kept threatening to arrest me and destroy our business.

On June 25, 1982, Mohamed Ali, a captain in the NSS, came to the hotel with six or seven soldiers and told me to get into their jeep. Two of my uncles protested; they too were arrested on the spot. There were seven other civilians in the car already − all prominent businessmen and elders from Hargeisa, as well as a number of government employees. There were 25 men and myself.

We were taken to the headquarters of the *Gulwadayaal*, the Militia Building.

Later that day, we were visited by Gani, Daud, Chief of the NSS, Dahir Idd, head of the *HANGASH*, Ibrahim Abdi Nur, "Af Gaab", the Governor and Jama "Green." Gani announced that we had all been "sentenced" to 10 years in prison and the others applauded. We were never taken to a court. Immediately afterwards, we were taken in military escort to Mogadishu. Four nights later we reached Mogadishu. We were given no food during the entire four days. We were blindfolded shortly before our final destination.

We were detained in the former Libyan embassy, an empty, dusty old building. We were chained two by two. We were in a terrible condition when we arrived − hungry, dusty, dirty and exhausted − and frightened, of course. We were given some food on arrival and soap. Each one of us was guarded by three armed soldiers. At around 5:15, the day of our arrival, the 12 government employees were taken separately in one car. The other 13 men in another car and I was taken in a third car − all escorted by armed soldiers and we were taken to the *Godka*, (The Hole), an NSS prison.

I was interrogated by Adan "Cirday" who was in charge of the *Godka* and told to "confess." I said I had not committed any offense, so what was I expected to confess to? "You know what you have done," he replied.

58

I was taken to an underground cell, where there were four other women and two girls. All this time our families in Hargeisa had no idea what had happened to us. I later found out that my mother spent a lot of money on false leads from soldiers. It was difficult for our families to find out anything, because since the 1982 demonstrations and political tension, communications with Hargeisa had been cut off. All flights were suspended and telephone services were interrupted.

After about three weeks, one kind soldier offered to inform our families of our whereabouts and he did. My mother and my aunt came to Mogadishu. I was only allowed to see them for five minutes, in the company of six armed soldiers. Later, the soldiers asked me to hand over the clothes they brought for me.

Eventually, I was taken to see the President. The President started talking politics straight away. He launched into an attack against Isaaks and against me. He had no kind words to say in spite of our ordeal. He commented, "What you Isaaks deserve is not to be detained but shot on the spot after you commit such offenses." I asked him, "What have we done?" I said I was not aware of anything illegal that I had done. He emphasized, again and again, the "arrogance" of the Isaaks. He accused me of having organized anti-government meetings in our hotel. In reference to Elizabeth Blunt, he said that I invited and paid white people to come and report negatively on Somalia. He said I had paid people money to throw stones in February. He accused me of instigating people to leave Somalia in order to destroy the country's political system. He held me responsible for all sorts of important political events, which I could not possibly know about, never mind organize.

I asked him, "Even if we were guilty, don't we deserve to be heard in a court of law?" We had received 10-year sentences, a heavy punishment, without any opportunity to defend ourselves or even to hire a lawyer. He replied, "You people deserve to be shot on the spot, not detained, never mind to be heard in a court." He said he had decided to pardon me now "because my father had been a patriotic man." However, "I must work with the government." I asked, "what kind of work?" He replied, "to report anything that could injure the security of the country." In a more straightforward manner, he said I should join the NSS. I told him that I couldn't work in government, as I was responsible for 20 people in my family who all depended on the business I ran.

Khadra was then released but ordered not to leave Mogadishu for five months. She had to report to the NSS every Saturday. "I felt I was still a prisoner, only I was not in prison." After the five months passed, she was allowed to go to Hargeisa but was forbidden to leave the country. She left for Hargeisa immediately.

I started working in the hotel again. Straight away, soldiers began coming, always threatening me, accusing me of working for the SNM. After a year and a half of this hell, I stopped working. Even then, soldiers came to the house late at night, repeating the same threats. Finally, I decided to escape. I left secretly, for Saudi Arabia.

In early 1984, after she had been away for over a year, Khadra's mother fell ill and she came back to Hargeisa.

After only six days I was arrested. I was interrogated: "Where had you been?" I told them I had gone to Saudi Arabia to get married. I was released only after my family paid U.S. $1000 plus 600,000 Somali shillings to the men in charge of my case — Ahmed Aden and to Captain "Hidde" of the police. I was released and left again for Saudi Arabia after six months. I stayed away for three years.

During that time, even though my eldest brother and I were both away, the constant harassment of our family continued. My younger brothers and sisters were arrested, detained and subjected to constant intimidation, partly to extort money. Because of this, our business declined and I had to come back. I returned to Hargeisa in September 1987 and was shocked to see how much things had deteriorated and how much the people were suffering. There was a curfew imposed. I was pregnant at the time and so I decided to stay in a clinic for a whole month, for fear that there would be no transportation when I went into labor. Aden Bulle, the Governor of Hargeisa, came to the clinic to visit someone and recognized me. He laughed sarcastically and said, "Why are we allowing one *qurmis* to give birth to another *qurmis*? What's the use of that?"

On March 21, 1988, Ahmed Abdillahi Hareed, known as "Weerar" and Shab'an Ali Dualeh were arrested in Gebiley while burying an elderly man who had died in his late 80s of natural causes. The deceased, who was highly respected in Gebiley, had been constantly subjected to harassment, despite his age, and accused of encouraging an anti-government attitude within the community. Six of the men at his funeral, including Ahmed and Shab'an, were arrested on March 21, 1988, just prior to the President's visit to Gebiley. They were transferred that same day to Hargeisa Central Prison. (Anyone arrested in the Gebiley region was transferred to Hargeisa.) They told Africa Watch when we interviewed them in Djibouti on August 10, 1989, that they were never asked any questions, apart from their names. No charges were ever brought. They were released on February 7, 1989 in an amnesty for political prisoners announced by the government in January 1989. They told Africa Watch that, in spite of the amnesty, many were still detained in Hargeisa Central Prison on suspicion of association with the SNM. They include:

- Mohamed Arab Ismail, accused of association with the SNM as far back as March 1981. [The SNM was launched in April 1981.] He was sentenced to 24 years in prison.

- Sheikh Mohamed Farah, arrested in Hargeisa and sentenced to 14 years in late October 1987. He was accused of being anti-government and an SNM "agent"; the only "evidence" was an allegation that he had criticized some people for joining the government-organized celebrations for the anniversary of October 21.

- A group of 17 nomadic men who were arrested in late November or early December 1987 in the Gebiley region. One of them had lost some camels and the others who lived in the area were helping in his search. They were accused of being scouts for the SNM. They are mainly young men in their twenties, among whom is Ismail Aw Mohamoud. They became known in the prison as the "Camel group."

Ahmed and Shab'an testified that about another fifty civilians arrested on political grounds were still in that prison, arrested both shortly before and immediately after war broke out. According to what they learned in Djibouti, there were, at the time of the interview, also alot of people detained in Borama.

Once a person was arrested, the entire family was vulnerable.

Amina Mohamoud Hussein, interviewed by Africa Watch in Newport on July 7, 1989, told of the predicament of the families:

> Men would be arrested in their homes or stores. Then their wives or daughters would go to the police station to take them food and then they themselves would be arrested.

4. EXTRAJUDICIAL EXECUTIONS

According to all the refugees interviewed by Africa Watch, the policy that particularly galvanized opposition to the government, both among nomads and city-dwellers, was the system of indiscriminate killings that followed SNM military offensives. The military apparently assumed that if the SNM was active in an area, local residents must be supporters of the rebels. Hundreds have been executed and subjected to other reprisals on the basis of such suspicions.

The killings started in earnest in 1984, after the SNM intensified its incursions into the cities. Whenever there was an encounter between government forces and the SNM, or the SNM took an initiative against its military adversaries, the army would conduct a sweep of the area where the incident occurred. Massacres followed, as did the killing of livestock, the use of landmines to blow up reservoirs, the burning of huts, arrests and detentions. The entire population in the area was regarded as "the enemy."

The following are some of the numerous episodes of the executions of Isaaks on which Africa Watch has gathered information.

October 15, 1984

On October 15, 1984, Habiiba Yusuf Liibaan, a farmer's wife, was arrested in Gogol Wanaag, near Arabsiyo, accused of having given shelter to an SNM fighter.* In addition to arresting her and several others, six men were executed on the spot. They included two elderly brothers, their two sons and the son-in-law of one of the elderly men who had just arrived on a visit from the Middle East where he was living. Their huts were burned and their animals killed. They were accused of having assisted Habiiba Yusuf Liiban to shelter the SNM fighter. The sixth man was charged with being a member of the SNM

---

*   For details of her arrest, see Chapter Seven.

and accompanying the SNM fighter, who was reported to have escaped. The villagers were not allowed to bury the dead men for five days.

Fardoosa Mohamed, the daughter of one of the elderly men, a young woman in her twenties, was also arrested and transferred to Hargeisa Central Prison where she was held for two years. Reportedly, she became mentally disturbed from the shock of seeing so many close family members executed in front of her.

Many others were arrested in the same incident. Another group was apparently taken to Gebiley. Their subsequent fate is not known by Africa Watch.

November 17, 1984

Twenty-six Isaaks, nine civilians and seventeen SNM fighters were captured in Boqol Jirreh, a section of Hargeisa neighboring a military compound. Twenty-four of them were accused of association with the SNM and the other two, Abdillahi Abdi Good, a businessman, and Ismail Sheikh Ibrahim Muse, also a businessman, were charged with assisting them. (See Appendix Three for the identities of some of the victims.) Many of the victims were nomads. They had been caught in ambushes set in different places and were sentenced to death by the mobile military court.

On November 17, when people began to file out of midday prayers, many of Hargeisa's most respected elders were seized by the NSS. Among those seized were Imams (religious leaders), including Sheikh Idris, Imam of a leading mosque opposite the Central Bank in the center of town. The elders were taken to witness the "proceedings" of the court, so that they would "talk sense" to the residents of Hargeisa. The elders were seized at about 12:45 p.m. after which the proceedings started. The men were executed between 3:15 and 3:30 p.m. Their property and assets were also seized.

Africa Watch learned the following details about the arrest and death of one of the victims:

> Abdillahi Abdi Good's family was expecting him for lunch after Friday noon prayers when word came that he had been picked up near the main mosque. He had organized a lunch

64

party that day and told his guests, who were with him at the time of his arrest, to proceed to his house and he would join them there. "There must be some misunderstanding", he told them. The next they heard was of his execution. Soldiers were posted around his house to prevent the family from mourning his death and to deny access to friends and neighbors who came to offer condolences.

Massacre of 43 Men in Burao in December 1984

Most of the forty-three victims had been detained in Burao Central Prison for some time, charged with different offenses. The majority were kat traders, accused of importing kat. (Kat is a mild stimulant chewed as a leaf. It is very popular in Somalia and plays an important role in the economy of the northern region.* Some were charged with theft and others were accused of political crimes.

In December, when the authorities became alarmed by the presence of the SNM in the mountains around Sheikh, the charges against the 43 were dropped, and they were all accused of association with the SNM. (A number of the victims were residents of Sheikh, arrested there on December 6th and then transferred to Burao.) They were "tried" before the Mobile Military Court and executed the same afternoon. Forty-five men were due to be executed. At the last moment, two wealthy men, "Kofiyadheere" and "Indaderro," were spared, apparently because of the size of the loans they owed to the banks. (See Appendix Four for a list of some of the victims.)

After this massacre, according to residents of Burao interviewed by Africa Watch, anyone arrested there on suspicion of sympathy for or involvement with the SNM was simply shot; there was no pretense of a legal proceeding. The majority of the victims were nomads, especially from the Gebiley and Tug Wajaleh districts near the Ethiopian border, where the SNM was particularly active, or men involved in the kat trade. They were apparently targeted on the theory that, without the material and political support of these two groups, the SNM could not survive.

---

*   See Chapter Six for a more detailed discussion.

Gebiley and Tug Wajale, March 14, 1988

Abdillahi Mahdi, Shab'an Ali Dualeh and Ahmed Abdillahi Hareed, "Weraar", interviewed by Africa Watch in Djibouti on August 10, 1989, provided details about the execution of twenty-five men in the Ghaas Dheere district of Gebiley in March 1988 and in Tug Wajale, the same day they were sentenced to death by the Mobile Military Court. They were apparently shot as a reprisal when a major military offensive against the SNM in the vicinty failed. Some of the victims were very old men. (See Appendix Five for a list of those killed in these two incidents.)

The massacres of 1984/85 tapered off in 1986 and most of 1987, after the tranfer of "Yusuf Dherre," the special prosecutor of the military court. Executions took place in smaller groups. Killings on a large scale became widespread again at the end of 1987, when he was reinstated. Some people were shot because they dared to challenge an act of cruelty on the part of the military. Many residents of Burao remembered the killing of "Dimbiil," a young student at Burao Technical Institute:

Ahmed Saeed Elmi, interviewed by Africa Watch in London on June 14, 1989, told us that:

> In 1985, a young student at Burao Technical Institute, known as "Dimbiil," 25, was shot when he protested the way soldiers were treating a woman they had arrested. Marian "Gaabo" was a widow and the mother of eight children. Her husband was among the group of 43 men killed in December 1984 (see above). Two soldiers banged on the door of her house. She refused to open. They broke the door down and dragged her out, pulling her by the hair. Dimbiil, who witnessed this, pleaded on her behalf. One of the soldiers turned around and shot him on the spot.

Africa Watch also heard numerous accounts of people killed simply because they were not quick enough about handing over a watch or their car keys, when ordered to.

Mohamed Saban Saeed, a seaman, interviewed by Africa Watch in Cardiff on July 7, 1989, recalled an incident in Hargeisa in 1985 when he was there on holiday:

A young boy was driving a car when soldiers stopped him and asked him for the keys. He refused. They just shot him as he turned into a garage at a house on the road between the main prison and the headquarters of the *Gulwadayaal.*

Abdi Kahin "Hadliyeh" testified to Africa Watch in Cardiff on July 6, 1989, about an incident in Arabsiyo in May 1988:

Aw Ahmed Daud Yusuf, a carpenter, went to visit his family in the countryside. He was arrested just before he reached his house and brought back to Arabsiyo. He was interrogated and searched. They found 2,000 shillings on him and a watch. He pleaded with them not to take them. They were furious that he had the gall to argue with them, so they just shot him. When we went to his funeral, two other men and I were arrested and taken to the police station and questioned about the SNM. We were released when a soldier who recognized us intervened on our behalf.

5. EXERTING POLITICAL CONTROL

Apart from killing and arresting opponents, the government has at its disposal a formidable range of extra-legal sanctions to exert control. The most simple acts, such as mourning the death of a relative, became subject to "political" controls. Military checkpoints, curfews, "the *tabeleh* system" (see below) and house-to-house searches, crippled freedom of movement and devastated privacy.

The "Tabeleh" System

The *tabeleh* system was the center piece of the system of control and was in effect only in the northern region. A leader, known as a *"tabeleh,"* was appointed for every twenty houses. The *tabeleh* was a member of the Party and worked closely with the NSS. He was required to submit to the NSS a list of all family members living in each household. If members of the household travelled, the NSS had to be notified. Visitors had to be reported, even close family members. A Party member frequently accompanied the *tabeleh* to double-check the lists and to look out for visitors. The objective apparently was to discourage SNM fighters from visiting their families and having contact with urban dwellers. (As intended, SNM fighters reduced visits to their families so as not to endanger them further according to the accounts we received.)

The *tabeleh* system was socially and psychologically divisive, forcing neighbors to spy on each other since their own well-being depended on how much information they passed to the *tabeleh*.

Amaal Jama, interviewed by Africa Watch in London on July 19, 1989, said:

> The government was stealing people from each other within the community by making neighbors spy on each other.

Sahra Arteh, interviewed by Africa Watch in London on June 17, 1989, described the system as follows:

The *tabeleh* was always accompanied by soldiers who would stand outside while he went indoors to count the members of the household. Sometimes the soldiers would go in after he finished and also count. If there was a discrepancy between his number and theirs, he was in trouble. If you failed to report a visitor, difficulties were in store for you. If the "guest" was male or a nomad, interrogations were endless. "How did he get to here? What car did he come in? Then they would check all the cars that arrived the same day to see if this was true. If we could not prove our story, the consequences for the household were very serious.

Hassan Ismail Omaar, who had been living in Saudi Arabia until January 1987 and was interviewed by Africa Watch in Cardiff on July 8, 1989, was one of the many people caught unawares by the *tabeleh* system when he returned to Somalia:

As I was new to the country I did not know about the system. In early 1988 my brother Ibrahim, living in the countryside, came to visit me. The NSS came at midnight. They took their file out and pointed out that there was an additional man in the house. I explained that it was my brother. That did not matter. He was arrested and I had to pay 5000 shillings to secure his release.

Yassin Karshe Mohamed, a resident of Cardiff where he was interviewed by Africa Watch on July 7, 1989, was in Hargeisa from October 1987 to April 1988. He discussed the difficulties of the *tabeleh* system and the way it disrupted family ties:

I never slept peacefully during those six months. I was always tense, afraid that a soldier would come to arrest me or a family member. Many people in our neighborhood, Goljano, had suffered punishment because they received visitors. There was a suspicion that every visitor was a member of the SNM. There was no alternative but to report visitors, no matter how close a relative. Sometimes, visitors came late at night. If the NSS center was closed at that hour and there was nowhere else to submit your report, you would have to send your visitors away, even if he were your own father. The tabeleh was not always available. Our community is a close-knit one and there are always visitors. It became a full-time occupation just to report all these comings and goings. You had to choose between working to support a family and reporting your visitors.

Other Constrints On Freedom of Movement and Expression

At the end of 1986, when Morgan became the new military commander, identity cards with photographs were introduced to enable the authorities to monitor people's movements. The cards were necessary even to travel short distances. It became such an intrusion that only people who had to travel obtained the cards. If people traveled without their card and were caught, they were taken to NSS headquarters and released only after a payment.

The military in Hargeisa made it compulsory for car-owners to obtain a card that authorized them to drive within Hargeisa. They had to secure a second card permitting them to visit another town. It was necessary to get such a card approved for the return journey, otherwise the car would be turned back at the first checkpoint.

Ever since the Siad Barre government came to power in 1969, freedom of expression had been tightly controlled; the controls had been particularly rigid since the end of the Ogaden war with Ethiopia in 1978. People did not trust using the post. Even letters that did not have a political content were entrusted to people who would hand-carry them. In the north, all letters had to be taken to the NSS to be read and then sealed with an NSS stamp; letters without an NSS seal were confiscated at the airport. The same procedure applied to cassettes; people had to take a recorder along so that the NSS could listen to the tapes. (Because of the high rate of illiteracy and the substantial diaspora, tape recorded messages are an important means of communication between Somalis at home and those abroad.)

The neighborhood committees of the Party organized compulsory attendance at public events, such as welcoming a visiting government delegation. To avoid arrest or a fine, people who did not want to attend these events had to bribe committee members.

71

Listening to unauthorized broadcasts was strictly forbidden.

Kalthoon Iggeh Isse, interviewed by Africa Watch in Cardiff on July 8, 1989, said:

> Soldiers came to our homes to eavesdrop and see if we were listening to the SNM radio. We did not dare to talk openly in our own house. As soon as night fell, we would turn the paraffin lamps very dim so that the soldiers would think we were asleep.

The intimidating behavior of senior government officials was intended to frighten the local population. Amaal Jama commented that:

> Gani was obsessed with showing his power and making sure that people knew who was in control. He would go through the city, intimidating everyone, even old women and petty traders. For a senior official, his behavior was shameful. He would demolish the little huts built along the main road, denouncing them as "rubbish" and declaring that he couldn't have visiting delegations see such ugly things. He said he wanted them replaced by nice looking houses. For poor people, that was the end, unless they were related to someone who had connections to high-ranking government officials who could intervene on their behalf.

> He went into every alley of Hargeisa to check. He visited even the little makeshift open markets where people sold an assortment of odd bits and pieces. He would kick over the stalls and the milk or gas containers, insulting the people and accusing them of making the streets ugly. Why did he have to do this? After all, there was a local government to run and control the city.

The government was apparently anxious to limit the interaction between Somalis and foreigners. Siegfried Koch, a Swiss national fluent in Somali, worked for Christian Refugee Aid, a Swiss non-governmental organization. He taught agriculture at an orphanage, *Dhalinta Ka'anka* in Hargeisa, from November 1984 to May 1988. Interviewed by Africa Watch in London on August 21, 1989, he described the government's nervous reaction to exchanges with foreigners:

The authorities were hostile to any interaction between foreigners and Somalis. They would become very suspicious if we went to the homes of Somali friends and of course the consequences were much worse for our Somali friends. Once I was talking to a friend in the Ganad area. I was summoned to an NSS center to explain what we had been discussing.

There were other ways to ensure that the presence of foreigners did not compromise the government's attempts to maintain a blackout of information on human rights conditions.

Siegfried Koch continued:

Foreigners, especially the heads of the agencies, were sometimes "invited" to important meetings, so as to "educate" the foreign community. The message was always the same: "There is no problem, only a bit of minor friction. So don't exaggerate and tell lies to people outside the country. Don't write about political developments in Somalia." Our mail was under surveillance. There was an incident in which they found a letter written by a member of the foreign community which they described as "subversive," though people who read it said it was harmless. The incident was used to intimidate the rest of us. We were warned and told to be careful about what we wrote. They even began to monitor the pouch and they would confiscate letters at the airport.

The Curfew System

The curfew was first imposed after the February riots of 1982. [Riots broke out in Hargeisa at the time the Hargeisa group were due to be brought to trial].* Before the government introduced the curfew system, there was another form of control in effect. For an offense known as "Staying up late at night" ("*Maseexdo soojeed habeenimo*") people were liable to be arrested if they were found walking late at night. If arrested, they would be accused of "Wasting a soldier's time" ("*Lugooyo askari*"). The punishment was 24 hours of detention.

A curfew, followed by dragnet arrests, was the government's response to political events ranging from student demonstrations to the break-in at

---

*   For further details, see Background chapter.

Mandera jail by the SNM in January 1983, to the assassination of government officials. Periodically, it would be lifted and then re-imposed after political disturbances. After 1984, when the SNM stepped up military attacks, curfews became an increasingly prominent feature of the government's apparatus of control.

Anyone caught breaking the curfew regulations was taken to the police station and released only if they paid 1000 shillings. For second time offenders, the punishment was imprisonment, a minimum of six months and up to two years; the sentence was not imposed by a court of law but typed out at the police station. No other formalities were necessary. A man caught during the curfew had half his head shaved to show him as a marked man. As for a woman, if a soldier or security officer liked her, she may not be released, even if her family paid a ransom. During the curfew, no doors were allowed to be opened.

Basra Aw Ali, interviewed by Africa Watch in Cardiff on July 6, 1989, told of the effects of the curfew:

> Once the curfew started, no one dared to put a foot outside, even to put your animals in the shed. Children would be shot near their homes and mothers would not dare even to pick up the body because they would be shot too, and that wouldn't do anyone any good.

Amaal Jama, described the selective way that the curfew was enforced:

> The number of people killed because they got caught during the curfew hours is incalculable. Non-Isaak people who got arrested were automatically released. When they recognized the person as a non-Isaak, they would get embarrassed and say to each other, "It's one of us. How did this happen?" Some Isaaks learned the accent and would use it to get out of trouble.

Many residents of Hargeisa told Africa Watch of the case of Saeed Ismail Gabas, about 27, who was wounded fatally at the corner near his home. The incident occurred just before curfew, at 5:00 p.m. A group of soldiers stopped him and asked him to hand over his watch. He refused. They kicked him to the ground and then stepped on him with heavy boots. He screamed for help but no one dared to lift a finger. He died ten days later. The military doctor insisted that he had died of a liver disease, but doctors at Hargeisa General Hospital stated that he had died from the wounds inflicted by the soldiers.

A refugee from Hargeisa who requested anonymity when interviewed by Africa Watch in Djibouti, described an incident in 1987:

> One afternoon in April 1987, soldiers stopped a public bus in front of the headquarters of the Victory Pioneers. It was making its last trip before the 5:00 p.m. curfew. The driver failed to pay the required bribe. The bus was sprayed with bullets and several passengers were severely injured. The driver and the victims were taken to the police station and charged with violating the curfew. They were not allowed to be taken to the hospital. Several hours later, when their cries of pain from the bullet wounds became too loud to bear, they were permitted to leave. The guards at the hospital turned them back, telling them that it was past curfew time. The case was never investigated and protestations were met with threats of arrest.

Abdi Kahin Hadliyeh, a seaman interviewed by Africa Watch in Cardiff on July 6, 1989, described the curfew in Arabsiyo during a visit in March 1988:

> No one was living in peace. There was a curfew which started at 4:00 p.m. Anyone caught during the curfew hours was taken to the *Dagaha Madoo* (Black Stone), the military headquarters. Either you paid the required ransom or you were automatically taken to Hargeisa to be detained there. People from abroad were the first target because they thought that we had money and valuables — and also because they thought that we came with the wrong attitudes and needed to understand the local reality.

The following cases are typical of the abuses facilitated by curfews:

Siraad, (not her real name), told Africa Watch when she was interviewed in Djibouti on August 3, 1989:

> I was arrested in April 1987 in Burao. I arrived at our shop at 4:50; the curfew started at 5:00 p.m. Still, I was found guilty. Twenty-seven of us, all young women, were locked up at the main police station. We spent the night there. As there were no toilet facilities, the men urinated into a curved corridor outside the male section of the station. The police collected

75

the urine in buckets, mixed it with water and threw it at the women. In the morning, my brother came, paid 1,000 shillings and I left. Everyone had to pay the 1,000 shillings.

Hassan Ismail Omaar reported:

The curfew system was one of the worst problems I found on my return to Hargeisa from Saudi Arabia. The curfew started legally at 8:00 p.m. But the army, which was a law onto itself and eager for ransoms, arrested people starting 5:00 p.m. They kept them in a detention center and said, "Either we hand you over to the police charging you with curfew violations — you know that no one will ask you any questions or listen to what you have to say — or you pay us now to release you, and no one need know anything."

Muse Saleh Ali, "Geldoon," used to be a seaman in Cardiff, where he was interviewed by Africa Watch on July 6, 1989. He described a return to his home in Burao:

My family is from Burao and had been living there for two years before the war broke out.

One of the worst things was the curfew. They would announce the curfew and then arrest people long before it was supposed to take effect. When I was arrested, the curfew was supposed to begin at 8:00 p.m. but I was detained at 5:00 p.m. People were arrested at different places and collected together. If anyone said that the arrests had taken place before the curfew fell, they were beaten. The detention centers and police stations were like marketplaces. People were priced and sold like animals. In my case, they kept raising the price till I finally offered them 7,000 shillings.

If you didn't pay at once, you would just rot in prison. There was no prospect of release through the legal system. Anybody who tried to visit a relative in prison ran the risk of arrest themselves. When I could no longer bear the hardship in Burao, I took my family to the countryside, near the Ethiopian border, where we had relatives.

An expatriate former relief worker in Hargeisa, interviewed by Africa Watch in London on October 27, commented:

I knew from our local employees how frequently people got arrested. In the end, we made ID cards for all our local workers. It helped them when they got caught up during the curfew hours. The curfew got much worse after December 1986, following the assassination of the local NSS chief. They tried to show a nice face to foreigners for fear of bad publicity, but they couldn't hide the truth from us. We knew how much people suffered from the curfew and all the other restrictions.

The curfew system had another disastrous consequence for the rural population coming to town to buy food; it denied them access to food supplies. Many travelled long distances only to return home empty-handed. It was difficult to avoid the arbitrary restrictions imposed by the curfew system.

The curfew was not only a means of political control; it was apparently part of a broader strategy to injure the pride of the community. Numerous refugees told Africa Watch that the soldiers would taunt men: "We've made idle women out of you, forcing you to sit out at your verandas and spend your day chatting. We've left you nothing."

Mohamed Karshe Mohamed, a seaman living in Cardiff where he was interviewed by Africa Watch on July 6, 1989, visited his family every year in Hargeisa. He reported:

It was distressing for the whole community to see active young men cooped up and forced to pass their time chatting because you can't go to bed at 5:00 or 6:00 p.m.

A Somali resident abroad who visited the camps in Ethiopia met with Tahir Abdi Nur, who recalled an encounter with government troops in the village of Tug Wajaleh. He was picked up for curfew violation late one afternoon in early 1988 and, together with a large number of other men, was taken to the dry river-bed in town. They were ordered, at gunpoint, to swim in the mud. One by one they jumped in, dipping their heads in the mud. The soldiers started laughing and then left them.

Military Checkpoints

Difficulties were not confined to the cities. Travel between cities was a nightmare. The roads were littered with "security" checkpoints manned by

77

soldiers where passengers were searched. Frequently, their belongings were confiscated. It was common for the guards at such posts to demand bribes from the owners of vehicles, the drivers or whoever was in charge. They threatened trumped-up charges about some form that had not been filled out properly or some other regulation they had failed to obey.

Muse Saleh Ali, "Geldoon," described his experience:

> I was travelling with provisions for my family. The soldiers stopped the truck. This time they decided to confiscate the truck itself. All the passengers had to disembark and make their own arrangements. It was difficult. Remember, this was in the countryside. Cars are not frequent and when they pass, they are already full, both of people and goods. It took me two days to find camels to transport the food to my family and then another two days to reach home.

There are apparently nine checkpoints between Burao and Berbera, a distance of ninety miles. Vehicles are stopped and bribes must be paid at each point. Frequently, the documents proving that the passengers had been searched were confiscated, leading to additional searches.

Asha Ibrahim Haji Hussein, who travelled from Hargeisa to Sheikh in March 1988, was interviewed by Africa Watch in Newport on July 7, 1989. She reported:

> You could see one military checkpoint from another, they were so close together. They even confiscated personal letters that people had entrusted to the passengers.

Abdi Kahin Hadliyeh, described his experiences in Arabsiyo:

> I left Cardiff on February 23, 1988 with my wife. I got to Arabsiyo on March 16. All the way from Djibouti to Arabsiyo, every time we were stopped at a military checkpoint, the driver descended and collected money from the passengers, so that he wouldn't be searched. We had to pay 25,000 at each control point. Life was unbearable in Arabsiyo. Everyone seemed to be waiting for his turn to be killed or detained.

Mohamed Ismail Kahin, a resident from Hargeisa, interviewed by Africa Watch in Cardiff on July 6, 1989, recalled :

78

I lived in Saudi Arabia from 1978 to February 1984. On March 3, I returned to Hargeisa and decided to open a business as a wholesaler. My first encounter with political reality in Somalia took place on July 20. We had transported some goods to Mogadishu and brought other wares on our return. We were stopped at a military checkpoint in Goa village, by the forces of the *Dabar Goynta Isaaka*, ("Isaak Exterminators"). They threatened us with bazookas. They ordered the driver to hand over the keys of the truck. They said that we had broken the 6:00 p.m. curfew, although it was only 5:00 p.m. Since I was new to the country, naively, I protested. I didn't know that this was the routine. The driver handed over the keys quietly. They started shooting at our feet when I became really angry. The three of us in the front cabin, two passengers and the driver, were tied up in the "MIG" position and one of them pushed his gun against my throat. There were more than thirty passengers in the truck. No one uttered a word because they knew of the consequences. They accused us of helping the SNM and threatened to arrest us unless we paid them 20,000 shillings. The driver paid.

I couldn't bear the situation in Somalia, so I left and returned to Saudi Arabia on July 26. Then, on reflection, I decided I should return to my country. I couldn't just leave in anger. I came back on October 13 to resume my business.

Leaving the country was equally complicated, because myriad forms had to be filled out and there were endless bureaucratic procedures to comply with.

House to House Searches

Claiming that it was looking for SNM fighters and weapons, the military conducted systematic house-to-house searches. A particular area would be targeted, sealed off and sweeping searches would be carried out. Terrified residents would be woken up at 2:00 or 3:00 a.m., the house ransacked, valuables stolen and males would frequently be arrested on the spot. Often what they could not take, they destroyed. Many refugees commented to Africa Watch on the vindictive behavior of the soldiers: mirrors would be smashed and sacks of charcoal emptied on carpets and beds. Searches that accompanied arrests were particularly menacing; the entire house would be ransacked.

Because the government sometimes checked people's bank accounts, increasingly, people buried cash and valuables in their backyards, in the rubbish heaps, or among piles of coal to conceal from the soldiers when they came to search.

Leila Awad, a resident of Hargeisa told Africa Watch, when we interviewed her in Djibouti on August 2, 1989, of the fear that came to be associated with the sound of footsteps:

> Long before the war broke out, we became extremely alert to sound; it meant fear. Once the sun fell, and especially at nightfall, the only sound you heard was the soldiers' cars, their voices and footsteps, as they came to search and loot your home and arrest you or your relatives.

Amina Mohamoud Hussein, a mother of small children, interviewed by Africa Watch in Newport on July 7, 1989, described her experiences in Burao:

> 1987, when the SNM was operating in the Burao area, was probably the worst year for us.
>
> Night searches were terrible; they were particularly bad that year. There was no man in the house so I was really terrified. There were just me, my mother, my children and our maid. Behind our closed doors, we could hear the cries of women and the groans of men from the neighboring houses. Every time I heard that, I immediately opened all the suitcases and cupboards to avoid confrontation and the wrath of the soldiers who were violent at the slightest pretext. One night, I heard them in a neighbor's house. I got everything ready. When they came, they took my husband's shirts and among other things, some of my dresses for their wives.

According to Muse Saleh Ali, "Geldoon," of Burao:

> After the curfew fell, when there was no one in the street to lay their hands on, they went to people's homes to steal from them and do whatever they liked. They had their spies to tell them who was well off, who had recently received help from relatives and who owned what. They looked for any excuse to

80

harass that person in order to steal from them, including torturing and detaining them.

Similar experiences were in store for the residents of Hargeisa. Nura Abdillahi Farah, testified to Africa Watch in an interview in Djibouti on August 2, 1989, that:

> The 24th Sector of the army was the worst for house-to-house searches. They would steal right in front of you and you wouldn't dare say anything. When people heard of troops of the 24th Sector coming, they knew terror was in store. They kicked people out of bed. If they saw a man who looked very tired or covered in dust, automatically he was accused of being an SNM fighter. That was it for him. When they took men away, they kicked them with their heavy military boots all the way to the detention centers.

Sahra Ahmed Arteh, a housewife, the mother of eight children lived in Dulmegag Darea district of Hargeisa. She told Africa Watch when she was interviewed in London on June 17, 1989:

> We buried valuables and money for household expenses in the back of the house, under a tree or among the coal sacks. You would be woken up between 2:00 and 4:00 a.m. by soldiers and the house turned upside down. Adult men would be arrested. They were especially looking for young, able-bodied men, the flower of our community who they feared would defect to the SNM. Sometimes they arrested the mother too. You just watched in despair, helpless to do anything about it. In the morning, neighbors would exchange stories about who was arrested last night.

81

6. UNFAIR ECONOMIC PRACTICES

After 1981, when Isaaks became a constant target for intimidation, it became difficult to separate the government's economic motives from its political goals. Isaak businessmen, both in the north and in the south, suffered from discriminatory practices. Lines of credit at state banks were severely restricted, which was a major blow to businessmen as there are no private banks in Somalia. No Isaak could participate on equal footing in government tenders. Nor could Isaak businessmen obtain loans from banks, unless this was facilitated by a non-Isaak crony of the authority.

The government's policies had a drastic effect on the pastoral economy of the north, based on the export of livestock, primarily to the Middle East. Though the Isaaks contributed significantly to the livestock trade, and 90-95% of all livestock was exported through the northern port of Berbera, the cooperative set up to control the export of livestock did not employ Isaaks in senior positions.

Yusuf, a businessman in Hargeisa, interviewed by Africa Watch in Djibouti on August 9, 1989, insisted that:

> The only business persons who could survive were either those who were wealthy enough to buy their way with substantial bribes — something few could afford — or those who collaborated with the government by becoming informers. The others, those who couldn't master the survival tactics in that world, saw their businesses collapse, or just left the country. The message was clear: "You either buy the right to life and business or leave the country."

Restrictions which did not have general application but were directed exclusively against the Isaaks took many forms. Since 1981, if an Isaak businessman wanted to export goods, he had to have a pro-government non-Isaak partner to obtain a license. He could not get his goods through the customs unless he went through a well connected non-Isaak middleman. This applied to everything — cars, cement, rice, sugar, flour, matches and clothes. Permission to import became an important political tool to reward government supporters who resold the license to an Isaak businessman — at a profit. Many of the Isaaks who did not "cooperate," had their goods confiscated, and would be accused of bringing in "contraband" items. Everything became an opportunity to profiteer by government supporters — frankincense, cigarettes and matches.

Mohamed Ismail Kahin, a resident from Hargeisa, told Africa Watch in an interview in Cardiff on July 6, 1989, that:

> When I went to Berbera port to collect goods worth two million shillings, I was told openly that I would have to pay 1-1/2 million shillings on account of being Isaak. I had no choice but to pay a non-Isaak middleman 200,000 to collect the goods under his name. Businessmen were always being harassed to show documents and they would accuse us of selling "contraband" goods in order to confiscate and resell them.

The harassment of Isaak nomads, who reared the livestock the country depended on, further crippled the economy of the region. When nomads brought their livestock into town, they had to go through numerous military checkpoints where they had to pay exorbitant bribes. The government grew increasingly suspicious of the entire Isaak nomadic population, regarding it as a fifth column for the SNM. Often, their livestock was confiscated, on the allegation that it fed the SNM and the proceeds financed the movement. Soldiers sold the animals in town and kept the profits.*

Isaak petty traders, men and women, did not escape control and discrimination. Traders of coal, firewood and limestone had formed small associations to collect the raw material from the countryside and sell in the towns. The military confiscated and resold the goods. In the marketplace, petty traders had to pay for the "privilege" of using the ground where they spread their wares.

Safia Ali Mataan, interviewed by Africa Watch in London on August 17, 1989, provided details:

---

*   For details about the persecution of the nomadic population, see Chapter 7.

In the marketplace in Hargeisa, women who had sewing machines had to pay 10 shillings a day and 3000 shillings every six months. Even women selling milk did not escape. They paid 10 shillings for the spot on the ground that each container occupied and 3,000 shillings every six months. Of course, all these regulations affected principally Isaaks. When the odd non-Isaak was affected, once it was established that they were not Isaaks, he or she would be compensated.

In town, it was common for the soldiers to confiscate goods in a shop on the basis that "the army needs them." At best, the shop owner was given a worthless piece of paper saying how much the army owed him. Sometimes the shop owner was accused of inflating the price and threatened with arrest unless he paid even more; or, if he demanded this piece of paper, he might be arrested on the grounds that he showed "a lack of trust in the government." Refugees interviewed by Africa Watch stated that, frequently, high-ranking officials walked into shops and told the owner that "he had been ordered to give x percentage of his profits to the government." If the owner argued or failed to pay, the consequences were serious.

According to Khadija Jama Sugal, interviewed by Africa Watch in London on June 12, 1989 it was not only Isaaks in the north who suffered economic discrimination. Isaaks in Mogadishu were also at a severe disadvantage. She described the example of Hashi Afboor, who tried to obtain money from his bank account in Mogadishu in 1986. He was told he could withdraw the amount he requested on condition that he gave four non-Isaak men the money with which to start a business.

Kat, a leaf that is chewed and acts as a mild stimulant, is extremely popular in northern Somalia and plays an important role in the economy of the region. In addition, kat sessions are the most important gatherings among men to discuss private issues as well as social and political questions. Kat is grown principally in Ethiopia where the SNM had its bases. As a result, the kat trade acquired political significance. Kat businessmen traveled back and forth and were a useful conduit for information between the SNM and the townspeople. The government's decision to ban kat in March 1983 was essentially a means of limiting the flow of information between the SNM and their supporters in urban

85

centers. Another motive was to deny opportunities to air political and social grievances. Severe penalties were imposed for selling and possessing kat, which were made even stiffer in 1984. If a kat seller was arrested, he was accused not only of contraband activities but also of SNM links. A consequence of the ban on kat was to undermine the economy of the north.

When the ban was announced, kat farmers were promised compensation, such as new machinery, seeds and other material aid, but nothing was provided.

In spite of the ban, neither the availability nor the use of kat decreased. The military sold it illegally and established a highly lucrative black market. The penalities provided by law were used as a political tool. The new system made kat far more expensive. The fine for possession of kat was 100,000 shillings for the first offense and much higher fines for subsequent offenses. The military sold it; and then they, the NSS and the police arrested those who bought it. While the penalty for possession was severe, government officers who sold it did not suffer consequences.

Jama Osman Sugule, interviewed by Africa Watch in Djibouti on August 9, 1989, explained:

> In Burao, the sector commander [of the army] made it legal for civilians to sell the kat, in order to make it possible for soldiers to be an integral part of the trade and supplement their incomes, and also to encourage suppliers coming from Ethiopia to report on SNM activities. (He himself got the revenue and all the kat he wanted.) Many other military commanders wanted to adopt the same system but those in administration would not agree.

The new system facilitated political persecution by providing a pretext for charging people with "political" offenses. Often the military would target someone they wanted to arrest, sell them the kat and then arrest the person. Many were arrested in this fashion by NSS and soldiers to settle personal scores. Africa Watch heard several accounts of soldiers and NSS officers asking an unsuspecting civilian for a lift, dropping kat in their car, asking them to stop in front of the NSS office, only to have their car searched, to be arrested and their car confiscated.

86

7. THE WAR AGAINST THE NOMADS

Nomads, who lead a pastoral or semi-pastoral life in the countryside, constitute close to 60% of the population. Their principal economic activity, rearing livestock, is Somalia's main source of income, employment and exports. It generates more than 80% of the country's total exports and foreign exchange earnings and accounts for 60% of the labor force.

Isaak nomads have borne the brunt of the government's campaign against the Isaaks. Because we did not obtain government permission to visit northern Somalia, where the nomads live largely as displaced people who fled their homes, most of the refugees we interviewed were urban dwellers. This hampered our ability to obtain direct testimony from nomads. Nevertheless, because of the close family ties between many nomads and family members living in the towns and abroad, including regular and extended visits to relatives in the countryside, we were able to gather substantial information about patterns of repression and on individual cases of abuse. Among those we interviewed were many retired seamen who had lived in Cardiff and London, who had wives and children settled in the Somali countryside, who they had gone to join when they retired. Now that their families were refugees, they had returned, to make it possible for their families to come to Britain. [Since long before World War II, there have been communities of Somali seamen living in London, Cardiff, Sheffield and Liverpool.]

Without exception, every refugee we spoke with emphasized the hardships and casualties suffered by the nomads. They were politically and socially victimized because the government regarded them as the economic and manpower base behind the SNM. The fact of being an Isaak nomad aroused suspicion and was itself treated as grounds for harassment. It was determined to subdue the nomads and, thereby, to make the countryside inhospitable to the rebels. The government apparently saw terror as the best means of discouraging nomads from providing food, shelter or other logistical support to SNM fighters.

In fact, however, the government's policies turned its fears into a self-fulfilling prophecy. Radicalized by their experiences of military outrages, Isaak nomads now form the backbone of the SNM, both as fighters and as providers of shelter and food.

Nomads were apparently an easy target, vulnerable to extortion because of their lack of familiarity with the world of officialdom. Unable to master the art of arranging identity cards, filling out forms and understanding the corruption, overt and subtle, that characterized public life, they were an easy prey. They were more readily intimidated as they lacked access to information about their rights, or knowledge of bureaucracy. In addition, there are the problems of illiteracy and of nomadic culture, where there is no history of a relationship with any central government, let alone negotiating their right to live the way they want with the armed forces.

The nomads in the western coastal zone suffered less because they lived in regions traditionally also inhabited by non-Isaak clans, especially the Isse and Gadaboorsi. This gave them a measure of protection against indiscriminate attacks. But in the Gebiley and Tug Wajale area and the region bordering Ethiopia, there were only Isaaks. In these regions, only they would be affected by government terror. Moreover, this region was close to Ethiopia and was, therefore, close to SNM bases. There was a significant military presence to "contain" SNM activities, facilitating abuses.

Nomads went into towns primarily to sell their livestock and to buy goods such as sugar and rice. It became increasingly difficult to undertake these journeys because of the numeorus military checkpoints along the way. At each stop, both the passengers and the driver had to pay bribes. To operate at a profit, the driver had to raise the fare he charged his passengers. The goods they bought would have to be displayed on the return journey at the military checkpoints, and were sometimes confiscated on the grounds that they were being taken to the "bandits" in hiding. The system discouraged urban dwellers from sending goods to their relatives in the countryside, which further penalized the nomadic population. The required bribes were often higher than the price of the goods being sent.

Dabar Goynta Isaaka ("The Isaak Exterminators"), a well-mechanized section of the army which consisted entirely of non-Isaaks, widely regarded as one of the most abusive forces engaged in counter-insurgency activities, was responsible for "dealing" with the nomads. They, and other branches of the military terrorized the countryside.

Yusuf Hussein Siarak, a resident of Burao and a former seaman interviewed by Africa Watch in Cardiff on July 8, 1989, described the attitude of the military:

> They knew these people were civilians but their attitude was "You are all Isaaks, that's enough." As soon as there was a confrontation with the SNM, the people in the area, who had nothing to do with the SNM, paid with their lives.

The following accounts describe typical abuses that resulted from the military's apparent belief that, if the SNM was operating in an area, the residents must be actively supporting them.

In an interview on October 27, 1989, Safia Hashi Madar, a former political prisoner, told Africa Watch about the case of Habiba Yusuf Liiban, who was in Hargeisa Central Prison at the same time as Safia.

> Habiba is a farmer's wife in her fifties, arrested on October 15, 1984, in Gogol Wanaag, a small village near Arabsiyo in the northwest, accused of having allowed an SNM fighter to sleep one night outside their home and giving him food. Her husband, aged 65, who was just returning from a visit when the soldiers arrived, was also arrested. Their hut was burned and their livestock killed.

> They were detained for four nights in a nearby military compound, then taken towards Arabsiyo. Between Arabsiyo and Gebiley, she was sentenced to life imprisonment while standing under a tree. The "sentence," which was never confirmed by a court of law or even a military tribunal, was imposed by the military commander in charge of that district. She was then transferred to Hargeisa Central Prison. Her "sentence" was commuted to 15 years imprisonment in October 1986. A soldier living in the vicinity and one of the men working on their farm told the soldiers who arrrested her that her husband was away at the time of the incident. He was beaten, and

detained for about seven months. She was released in August 1989.

In an interview with Africa Watch in Cardiff on July 6, 1989, Abdi Kahin Hadliyeh, a retired seaman, recalled during incident in Arabsiyo:

On May 18, 1988 a military car exploded because of a land mine in the Arabsiyo region. Sixty-five farmers were arrested and taken to the army headquarters. They were interrogated and ordered to clear out of the area within ten days. These were settled farmers, not nomads. They moved nearer to the Ethiopian border, but of course they lost their farms, their source of livelihood.

Jama Osman Sugule, interviewed by Africa Watch in Djibouti on August 9, 1989, provided another vivid example:

In early November 1987, the SNM ambushed two fuel tankers en route from Djibouti to Garoe. The ambush took place near Burao. The tankers were released but the army learned of the incident and a clash with the SNM followed. The military brought the tankers to Burao. A Djibouti national who owned the tankers went there and claimed them. Instead of getting his property, the army asked him to compensate the loss of their men and equipment. The military commander confiscated 150 camels from nomads living in the area who, he claimed, were the same clan as the SNM fighters responsible for the ambush. The owners complained to the military authorities in Hargeisa. For once, inquiries were made. The army found out that the families who owned the confiscated camels were not the same clan as the SNM fighters identified by the army. They chose another group of nomads who they claimed were the same clan and ordered them to reimburse the camels, though there was no evidence that these civilians had any involvement with the ambush or that the information about the identity of the SNM fighters was reliable. War broke out in May 1988 before the case was settled.

He also told Africa Watch that:

In late June or early July 1987, the governor of Las Anod was killed by the SNM. The military demanded that Isaak civilians living in the region pay 120 camels "in exchange," although they had nothing to do with the killing.

Mawliid Nuh, interviewed by Africa Watch in Djibouti on August 11, 1989, reported that:

> Shortly before the President's visit to Gebiley, the SNM had hijacked a water tanker belonging to the government near the village of Kalabeyd. In retaliation, the government confiscated 10 water tankers belonging to Isaaks, and 18 people, the drivers and their assistants, were arrested. Government forces surrounded the stream where people congregated to fetch water and to water their animals. The authorities accused the residents of gathering at the stream in order to assist the SNM and facilitate their ambushes. Three people and many animals were killed; countless others were wounded.

The soldiers themselves called on wealthy families and left their tracks. They would return shortly afterwards and insist that SNM fighters had left the tracks. If the nomads proved recalcitrant in meeting the soldiers' demands for "compensation," or at times irrespective of this, many were killed, some arrested and their animals confiscated. Apparently, many in the military were intent on using the nomads as a source of personal enrichment.

Long before war broke out in May 1988, significant numbers of nomads had fled as a result of these practices, and had sought sanctuary in Ethiopia.

Mona Ahmed Yusuf, "Qulumbe," interviewed by Africa Watch in London on July 2, 1989, discussed the reasons for the flight of nomads:

> The village of Haji Saleh [near Burao], inhabited by Isaaks, was burned down in 1983 on the basis that it was too close to SNM bases in Ethiopia. All the water reservoirs were blown up by landmines and the people were ordered to evacuate the place within three hours. They took what they could and then the whole village was burned. Nothing was left to stand. Until the refugees from the war started to pour in, there was not a single person, not even a goat, living there from 1983-1988.

To test where the sympathies of the local nomadic population lay, the military sometimes dressed in "guerrilla" uniforms and posed as SNM fighters. They enquired, "Have you seen anything of the SNM lately?" If they detected pro-SNM sympathies, the nomads would be punished accordingly.

Punishment took many forms.

91

Destruction of Reservoirs

One of the common methods of forcing nomads to abandon their settlements was to deny them access to their reservoirs. Reservoirs, known as *barkad* in Somali, are square or rectangular underground storage-tanks with cement lined stone or concrete walls, built for collecting water during the rainy season, to be used for human and animal consumption during the dry season. They are a valuable asset in a country that is dry for much of the year and which has often been afflicted by droughts. Though a calculable investment, they are expensive to build. They are usually constructed with the financial assistance of relatives working abroad or in the cities.

Because of their importance to the survival and economy of the rural population, reservoirs were a special target of the military's campaign against the nomads.

Muse Saleh Ali, "Geldoon," described the behavior of the military in an interview with Africa Watch on July 6, 1989:

> Soldiers either passing through or with temporary barracks in the area came and helped themselves to the water and the owner couldn't say a word. If they found the owner, they simply asked for the keys and the reservoir was theirs. If the owner uttered a word, he might be shot on the spot. Frequently, they didn't even wait for the owner, they just forced their way in.

> Often, they also burned down the houses of the farmers. This happened to Farah Mohamed Awad and Abdillahi Jama. In 1986, the villages of Dagah Dheer, Bayda and Gool Allahleh were burned and reservoirs mined and blown up.

When the army learned of the presence of large herds in a certain area, they surrounded the settlement and took the livestock they wanted to their compounds. What they didn't need for themselves, they "sold" back to the owners.

Yassin Karshe Mohamed, interviewed by Africa Watch in Cardiff on July 7, 1989, reported:

> After spending so much money in constructing reservoirs, the owners were often not even allowed to drink from them, never

mind their animals. If there were soldiers living in the area, the reservoirs became theirs. In early 1988, Wais Aw Hassan was refused permission to draw water from a reservoir he owned in Warabeye in Burao region. When he inquired if at least the family could drink from it, even if the animals could not be brought there, he was arrested and detained for eight weeks in a nearby military compound. He was only released after his family gave some camels to the soldiers and he agreed to give up title to the reservoir, handing it over completely to the military. He was warned that he would be arrested if he tried to reclaim his property.

Yusuf Hussein Siarak, spoke of his family's problems:

My brothers owned a reservoir in Ballidhiig. They weren't allowed to use it for seven years. The government took it over without any compensation. There were 180 reservoirs in the area and very few people were able to use any of them. The army confiscated most of them and resold the water to the owners. The owners did not dare to claim them, for fear of being shot. Many of them fled out of fear.

Ismail Dualeh Mohamed, a former seaman interviewed by Africa Watch in Cardiff on July 6, 1989, elaborated:

When there is a drought in the countryside, water is brought in tanks which are loaded onto trucks. Frequently, the government confiscated the tanks in order to force people and livestock to come to the wells near the cities. That way, it was easier for the army to confiscate the livestock, with the rationale that everyone in the countryside supported the SNM or, even worse, had family members involved in it. But the people were often afraid to come to the cities, in spite of the drought.

The rape of women in the countryside was common. Women tended the animals in remote areas on their own. The isolation facilitated rape.

Soldiers in military compounds in the countryside, went to "look for food." During the day, many identified families with means, or with attractive daughters as their prey for that night.

When confronted by the military, refugees told Africa Watch, nomads would be extravagantly generous, hoping that would appease their "guests" and they would be left in peace.

Yusuf Hussein Siarak explained that, sadly, that was of no use:

At the end of 1987, some soldiers visited Aw Harrir Nur. He was very hospitable. They repaid him by raping his daughter and ill treating his wife. When he protested, they beat him.

Nomads were also subjected to double "taxation." Everything they brought into the cities —- milk, ghee and animals —- was taxed. Then they would have to pay a tax on the goods they bought, such as rice and flour.

Land Mines

Africa Watch heard from many sources that land mines have been used extensively by the government since the end of the Ogaden war, as part of its strategy against incursions by the Ethiopian army. However, from 1984, the indiscriminate use of land mines became a central feature of its counter-insurgency policy against the SNM. The mines used were apparently imported mainly from Egypt, though it is not clear if they were actually manufactured in Egypt. They also included American and Italian-made mines. Africa Watch has not been able to conduct its own independent investigations on the question of the use of landmines.

According to the information we received, land mines have been used to blow up:

1. Reservoirs

2. After 1984, when the SNM began incursions into the cities, the government started to mine a number of the main routes leading in and out of cities.

3. Roads leading to army compounds, no matter how temporary the barracks. The army would use other roads in order to avoid the mines, but many soldiers were killed by the mines they planted.

4. Once the army suspects the SNM to be in a particular vicinity, the roads that it thought the SNM might use were mined.

Hundreds of non-combatants were killed and maimed as a result. In addition, thousands of camels and other livestock were killed and wounded. In turn, the armed forces engaged in severe reprisals against civilians when its personnel were victimized by landmines.

In January 1989, Community Aid Abroad, an Australian agency operating in the Sanaag region reported that:

> Widespread massacre occurred after 2 soldiers were blown up with a landmine in Elafweyn District. In reprisal the military commander of Sanaag ordered the deaths of 200 nomads. One hundred and three men, women and children were slaughtered the following day."*

Jama Osman Sugule, testified that:

> Before the war, the soldiers placed mines around their settlements and if a camel was blown up by a mine, they asked the owner to compensate them for the cost of the mine.

Ahmed Abdillahi Hareed, "Weraar," told Africa Watch in an interview in Djibouti on August 10, 1989, that:

> In August 1985, an army truck was blown up on a two mile feeder road that connected the main asphalt road to the military barracks near Arabsiyo. The driver was killed. The army responded with massive retaliation against the residents living within 30 kilometers of the area; many residents were shot, livestock confiscated and many huts burned.

> Since 1982, the army mined the areas along the main roads, several kilometers from their compounds, to ward off the SNM, but hundreds of unsuspecting civilians and animals were killed. No signs were used to warn civilians.

Ahmed Mohamed Hawsi, "Kirih," interviewed by Africa Watch in London on July 9, 1989, recalled, among the victims of landmine explosions in the period before the war:

> Mohamed Ali Guled, who died in early May 1988 outside Hargeisa and Mohamed Ogle, whose car was blown up by a land mine near Geedbalaahd in 1984.

---

*   Community Aid Abroad, Agency Statement on Somalia, January 12, 1989.

8. THE WAR AGAINST STUDENTS

The arrest of the Hargeisa group and their trial in February 1982 radicalized the student community and turned schools virtually into a war zone between the government and students. (The students were secondary and intermediate school students, not university students). The unrest that erupted on February 20, when the Hargeisa group was due to stand trial, lasted a week. The trial had to be postponed for a few days because of the violent protests spearheaded by students. Outraged by the detention of men, including their own teachers, who they looked up to as role models, students in school uniforms took to the streets of Hargeisa to express their anger. They lashed out at every symbol of government — throwing stones at soldiers, government buildings and vehicles and tearing school books. Hargeisa came to a standstill.

The military turned the full force of their weapons against the demonstrators. They responded with excessive and indiscriminate use of live ammunition, killing five, including students. Hundreds of students and others were arrested. Eighteen female students were sentenced to six months imprisonment at Hargeisa Central Prison, and two hundred male students were sent to Mandera Prison. Many businessmen were arrested after the riots, on the grounds that they were responsible for the disturbances; most spent as long as seven months in Mandera prison. The memorandum* submitted to President Barre shortly after the riots by a group of elders made the following comments about the behavior of the army.

> It is true that when some women and children began to throw stones, the commander of the 26th division who is considered by members of the public as the real Regional Chairman ordered his men into the city, complete with heavy equipment including armored cars; that the unarmed people on the streets were fired upon. This extreme measure was taken

---

*   For details about the memorandum, see Background chapter.

without verifying first whether the police force could deal with the situation themselves. It is certainly true that the gravity of the unrest was not such as to warrant the use of heavy armor. So far no enquiry has been ordered to identify those responsible for the deaths and the people are waiting for such enquiry to be instituted in the interest of justice.

Yunis was a 15-year-old student at the time, at Ga'An Libaah Secondary School. Interviewed by Africa Watch in Djibouti on August 2, 1989, he described the effect of the arrests on the students:

When they imprisoned our teachers, doctors, engineers and our intellectuals it became clear to us that the government did not want the north to develop, educationally or economically.

Ibrahim Hussein Abdi, also 15 at the time, was interviewed by Africa Watch in London on July 26, 1989, echoed the same feelings.

We saw the arrest of the Hargeisa group as a proof of the government's determination to suppress the north, because these men only wanted to improve local facilities.

Students were singled out as a special target of government hostility because of their effectiveness in galvanizing public opposition to the arrest of the Hargeisa group. Their defiance unsettled the government. In the absence of an internal opposition political party or dissident movement, students constituted the sole visible challenge to military authority in the north and as such, were to become the focus of the government's determination to quell unrest in the region.

The government's response to student unrest was a campaign to undermine their effectiveness. The military and security forces adopted tough measures to break the student protests. After 1982, the presence of heavily armed soldiers became a feature of school life. At a hint of "trouble," or simply to cow the students, they stormed on to school premises, fired live ammunition and then arrested the students as they ran for cover. Many students were killed in these confrontations and many more were injured. The government's violent response only made the students more radical.

At first, the students were united in their anti-government stand. To counter their cohesion, the government established "committees," composed both of ordinary students and adults planted in the classrooms, representing the NSS and the Party, to discourage meetings and discussions. The effect was to drive student protest underground.

Motivated initially by a limited objective, the release of the Hargeisa group, the subsequent politicization of the student community turned into a challenge to the totality of government policy and to the basis on which its authority rested. Increasingly, students voiced the grievances of their parents and the community at large. They condemned the killings, the arrests, the detentions, the neglect of public facilities, including schools, the curfews and the house-to-house searches.

According to both former teachers and students, the government used education as a political tool, a policy that became increasingly apparent after February 1982. Isaak students were accused of SNM involvement.

Ismail Hassan Yusuf, now 23 and living in London, where he was interviewed by Africa Watch on June 9, 1989, was a student in Hargeisa until 1984. He was at Farah Omaar Secondary School. He was a member of the United Somali Student Organization (USSO), created after the arrest of the Hargeisa group. He explained why the students felt it necessary to organize public demonstrations and to distribute pamphlets critical of government policies:

> Our initial aim in creating USSO was to ensure proper teaching after the chaos that followed the arrest of the Hargeisa group. We wanted to explain our concerns to the government, especially our feelings about the arrest of our teachers. We realized there was no justice. We had to be secretive because if our meetings became publicly known, we would be arrested. Our first priority was to become strong from within. Once we had achieved that, then we could openly challenge the government. We decided on a secret campaign to mobilize the public.

> In the midst of getting established, we learned that the teachers and the doctors group were to be brought to court on February 20, 1982. There was a rumor that some of them would be condemned to death. Many schools organized a big demonstration to coincide with the trial dates. The court was surrounded by soldiers. There was a confrontation. At first

they fired warning shots but the use of live ammunition started very early on. The soldiers chased us. Many students were arrested. Civilians got killed and wounded. About 300-400 people, overwhelmingly students, were arrested. For a month, there was a curfew.

Luckily, none of the members of the USSO were arrested. Around April, life became somewhat normal. We returned to schools and continued our meetings. We also distributed leaflets, encouraging people to demonstrate. People were very scared. No one would dare to act on one's own. So people had to be encouraged by showing them that they were not alone.

Our leaflets began to go beyond narrow questions that affected only students, and started to address the wider problems in the community, such as the arrests, restrictions on food supplies either through the tax system or confiscation by the army. This led to shortages and inflation and meant poor people going hungry. For example, during the month of the curfew, no new food shipments entered Hargeisa.

After April, soldiers started to search people's homes, looking for weapons. They came at 3:00 a.m. and turned houses inside out, terrifying the residents.

From April 1982-1984, we continued to distribute leaflets. We intensified our leaflet campaigns around February 20, the anniversary of the 1982 demonstrations. [The commemoration of the demonstrations, known popularly as "Dhagahtur," "Stonethrowing" became important political events and were the occasions for vigilant confrontation between the army and civilians, especially students.]

During this period, killings, arrests and torture increased. The quality of teaching deteriorated as teachers became intimidated. School was no longer safe. Whenever soldiers wanted to arrest students and teachers who they thought were anti -government, they came to the school as it was easier to find them there. The teachers even stopped coming to school. So there was not much point for the students to come either. Non-Isaak students were encouraged to spy for the government. In spite of all that, our organization grew stronger as our ranks swelled and our organizational ability improved.

In July 1984, one of the members of our organization, Mohamed Ismail, was arrested accidentally. He was together with a group of students in a tea shop when soldiers came to arrest them. He was taken to the NSS Headquarters and tortured very badly. So of course he confessed and identified the other members of the USSO. Three members of our organization, the oldest of whom was 19 or 20, were arrested that night in their homes. The next day, when the rest of us found out what had happened, we fled. About 15 of us left, some towards Djibouti and others towards Ethiopia.

The three who were arrested were Nur Hussein, Mohamoud Sheikh Ibrahim and Mohamed Bashe. The last two had been particularly active members of the organization. They were both subsequently sentenced to death in October 1984. Nur Hussein was released after few months but he was badly tortured while in custody. He had not been that involved so he couldn't give them a lot of information.

The families of the students were not spared. The relatives of those who escaped had to pay the price.

Ismail continued:

The father of Mohamed Hashi was arrested and ordered to bring his son; otherwise they threatened to kill him. When he couldn't, he was sentenced to twenty years in prison in October 1984. He was a wealthy businessman. His cars and property were also confiscated. Many others suffered a similar fate. Ibrahim Ali Askar's brother was arrested and tortured to reveal his brother's whereabouts. He was tried in October 1984 though later released.

Ibrahim Hussein Abdi, described government tactics to control the students and their consequences:

Education deteriorated year after year. After only two hours at school, the teachers would leave. Those were the conscientious ones. The others simply never turned up. The students could see that both the living conditions and the political situation were getting worse every year. Soldiers came to the schools with their tanks and fired into the air. Students ran and then they would be arrested and beaten. Those who really could not tolerate the situation left to join the SNM. Soldiers

101

were enrolled into the schools as "students" to spy on us and discourage meetings. Some of these were obvious, but not always. From September to October 21, it became compulsory to attend rehearsals for the October 21 celebrations. Students who refused to participate were arrested. Many of us took part in demonstrations to show our opposition.

Many politically active students, like others taken into custody for "political" offenses were tortured. Interrogation of political suspects in Somalia is routinely accompanied by violence to extract a confession of personal guilt and to elicit information about collaborators. Students were not spared, in spite of their youth.

Bombs had exploded at several places where local government officials used to meet, including "Harunta Hisbiga," the Hargeisa headquarters of the SRSP.* Despite the damage to property, there were no reports of civilians killed or wounded. The SNM claimed responsibility for the bombs and announced this on their radio. Nonetheless, students were accused of being involved.

On June 26, 1984, Hargeisa celebrated the anniversary of northern Somalia's independence from Britain. The authorities interpreted the celebrations as an act of disloyalty. The authorities, who had been keeping a close watch on schools, suspected students of inciting the public against the government and being behind these activities. In addition, a number of Isaak elders recived leaflets, warning them against collaboration with the government. The government accused students of having distributed the leaflets. The HANGASH (Military Police) visited secondary schools, warning the students of the consequences of their anti-government attitude.

Abdirizak Ibrahim Koshen, a student at 26 June Secondary School, was arrested in July 1984 and tried on September 29. Interviewed by Africa Watch in London on June 7, 1989, he provided details of the torture.

According to Abdirizak, he was in a tea shop with two school friends, when, at 11:00 a.m., on July 1, a group of soldiers arrived from the *HANGASH* approached him. They ordered him into a land rover. He was taken to the

---

*   Somali Revolutionary Socialist Party.

Qaybta, the headquarters of the regional military commander, notorious for ill treatment of detainees during interrogation sessions.

I was left alone in a dark cell. I was not given any food or drink all day. At 3:00 a.m. I was taken to a room full of soldiers in full military uniform, sitting around a table. They asked me my name, my school and other details. One of them took out a list and asked me if I knew any of the names on the list. I recognized one or two, students in my school. He kept going through the list, saying, "But you must know so and so. Isn't he a friend of yours?" I replied that I didn't know the name. "But he knows you," they replied, "so you must know him too." Then one of the group, who seemed to be the leader, said, "Bring him to me once he confesses to knowing these people." While I was being interrogated, I heard the screams of people being tortured.

Then I was taken to another room, also full of soldiers. Some of them had their faces covered; only their eyes were visible. As I entered the room, I saw chains, ropes and clubs on the floor. They slapped and shouted at me, demanding that I confess. I told them that I didn't have anything to confess. They hit me with clubs. I was told to strip and again they beat me with the clubs, this time very hard. I fell to the floor. One of them leaned over me and said, "Why don't you confess to what they are demanding from you." Another one took a rope and tied my hands together and then my feet. The others kicked me with their heavy boots. The most painful thing was when one of them squeezed my penis. The pain was excruciating. I lost consciousness.

Later, I woke up in a dark room. After a while, the door opened and a soldier gave me some rice in a tin. I was still tied which made it difficult to eat. In the middle of the next night, they took me a short distance by car. Another interrogation session began. One of the interrogators put his cigarette out on my left hand. Again the same questions and the same answers. Then they brought in a group of men who looked sick and exhausted. They had obviously been beaten. Their eyes were swollen, their faces puffed, and they had wounds on their foreheads. The interrogators asked me if I knew any of them. Even if they were people I had known previously, it was

103

difficult to recognize them in their present condition. I eventually recognized one of them, a schoolmate. They asked me and then them if we knew each other. Only he recognized me. They were taken out and I was warned about my obstinacy. I replied that I was not being obstinate — after all, only one of them had recognized me.

I was taken to the torture room. This time I was really terrified because I knew what to expect. They kicked and beat me with the clubs, repeating, "Why don't you confess? You are a young man with a future to think of." They tied me in the MIG position. Then they hung a rope from a hook in the ceiling, tied the rope around me and beat me with a club while they swung the rope continuously to accentuate the contorted position. You cannot control your body in that position and you start to urinate. It is physically painful and humiliating. Then they released me and I fell straight on to the floor. They untied the ropes and told me to stand up. But I couldn't. They kicked me so I tried to get up but I couldn't. Some of them half-lifted me and dragged me back to the interrogation room. Again, I could hear screams coming from some of the other rooms. I was seated down and one of them said, "Now, I think you will recognize your friends." I gave the same reply as before. I was left in a room where I stayed for a whole day with no food. Then a third night of interrogation and torture started, with the MIG and the whole routine. At the end, I confessed to knowing all the names they showed me.

The next day I was given some rice in a tin, only once. When night came, I was taken before the same soldiers. They asked me if I knew of an organization called "SSN," or "Victory,"* and the names of several other organizations. I replied no. Then they showed me pamphlets dating back to 1982 with the names of these organizations. They asked if I had been involved in these organizations or in distributing the pamphlets. "Weren't you involved in those bombs?" I said no, that I was merely a secondary school student. For the next three months, I was tortured and interrogated regularly at night. On three

---

*   Africa Watch has learned nothing of these groups and is unable to determine whether they ever existed.

separate occasions, I was taken out in the middle of the night, blindfolded, with my arms and hands tied, and driven in a car. In the middle of nowhere, I was placed in a sack and immersed in a hole, very deep, full of water, thorns and scratchy leaves. The thorns bit into my skin. Some of them are still in my body, especially in my feet and thighs.*

After a while a new person was taking the lead in the interrogations. He was Ahmed Aden, the new head of the NSS in the northern region. Then Gani [regional military commander] came to see me. For a few days, the beatings and interrogations stopped. Gani said that we were going to be tried soon. Two other boys had joined me in my cell. I did not know them. They turned out to be Isaaks, of course, studying at the University in Mogadishu. They had been arrested in Mogadishu and transferred to Hargeisa.

A few nights later, I was taken to a room packed with soldiers and one man in plain clothes. He said he was from the National Security Court [NSC]. He asked me to read a paper which he said was my confession. I read it. He asked me if this was what I had wanted to say. He encouraged me to tell him if it was not the truth, saying I could trust him because he was a "judge". Because of these words, I replied honestly. I said it was not the truth. He slapped me and subsequently participated in my torture. Then they forced me to "sign" the document. They took my thumb, pressed it on an ink pad and then on a paper which said that I had distributed anti-government pamphlets, that I was a member of the organizations they mentioned, that I was involved in the SNM, and that all these organizations were behind the recent bombings.

Abdirizak added that on returning to his room, he discovered that his two companions had had similar experiences. A few days later, twenty of them, all secondary school students, were transferred to Hargeisa Central Prison. They were kept in one room and not allowed out of their cells for a week. Their families brought them food, but they were not permitted to see them. No

---

* Africa Watch interviewer observed scars on Abdirizak that comported with his account of torture. He complained of lasting injuries that caused him pain.

105

medical treatment was available. During the first week, they were given papers specifying the charges against them, which ranged from seeking secession of the north, to plotting the assassination of government officials, to involvement in the recent wave of bombings and participation in distributing anti-government pamphlets. They were asked if they wanted their own lawyers or government-appointed lawyers. Abdirizak chose to have his own lawyer. He sent the charge sheet to his mother and uncle and they arranged a lawyer for him. He saw his lawyer once, briefly, when he came to ask him about the charges.

On September 29, the students were taken to the NSC. The president of the court, Ghelle, presided. The public prosecutor read the charges. Government officials and witnesses packed the court. Each defendant was allowed to have two relatives in the court. In practice, the court kept relatives out by stating that standing was not permitted in the court, and packing the court with militiamen.

The witnesses were mainly the military officers who had interrogated and tortured the students. The elders, whom they were accused of having threatened, were also present. Soldiers who testified for the government were unable to state that they had caught the students "red-handed." Their lawyers argued that the charges, based on confessions signed after interrogation could not be used as evidence. The elders denied that the students had given them the pamphlets. The trial lasted all day and night, then the court adjourned for the verdict. On October 3, the defendants were chained to each other and taken to the NSC. The court was surrounded by soldiers. Ghelle stated that he did not want to see any signs of emotion when the verdicts were announced. Then the sentences were read out. Seven students were sentenced to death, including Abdirizak, 9 to life sentence, 3 to 3 years and 1 to 15 years.

The students were transferred to Mandera Prison near Berbera. Conditions at Mandera are reported to be harsh. There is a military compound nearby, which ensures tight security.

The seven students condemned to death were taken to death-row, known as "Qabta," [This word is derived from the Somali word "to bang" and was probably used because of the steel doors.] This wing has eight small cells with steel doors and bars and no windows. Three of them shared a cell and the

106

other four shared another cell. They were chained together at night. Death row had its own special guards and security was tight. Food was scarce. Prisoners were given maize ("galay") or sorghum ("hadhudh") in a tin and water once a day. Once a week prisoners were taken to an outside toilet. The rest of the time, they had to relieve themselves in their cells.

When a political incident occurred, such as an SNM attack, prisoners were tortured. There was no medical help. They were not allowed family visits. Executions at Mandera were frequent, but prisoners did not know when their turn would come.

On November 24, 1984, a Somali Airlines passenger plane was hijacked by three civilians, two teachers and a member of the Somali Custodial Corps, to publicize the plight of the students and seek their release.

On January 28, 1986, the death sentences were commuted to life imprisonment after appeals to the president. Abdirizak and a number of the other students interviewed by Africa Watch believe that international publicity made the critical difference. They were transferred to a section called the "cellars," built like Qabta, but with more rooms. The "cellars" were apparently built initially as punishment cells for problem prisoners who could not be handled in the ordinary prison. They stayed there several months under conditions similar to Qabta. On March 20 1986, without explanation, one of the group, Abdi Dhama Abby, was executed by a firing squad, reportedly on Gani's orders.

After several months, the students were transferred to the ordinary section of the prison which was overcrowded. At one point, Abdirizak told Africa Watch, he shared a cell with 52 others. Conditions did not improve.

After the May 1988 SNM attack on Burao, heavily armed soldiers surrounded the prison. From May 27, prisoners were not taken out of their cells and were given nothing to eat. Additional soldiers were flown in from Burao; then some of the guards joined the soldiers in patrolling the prison.

Abdirizak and the other students were released when the SNM stormed Mandera Prison and freed all the prisoners on June 5, 1988. About 750 inmates were released, many of them political prisoners.

Mohamed Bashe Ali is another of the students arrested in July 1984, sentenced to death and sent to Mandera. Interviewed by Africa Watch in

Djibouti on August 3, 1989, his description of torture is similar to the testimony of other former students we interviewed:

> I was a student at 26 June Secondary school. I was arrested in July 1984, accused of involvement with the SNM. We were sitting for our exams when another boy and I were arrested. We were taken to the *Qaybta*. I was blindfolded and taken to underground cells and tortured in various contorted positions, the "MIG" and the "shilling."* I was beaten with clubs. I was brought face to face with what they described as a "witness" to my crimes, a poor boy who had also been badly tortured. On one occasion, they put a loaded gun in my mouth, threatening to blow my brains out.
>
> After all the pain and the isolation, you give in and confess to whatever they want. The worst was when the torturer grabbed my penis and pulled and pulled. The pain was unbearable. After that I admitted to whatever they accused me of.
>
> I was returned to my cell, but even when the physical torture stopped, the intimidation continued. They used food as a weapon to weaken and frighten us. They gave us only a bit of rice in a tin once a day.
>
> On October 3, 1984, we were taken to court. The prosecutor argued that it was essential to sentence us to death because, if we are so anti-government now, at this age, what would we be like later? He said it was important to discipline the young in the north. We were sentenced to death and taken the next day to Mandera Prison.
>
> At Mandera, we assumed we would be killed because so many people were executed during our time there.

When an increasing number of students left to join the SNM, this made life more difficult for those who remained behind. As the NSS learned the identities of the students who left, they approached their friends, interrogated them and frequently arrested them.

---

* The "shilling" is a form of torture practiced in Somalia where the victim's hands and feet are tied so tightly behind his or her back that when the victim is placed on the floor, face down, only a small part of the chest touches the floor. The word implies that the part of the chest that touches the floor is very small, like the coin for which this practice is named.

A group of six students and their former teacher were arrested in Hargeisa in July 1985, accused of involvement with the SNM. On May 31, 1986, three were condemned to death, three to life imprisonment and one to fifteen years. Many of their relatives were also arrested and spent eight months in prison. The group included a brother and sister, Fiaza Dahir Jama and Saeed Dahir Jama.

Hassan Osman Omer, was one of those students. He was also released on June 5, 1988 when the SNM overran Mandera Prison. He is now in Dire Dawa, Ethiopia. He described, in a written interview, the torture that he and other students endured.

> I was among several students...accused of political subversion and jailed in mid-July 1985. The national security court punished some of us to death on May 3, 1986. On September 28, 1986 the so called Government commuted the death penalty to life sentence. During my jail term and before, I had all sorts of torture, [which] made me to lose my left eye. It is [now] completely unfunctional and it affected some of my other senses. I have not had any medical [treatment] whatsoever during my stay in jail ...I feel we were in a concentration camp ...not in jail...I'm in Dire-Dawa, Ethiopia with another two of my fellow prisoners, Saeed Dahir Jama ...and Elias Qasa Farah who lost his limb during our torture. [Elias is said to be paralyzed in one arm].

Student trouble was not limited to Hargeisa. Similar student activities were also common in Burao during these years. Hundreds of students, male and female, were arrested and sentenced to long terms in Mandera prison.

Mohamoud Ahmed Isse, interviewed by Africa Watch in London on June 26, 1989, described the mood among students in Burao.

> I was at Sheikh Bashir secondary school in 1982. We wanted to show our solidarity with the students in Hargeisa, so there were sympathy demonstrations in Burao. In February 1982, teachers were also arrested in Burao, including Omer "Sugume" and Abdi Askari who were at our school. About 350 students were arrested. They spent four months in Mandera Prison. At first all the students were united. Then they began divide and rule tactics to poison the non-Isaaks

against the Isaaks. After that, soldiers disguised as students joined the schools to discourage political activity and discussions among the students.

Ahmed Saeed Elmi, was interviewed by Africa Watch in London on June 14, 1989. He had left school in Burao shortly before his arrest:

In October 1987, I was accused of distributing anti-government pamphlets in Burao. I was standing outside my father's shop when at 10:00 a.m., two security officers approached me and forced me into a car. They took me to the NSS headquarters. The head of the NSS, Abdiqani, came to see me at 11:00 p.m. I had had nothing to eat all day. He told me to confess and to name the others involved in distributing the pamphlets. I denied the accusations and told him that I didn't know of anyone involved. At midnight, I was blindfolded and driven to a place about 10 kilometers outside Burao. I was stripped naked and pails of water were poured over me. I was whipped with long strips of tire and beaten with heavy clubs. I was held in the MIG position. I saw Abdiqani again. He said that some of my friends at school had informed him that I was involved in anti-government activities, including distributing the pamphlets. He said that as they already had the "proof" of my guilt, all they wanted from me was the names of my collaborators. I didn't say anything. Frustrated, he threw his teacup at me, which cut my forehead. For the next two weeks, I was beaten every day. Then the beatings stopped. I remained in prison until May 27, 1988, when the SNM broke into the jail in Burao.

One of the other students in prison was Seke Osman Liiban, also accused of distributing anti-government pamphlets. He had been arrested in March 1987. He had been so severely tortured that when I came to prison, only six months later, he was mentally disturbed.

Omer Mohamed Geti, 13, was in Biyada'ay Intermediate School in Hargeisa when the war broke out. He fled with his family to Ethiopia and arrived in London in May 1989 where he was interviewed by Africa Watch on June 17. He described the difficulties of school life:

There was no proper schooling. The teachers got paid very little. The students had to collect money for them. Each

110

student in the elementary and intermediate school had to pay 70 shillings a month and students in the secondary schools 110 shillings. We had to give the money to the form master and he would share it out among all the teachers. If we didn't pay, either we couldn't sit for our exams or we were failed. If we were late with the payment, we were threatened with this kind of punishment.

Life in school was tense. There were leaflets distributed in the courtyard, saying "Down with the government" and writing on the walls saying the same thing. We didn't dare look for fear that we would be accused of having written the words ourselves. The headmaster, Hassan "Qahar," would burn the leaflets. He had to tell the Ministry of Education he had done this, otherwise he might be arrested himself. When this did not stop the leaflets, soldiers were sent to spend the night in the schools, to catch those responsible for distributing the leaflets. Still, there were leaflets everywhere because the soldiers did not sleep there as they were supposed to. They got into trouble for this. The mayor of Hargeisa visited and told us to stop these activities. Sometimes Gani and later Morgan came to the schools and gave us the same lecture. They criticized the headmaster in front of the whole school for being ineffective.

Often, we had to walk long distances to welcome some visiting government delegation. Most of the time, we stoned their cars instead and then the soldiers would shoot and arrest us. Once, a classmate, Abdillahi Omar Abdi, who was 12 at the time, was arrested and held for 15 days. After his release, he had to report to the Criminal Investigations Department (CID) every day and his parents had to report to the CID every day as well. They were told to discipline their son.

After the school disturbances began, for two years young teachers from the south were sent to northern schools, even though they themselves had graduated only from secondary schools. The students regarded them as government spies.

According to Omer:

They didn't know anything themselves. They were always asking us political questions, such as "Does anyone know the meaning of "faqash."* Innocently, someone would explain what "faqash" meant. During break time, the student would be asked to come to the teacher's office and reported to the NSS. He or she would be beaten and reported to their parents who would be ordered to change their children's attitudes. The soldiers were always calling us the sons and daughters of "qurmis".

Many former students commented that their classmates who belonged to Islamic study groups were among those arrested most frequently and subjected to the worst treatment. They would be taken to NSS centers and the girls, stripped of their veils, would have urine splashed at them, making them unfit to pray, and then beaten.

Parents were inevitably affected by the political activities that gripped the schools and the violence directed at schoolchildren. Yet they were helpless to protect their children against heavily-armed soldiers. According to Safia Ali Mataan, interviewed by Africa Watch in London on August 17, 1989 :

> Naturally, as parents, we were caught up in the "political" problems of our children. They would cook up charges, such as planting weapons in the schools, arrest and torture the children to reveal their own identities and to implicate others. Then the parents would be shown an impressive array of armaments that was meant to be "evidence" of their "crime."

The unrest meant anxiety for parents. Sahra Ahmed Arteh, the mother of five boys, told Africa Watch when we interviewed her in London on June 17, 1989:

> So many school children were arrested at school. The mothers would go to the school and wait outside to see if that day it would be one of theirs. We did not cook for our families during the day because we were standing guard over the children at school. We cooked a main meal at night instead. My two eldest boys became so fed up with the NSS coming to their school every day, accusing them of being pro-SNM, intimidating them with stories of "what happens to those who sympathize with the SNM," that they finally left Somalia in

---

*   Faqash is a derogatory term used by Isaaks for the government and their supporters.

1983 and went to Ethiopia. After they left, I dreaded the thought that they would try to visit us, which would endanger the rest of the family as well as our neighbors. It was too big a risk. It was out of the question for me to think of visiting them. As the mother of two boys who had left, I was under special surveillance and my absence, even for a night, would be reported by the *tabeleh* or spies in the neighborhood. No matter where I might have gone, it would be assumed I had gone to visit my sons and the whole family would be punished. I was torn between a longing to see my sons and the hope that they would not get too homesick and try to visit us. Luckily, they were grown up enough to know better.

One of our neighbors, Hussein Ali Abokor, was not so lucky. Two of his boys had also left for Ethiopia in early 1988. He was told to send his wife to bring the boys back. He offered to go if the government would pay for his transport as he was unemployed. He was prohibited from going because they said he too would join the SNM. He said he could not send his wife because she had just given birth. He had to report to the NSS every day and was arrested when the SNM attacked Burao. He was sent to Mandera Prison and released by the SNM.

Both teachers and students interviewed by Africa Watch emphasized the government's determination not to improve the glaring inadequacies in the educational system. On the contrary, it discouraged teachers from making any attempts to improve the situation.

Fawzia Ismail Jama, a former teacher in Burao was interviewed by Africa Watch in Djibouti on August 4, 1989. She commented:

> I returned to Somalia on February 12, 1984 after I completed my studies abroad. The situation in the north was far worse than I could ever have imagined. I looked at everything in disbelief. However, I was determined not to be discouraged. I established my own private school on August 11, 1986 in Burao. I was an English teacher there and that was when the security agencies started to keep a watchful eye on me. My tracks were closely followed. My school was searched thoroughly a number of times, and everything turned topsy-turvy. They listened to the tapes I was using to teach. Govern-

113

ment officers came with their bodyguards and wasted hours going through my books.

Government officials in Burao made it clear that they were against my teaching English to the children of the town. Of course many such schools were open in Mogadishu, but they did not want our children to be able to cry out for help in an international language. They tried everything to make me leave Burao and were angry when I did not pack up.

The government argued that the problem was essentially one of the maintenance of the schools and it attempted to shift the economic burden of repairs and the cost of running the schools onto the parents. To defuse the tension, parents agreed to assume this responsibility and to act as a buffer between the students and the government. A group of respected elders formed a "schools committee" in Hargeisa and collected money from the community which they organized on a sector basis — traders, taxi-drivers, market-stall owners and so on. Millions of shillings were collected to repair schools and to buy chairs, desks and equipment. In an effort to encourage decent teachers to remain in their profession, the committee also required parents to contribute monthly payments to supplement the teachers' meagre salaries. This system lasted until the outbreak of the war.

9. DESTROYING HEARTS AND MINDS: PSYCHOLOGICAL INTIMIDATION

The government had at its disposal, a formidable array of extra-legal sanctions that it used to wage a more subtle kind of political warfare. There was little direct inter-action between the Isaak population at large and the government. Their interests had to be represented by non-Isaak middlemen.

A system known as "Isaak Extermination" (*"Dabar Goynta Isaaka"*) was put into effect. Local officials competed for the most hard line policies.

Siegfried Koch, a Swiss national interviewed by Africa Watch in London on August 21,told us:

> Of course there were some decent individuals working in government, but the cruelty of its policies towards the Isaaks is beyond description.
>
> If you were Marehan, you were a king, but if you were Isaak, you did not count. No one believed your word, whereas the word of a non-Isaak was not disputed. This government has destroyed the cultural values of their society. They destroyed mutual trust and frienship. Friendship became a mask you wore when you needed something from the government. Otherwise you had no chance of getting anything done. Their policy was to keep the people impoverished, and then tempt them with money to act as informers. Even families were encouraged to betray one another.
>
> You couldn't be yourself because you had to suppress your emotions and your needs. If you didn't, you couldn't survive. There was no opportunity to let out steam. For me, it's very logical that one day it will explode if you always suppress and suppress. That's why the Isaaks are so anti-government. It's the policies of the government that are responsible. Instead of fighting tribalism, they "cooked" it. Siad Barre has a special gift for not solving problems but making them worse. From my years in northern Somalia, it is clear to me that only one thing

115

matters to him — to stay on his throne at any price. He does not care if 100,000 people die or if his country falls apart. If that's what it takes to remain in power, that is O.K. The Isaaks rebelled against this policy, so the government resorted to executions and torture. If I were Isaak, I would have stood up as well.

People really despaired. They lost hope in their future, both as individuals and as a community. The hostility built up and intensified, creating more resentment among the Isaaks and provoking more repression from the government. There is no way out, either for the Isaaks or Siad Barre. He has to leave or stay by force.

Most of all, I feel saddened by what has happened to the young people. The government of Siad Barre has destroyed the youth of Somalia by encouraging many negative attitudes. He created a situation which made everyone suspicious and un-trusting. People lost the belief in the virtue of getting things done honestly. You had to survive by any means. The young were not taught the discipline necessary for learning. Hard work through honest means was not encouraged. Frustrations led to a destructive form of life. It will take Somalia many, many years to recover from the destruction of Siad Barre's rule.

The need to hide the fact of being Isaak to escape discriminaton in one's own home town, at the hands of one's own government, bred a deep Isaak hostility towards the regime.

Yusuf, a former businessman interviewed by Africa Watch in Djibouti on August 9, 1989, expressed this anger:

It got to a point that the people of the region became invisible, no matter what their qualifications or qualities. They were worse off than foreigners; they became a people with no rights in their own country. Every group was encouraged to watch over the others, as the only way to protect themselves and the government. It destroyed community life. Neighbors became suspicious of each other.

Amaal Jama, a resident of Hargeisa, interviewed by Africa Watch in London on July 19, 1989, said that:

If an Isaak man needed something from a government office, he had to go through a woman because no Isaak man dared to go to a government office, act with dignity and exercise his rights. The only Isaak men who could walk into offices were "ass lickers" (*"Dabadhilif"*).

Isaaks had to rely upon the protective patronage of influential non-Isaak figures to safeguard their interests.

Mohamed Ali Abdillahi, a retired bank manager who worked at a number of banks, including the National Bank, the Commercial Bank and the Development Bank, interviewed by Africa Watch in Djibouti on August 3, 1989, discussed aspects of this policy:

An Ogadeni friend who came to Hargeisa as a refugee in 1978 wanted to take a bank loan and asked me to stand collateral for him, using my property. I agreed and there was no problem. However, when I asked for a loan, using the same collateral, I was turned down. I had to turn to the Ogadeni friend who I had helped. When I wanted an ID card for one of my sons, I had to go through the same friend.

Mona Ahmed Yusuf "Qulumbe," interviewed by Africa Watch in London of July 2, 1989, explained that these measures had the effect of depriving many Isaaks in Buroa of their livelihood:

The government deliberately put all power in the hands of non-Isaaks. By 1984, there was no Isaak in any position of authority in Burao. If you did not have good relations with non-Isaaks, you were finished. People who had lived for generations in the north had to rely on others or on outsiders to "facilitate" every aspect of their lives. This was used, as the government had clearly intended, to destroy the economic base of the Isaaks. If an Isaak had a business coveted by a non-Isaak or which was regarded as a competitive threat, he or she would be labeled a "trouble maker" and harassed till they got fed up and closed the business – better still, left town. If you refused to oblige, your license or merchandise was confiscated, or you were arrested, or both.

Aside from arrest and detention, there were more subtle ways to facilitate the departure of Isaak men holding senior positions in government,

117

the armed forces or in business. It was insinuated to a friend he trusted that he was on a wanted list, or that his name was being associated with known SNM fighters and activists. In the atmosphere of fear and mistrust that prevailed, it was impossible to distinguish a false and politically motivated rumor from a sincere warning. Neither the target nor his friends were in a position to discern the difference. But the risk of disbelief was too great and it ensured that an increasing number of Isaak government officials, businessmen, army personnel and professionals left the country, ironically, many of them to swell the ranks of the SNM.

Many high-level officials and military officers made it difficult for women to obtain jobs or documents from government offices. They would say, "I'll come to see you tonight, and we can sort it all out." The governor, Adan Buleh Mohamoud, was famous in Hargeisa for going to offices and if he liked one of the women employees, he sent his bodyguards to "collect" her from her home, if necessary, by threatening the whole family. Many women, including married women whose husbands worked abroad, left the country to escape this pressure and humiliation.

Amaal Jama noted that General Morgan's tactics centered on corrupting the community through women. He introduced social mores that were profoundly offensive to an Islamic society:

> In addition to the killings and arrests, his aim was to steal people's minds, to destroy the Isaaks psychologically. He wanted to humiliate their women, and in particular, married women with children, whose husbands had joined the SNM or were working in the Middle East, the people the government regarded as financing the SNM. That way he hoped to destroy the morale of the SNM.

> Beauty contests were held before Marehan and other non-Isaak military personnel. Dancing competitions took place every Friday at a military club. Only military men were allowed to dance with single women. The women would be encouraged to drink. Party members, both men and women, combed private homes to "select" the women for the beauty contests and dancing competition. Of course the policy backfired. It

simply made the whole community more wholeheartedly anti-government.

Yusuf elaborated:

They would confiscate your car, force your daughter into the car, and you could do nothing about it. Then they would call a meeting and humiliate you publicly, saying they were fed up with your daughter pursuing them, and that the Isaaks should discipline their womenfolk.

In an angry voice, he added:

They turned our cultural values upside down and then accused us of being responsible for our condition, the ones guilty of the rape of Hargeisa. It's indescribable what we have suffered. No one can believe it.

The regime has placed considerable emphasis on punishing people related to members of the armed opposition, their friends and associates. The "news" was announced on the radio, through loudspeakers and in pamphlets, that the wife and the wealth of anyone who had joined the SNM were "free for all." Their wives were not theirs any more, their families could be arrested anytime, and they are seen to have forfeited their wealth. Then they would mock the SNM, "While you are out there fighting, your wives belong to other men."

Yassin Karshe Mohamed, interviewed by Africa Watch in Cardiff on July 7, 1989, commented:

You can imagine the effect this has on an ignorant and undis-ciplined soldier who wasn't paid much to begin with. This encouraged them to rape, kill, arrest and loot.

Especially since 1984, Isaak men living abroad were afraid to visit Somalia, particularly if they were coming from the Middle East, for fear that they would be accused of involvement with the SNM. The NSS and Immigration harassed them at the airport for "problems" with their passport. They could be detained for several months, and as a result, their business suffered or they lost their jobs. Increasingly, Isaaks working abroad took holidays in foreign countries or did not travel at all.

119

If they went to Somalia, they avoided taking new clothes so as not to invite suspicion and, above all, avoided visiting government offices in order not to get into "trouble."

Omer Yusuf Isse, a seaman in his sixties, is a resident in Cardiff, where he was interviewed by Africa Watch on July 6, 1989. He went to Hargeisa for a holiday in 1985:

> As soon as I arrived, the military police (*Dhabar Jabinta*) followed me around. They pestered me to say where I got my clothes because they were not available in Hargeisa. I denied that I had ever been abroad. They persisted. Finally, I paid them something to get them off my back. I couldn't believe that I had to justify my shirt and trousers.

The government intruded into the most private aspects of people's lives. Nothing was too intimate to escape state control. Some of its initiatives were particularly vindictive. From 1985 onwards, officials working in the Ministry of Justice and Religious Affairs and religious figures close to the government, announced on the radio that women married to SNM fighters and the wives of political prisoners were entitled to consider themselves "divorced" and were legally free to marry other men. They stated that such men were no longer Muslims, but traitors to their religion and nation, and as such, the country's enemies. Consequently, their wives need not consider their marriage vows as legally binding.

Nor was anything too petty to remain a matter of personal choice. In early 1987 in Hargeisa, the government forbade men to wear a type of shawl popular in the north, on the basis that the SNM fighters who had assassinated the local head of the NSS in December 1986 had worn such shawls.

Constraints on Mourning Victims
Killed by Government Forces

A particularly cruel form of psychological harassment concerned mourning relatives killed by government forces. Those who expressed their grief publicly risked arrest themselves, as well as having their property and assets confiscated. Soldiers went to the homes in Hargeisa of some of the victims executed on November 17, 1984 to test their reactions and to watch for any public sign of grief. The wives of SNM fighters who died were themselves threatened with death if they wore traditional mourning dress. In Hargeisa, Gani threatened to shoot Mako Haji Ahmed Yusuf "Qulumbe," whose husband had been killed, if she wore mourning dress. He added that he hoped she would "redeem herself by not marrying a "qurmis" next time around".

Harassment was not limited to family members. Distant relatives, friends and neighbors were not allowed to pay condolence calls on politically suspect families. Soldiers guarded houses to turn people away. Neither did they respect the privacy of burial. As in the black townships of South Africa, the funerals of the victims of government violence became important political events themselves. The presence of so many people was in itself intended as a form of protest. The conduct of soldiers at funerals was confrontational and insulting. They would taunt participants that "Isaaks know how to bury their dead, but not how to take revenge." An angry response would be a pretext for additional arrests.

Africa Watch received numerous accounts that soldiers would kill somebody and then wait around to see who claimed the body. That person, in turn, would be accused of association with the SNM. Many bodies were not claimed out of fear.

Safia Ali Mataan, interviewed by Africa Watch in London on August 17, 1989, described another form of intimidation — leaving dead bodies in residential areas:

> From 1983 onwards, the bodies of people killed near their homes were left in another part of town, to intimidate the whole city. The body of Ahmed Mohamed Hersi was found at Sheikh Madar though his home was in another district. The body of Saeed Mahdi Buba, a bank employee, was killed at Ga'an Libaah, near the National Theater and his body discovered at 26 June district.

In late 1984, alarmed by the presence of the SNM in the mountainous region of Sheikh, the military apparently determined to teach the residents of Sheikh a lesson about the price of supporting the SNM.

Saeedo Haji Ahmed, whose husband was executed in Burao in December 1984, told Africa Watch during an interview in London on October 31, 1989, of an incident in Sheikh in November, shortly before his death.

> We were woken up at 6:00 a.m. by loud bangs. Soldiers herded us out of the house at gun point — including my elderly grandmother, the children, my husband and myself, in an advanced stage of pregnancy. The children were very scared. They claimed to have found an arm outside our house, which they insisted was an SNM arm. We had no idea what they were talking about. They said they were taking us to the police station for interrogation. My husband said that since they were after him, there was no reason to punish the rest of the family. One of the soldiers took pity on us and blurted out that the army itself had planted the arm there and should leave us alone.

Women whose husbands had joined the SNM were in a particularly vulnerable position. Unscrupulous NSS and military officers sought to take advantage of their weak position. One refugee, interviewed by Africa Watch in Djibouti in August expressed their predicament as follows: "She was lost if she accepted, she was lost if she refused." If they refused to be coopted, anyone could accuse them of an offense and the authorities would rule against them.

Once it became known that your husband had joined the SNM, there was intense pressure to have the marriage dissolved, sometimes by the family itself, both because the consequences of being regarded as an anti-government family were so great and because of direct government pressure. If the woman resisted, she herself would be considered "guilty."

Forced Witnessing of Public Executions

Part of the government's strategy to frighten Isaaks was to make it compulsory for everyone to attend public executions of men suspected of SNM sympathies, or captured SNM fighters or those who were being killed to serve as a "warning."

Sahra Ahmed Arteh, interviewed by Africa Watch in London on June 17, 1989, described being forced to witness public executions:

Nomads arrested in the countryside were brought to Hargeisa to be executed. These poor people would be forced to wear what the government described as "SNM uniforms" and were paraded in the National Theater. This was always a great occasion for the Party and the government to teach us all a "lesson." Party officers came to people's homes and ordered them to come to the *Badka* where executions took place. Everyone had to attend. Any shops found open would be forcibly closed. To avoid going, you bribed your *tabeleh*, so he would not report you. Buses transported people to the place of execution. We had to pay the bus fare ourselves even though nobody wanted to go. During the parade at the theater and the execution, we were warned about "what would happen to our boys if we did not control them." Spies watched people's faces to read their emotions. Anyone who showed signs of sadness was in trouble. Those who didn't applaud or who didn't show sufficient enthusiasm were accused of something themselves and punished.

Mohamed Ali Abdillahi, noted another tactic:

Whenever the military suffered a defeat in an encounter with the SNM, they killed some nomads in the area. Then they brought their dead bodies to town, saying, "We have killed some Ethiopians — come and see for yourselves."

Undermining the Standing of Elders

Undermining the moral stature, and therefore the social standing and political clout of elders was part of the government's way of destroying the cohesion of the community, leaving it bereft of its respected and experienced leaders. Through arrest, imprisonment, inducements that included corruption and the promise that the elders would not be subject to further political harassment, the community's traditional social fabric was compromised. To force the community to stem defections to the SNM, and to create divisions, elders would be publicly rebuked at meetings. There was pressure to become "informers." When "persuasion" did not work, elders would be picked up from mosques and their houses, forced to attend summary trials of "their boys," and witness executions of their nephews and cousins, apparently in an effort to frighten them into political acquiescence and through them, the rest of the community.

Rape

Rape by soldiers became common. It was particularly frequent in the countryside. Those who could send a daughter out of the country did so. From the accounts Africa Watch received, we conclude that this was not the unrestrained behavior of a few undisciplined soldiers, but a pattern by the military against both urban dwellers and nomads. Rape was not only a torment for the victims — but a source of pain and humiliation to Somali men as well, whose standing in the community is based to a large extent on the protection they are seen to afford their womenfolk.

People were understandably reluctant to reveal the identities of rape victims because of the shame that is associated with rape, no matter the circumstances.

Mohamed Abiib Muse, interviewed by Africa Watch in Djibouti on August 6, 1989, said:

> Often, when they came to search houses, they raped any attractive woman they saw, saying, "Instead of giving birth to a *"qurmis*," I will force her to have a pro-government bastard. It's better than what they give birth to anyway." Isaak men would constantly be told, "Go and get those prostitutes of yours" — meaning their sisters and daughters. These are the sort of things, the determination to deprive us of every shred of dignity, that really turned people wholeheartedly against the government.

Siraad (not her real name), interviewed by Africa Watch in Djibouti on August 3, 1989, said that the often "public" nature of rape was intended to shame the women and their menfolk:

> They would kick the man out of the house and soldiers forced him to remain outside while the women were raped by other soldiers. Just to humiliate the men, they did not even spare the old women. Sometimes women were gang-raped. This is really what made the SNM expand. So many storekeepers, traders and tea shop owners just locked up and left to join the SNM,

124

feeling that they couldn't just sit around watching this happen to their wives, daughters, sisters and the relatives of their friends and neighbors.

Amaal Jama, spoke of the rage that built up in the community as a result of its helplessness:

No matter what happened to the victim, she couldn't tell her family because of the shame and because they couldn't do anything about it anyway. If anything, they would say it was her fault, not because they believed it, but because they were so powerless to help her and to defend the family. They would say that she should not have gone out. But, of course, they knew that women couldn't stay indoors all the time like prisoners. They could do nothing for her and that is what made them so angry.

10. WAR BREAKS OUT

Eager to contain the unrest in the northwest region, President Barre ordered a number of Isaak men in Mogadishu to go to Hargeisa "to talk to the people". The delegation was presented with airline tickets and told to leave for Hargeisa. It included Jama Osman Samater, a businessman and Abdi Aden Qeys, a poet, both long-term political prisoners released only in February 1988. The President himself visited the region in March in an effort to encourage reconciliation, and met with Isaak elders, as a group and in smaller groups. Jama Osman Samater described the meetings to Africa Watch in an interview in London on June 1, 1989.

> The talks were extremely frank and during the first few meet-
> ings, he listened and seemed keen to learn about the problems.
> Elder after elder told him about the killings, the rape, the cruel
> behavior of the army and security forces towards civilians and
> the indifference of government agencies to the plight of the
> people. He was told point blank that it was his policies which
> were responsible for the expansion of the SNM. He replied
> that he was not aware of all this and promised to put an end
> to it. Then suddenly, after sometime, his attitude changed. He
> insulted everyone and became sarcastic and dismissive. We
> couldn't figure out what had happened. Then we learned that
> Somalia and Ethiopia had just signed a peace treaty. Obvious-
> ly, he felt that he did not have to listen to anyone or placate
> the population as the SNM was going to be expelled from its
> bases in Ethiopia. After that he left for Gebiley and Borama.

On his return to Hargeisa, the President held a public rally at the football stadium. A demonstration broke out and angry students threw stones at the president. The presidential bodyguards fired into the crowd, killing five students. Many people were arrested at the time and in the subsequent weeks. During the same visit, twenty-four Isaak men were summarily executed in Gebiley and Tug-Wajale, in reprisal for an SNM attack against government forces. (See Appendix Four for a list of the casualties) These incidents were not likely to convince the population that the President was intent on seeking peace in the northwest region.

On April 3, the government signed a peace treaty with Ethiopia; an important feature of the treaty was an agreement not to assist rebel organizations based on each other's territory. The Somali government was anxious to ensure the expulsion of the SNM from Ethiopia and the Ethiopian government, besieged at the time in both Eritrea and Tigray, wanted to end the Somali government's support for the guerrilla movements in both regions. Since the agreement, the return of the SNM was regarded as imminent, both by the local population and the government. In anticipation of "trouble," the curfew was renewed, and General Morgan sought to discourage assistance to the SNM by threatening severe reprisals. Nevertheless, the SNM attack on Burao appeared to catch the government by surprise.

The GAO report made the following comments about the political consequences of the peace treaty with Ethiopia:

> The peace accord was designed to ease relations between Somalia and Ethiopia and promote economic development by redirecting resources. Some observers believe it exacerbated the conflict. With peace between the countries, the Issak community saw little hope of removing Ogadeni refugees from its territory. Furthermore, the demilitarization of the borders enabled the SNM to infiltrate Somalia unimpeded.

Burao

The SNM attacked Burao on Friday, May 27. They captured the town in about two hours. Immediately, they took over the military compound at the airport where the largest number of soldiers were stationed, the military compound at Goon Ad located outside the city, as well as the central police station, another police station, the prison and various government offices, where they executed a number of military officers and officials. Such executions of those in custody or hors de combat are, of course, themselves gross violations of the laws of war and are condemned by Africa Watch.

128

The armed forces retreated to Goon Ad which served as their base. In the late afternoon, soldiers who had not been on duty when the SNM attacked, regrouped and entered the center of town. According to all the accounts we received, the soldiers went on a rampage on the 27th and 28th, dragging men out of their houses and shooting them point blank range. Whatever the violations that were committed by the SNM, these provide no justification for the military's attacks on civilians. Under the laws of war, each side has an independent duty to avoid abuses, regardless of the abuses by the other side. The military grossly disregarded this duty. They were particularly vengeful in the districts first conquered by the SNM. Civilians of all ages who had gathered in the center of town, or those standing outside their homes watching the events, were killed on the spot. Among the victims were many students.

There was also widespread looting by soldiers, and some people were killed as a result.

Khadija Jama Sugal, a businesswoman interviewed by Africa Watch in London on June 12, 1989, reported:

> If a shop was closed, they broke the door down. If they met with any resistance, they shot the owner on the spot. Mohamed "Baadle" was shot inside his shop. They also broke down the doors of the houses, threatening to kill the occupants unless they opened the doors. Once they came in, they helped themselves to whatever they wanted, and you handed everything over.

After the first two days, apparently frustrated by their inability to crush the SNM and angered by the extent to which Isaaks welcomed the SNM initiative, the military attacked the civilian population without reservation, as if it were the enemy. The military used heavy artillery and tanks, causing severe damage, both to civilians and to property. Bazookas, machine guns, hand grenades and other weapons of mass destruction were also directed against civilian targets in Hargeisa which had also been attacked as well as in Burao. The GAO reported the government's response to the SNM attack as follows:

> The Somali army reportedly responded to the SNM attacks in May 1988 with extreme force, inflicting heavy civilian casualties and damage to Hargeisa and Burao....The Somali military

129

resorted to using artillery and aerial shelling in heavily populated urban centers in its effort to retake Burao and Hargeisa.
A majority of the refugees we interviewed stated that their
homes were destroyed by shelling despite the absence of SNM
combatants from their neighborhoods....The refugees told
similar stories of bombings, strafings, and artillery shelling in
both cities and, in Burao, the use of armored tanks. The
majority saw their houses either damaged or destroyed by the
shelling. Many reported seeing members of their families
killed in the barrage....*

Under the Geneva Conventions, such attacks are by definition indiscriminate as they "employ a means or method of combat the effects of which
cannot be limited...and, consequently, in each such case, are of a nature to strike
military objectives or civilian objects without distinction." The obligation to
protect the civilian population against disproportionate attacks is clear, especially in areas where there is a high concentration of civilian population.

Refugees from different towns interviewed by Africa Watch described
the indiscriminate nature of the army's counterattack in strikingly similar terms.

Mona Ahmed Yusuf, "Qulumbe," 17, living in the Tuurta Turwa
district of Burao, interviewed by Africa Watch in London on July 2, 1989,
described what happened in her neighborhood:

Shelling with long-range weapons started on Sunday. It hit a
neighbor's house, the Abdirahman family of seven people. Six
of them died instantaneously. The only survivor was a little girl
who had been sent to fetch sugar. The mother had just had a
baby.

They were after civilians. Their scouts would direct them to
those areas where civilians were concentrated and then that
spot would be shelled. On Monday, the shelling intensified.
Two houses behind ours belonging to my uncle were hit.
Luckily, one was empty as the family had congregated in the
other house. It hit that house too and his daughter, niece and
sister-in-law were wounded. Our side was particularly targeted as it was one of the areas the SNM entered when they

---

*   GAO report on The Northern Somalia Conflict, May 4, 1989 at pp. 4 and 5.

130

first came into town. When the bombing started,the sight of the dying, the wounded and the collapse of houses was too much to bear.

Khadija Sugal, described how the government separated the non-Isaaks from the Isaaks:

> As soon as the fighting broke out, the government used loudspeakers to sort the civilians out into Darood and Isaak. They would shout, "Who is from Galkayo? Mogadishu? Las Anod? Garoe?" [Non-Isaak territory]. They appealed to the non-Isaaks to leave so they could burn the town and all those who remained behind. Most of the people from these towns left; the government provided them with transportion.
>
> The artillery shelling began immediately after the non-Isaaks had been evacuated. Everything seemed to collapse or to be on fire. Whole areas of Burao seemed to be lit up with gunfire. Our suffering until then seemed of no significance compared to the impact of the shelling. The effect of the shelling is indescribable. The shock made people sick — many pregnant women went into early labor and, without any medical help, gave birth to premature babies. The shelling forced everyone, even the wounded and the very old, to flee.
>
> On Tuesday, the aerial bombardment began. The smoke was overwhelming. You choked, and felt as if you were inhaling poison. It left a sharp pain in your throat and burned your eyes. After Tuesday, the city seemed to be burning. There was smoke everywhere. By Wednesday, we became desperate. I left home without even a head scarf, with only one shoe on. I headed east with some other women. There were so many dead people spread out on the road; it seemed as if someone had laid a giant cloth on the ground.
>
> Among the dead are: My brother, Suleiman, in his 30s, killed by soldiers as he fled; Mohamoud Jama "Ogleh," my children's grandfather, shot by soldiers. A friend of mine, Khadija Haji Abdi, a woman in her 50s, died when a bomb hit her home and the house collapsed on her.

Ismail Dualeh Mohamed, a seaman normally resident in Cardiff, where he was interviewed by Africa Watch on July 6, 1989, gave the following account of the war:

> If they had made any distinctions between SNM fighters and civilians, there wouldn't have been so many casualties and there wouldn't have been so much suffering. What they wanted, to put it simply, was to wipe us out. A hail of bullets came at you from every direction. As we fled Burao, my wife was hit by a bullet and badly wounded. My mother-in-law died when a bomb hit their house. My mother's niece was also killed. So many people have died in this war, including so many members of my own extended family. Only God can count the numbers.

Hargeisa

Hargeisa is the second city of the country. This, and its proximity to Ethiopia, has given it a central role in the military planning of successive governments. It was, therefore, critical, both in terms of military strategy and psychological impact, that Hargeisa should not fall.

When news of the SNM attack on Burao reached Hargeisa, all the banks were closed. Soldiers surrounded the banks to prevent people from approaching. Electricity and water-supply lines were cut. People had to fetch water from the stream. As it was the rainy season, they could also collect water from the roof tops. All transport was confiscated, apparently to control the movements of the civilian population and to put sufficient transport at the disposal of the military and government officials. Even taxis were confiscated. Top government officials evacuated their families to Mogadishu. Killings did not begin until the fighting actually broke out in Hargeisa on May 31. Between May 27-31, there was much looting and mass arrests.

The number of soldiers patrolling the city center increased day after day. There seemed to be thousands of soldiers everywhere, the refugees reported. They began systematic house-to-house searches, looking for SNM fighters. A curfew had been imposed on May 27 starting at 6:00 p.m.; the next day at 4:00 p.m.; the third day at 2:00 p.m.; and on the fourth day at 11:00 a.m.

132

Men did not dare go out for fear of being shot; only women went to look for what the family needed. Frantically, people stock-piled food, coal and other essential supplies in anticipation of fighting. The soldiers looted all warehouses and shops. The open market was one of their prime targets. Soldiers even raided mosques, where some people had hidden their safe-boxes. These were taken, as were the carpets and the loudspeakers. Later, people would be killed inside mosques.

A substantial number of civilians died as soldiers robbed them. Some who refused to hand over their watches, jewelry and money, or who were not quick enough, were shot on the spot. Food was another incentive for robbery, apparently because the soldiers were not being supplied by the government.

Sahra Ahmed Arteh, interviewed by Africa Watch in London on June 17, 1989, provided the following account of looting:

> I saw them go into a big shop in front of our house that belonged to Suleiman Amin, a wealthy trader, and empty the shelves of food, tins, clothes, everything they could lay their hands on. Suleiman Amin is at least alive. Others were looted and then shot.

Samia Sheef, an articulate young mother of three, interviewed by Africa Watch in London on June 3, 1989, described her experiences of the outbreak of the war:

> We were overjoyed when we heard that the SNM had attacked Burao. We wondered when they would come to Hargeisa. We spent the first nine days of the war in the Goljano area of Hargeisa. No one had any expectation of the hardship that was to come. All we thought about was the possibility of never having to see those soldiers again and never having to fear a government official.
>
> Immediately, the soldiers became tense and even more aggressive toward the public. Soldiers came with big trucks and walked into the stores and just took everything. No storekeeper could utter a word. The public also started to stock up on food and other essentials. Even after people paid for things and were transporting them home on donkey carts, soldiers stopped them, confiscated everything and they were forced to unload their shopping either at the nearest police station or

at the prison. Thieves took advantage of the fear and confusion and looted the shops as well. The army shot dead some of the looters.

Amaal Jama, interviewed by Africa Watch in London on July 19, 1989, described a similar reaction to the outbreak of the war:

When the SNM came into town, our morale shot up. It never entered our minds that the SNM would not win. We even thought the fighting would last only a few days.

Yusuf (not his real name), interviewed by Africa Watch in Djibouti on August 9, 1989, described part of the government's response:

The non-Isaaks who were in prison/detention centers were released and armed. Arms were provided to every non-Isaak willing to bear them, young and old, even schoolchildren. Many of them were taken to military compounds for crash training. Some of our non-Isaak neighbors came back after three days with arms and uniforms and started to use them. It's when they recruited non-Isaak civilians on a large scale to join in the war that the house-to-house looting became rampant. It's your neighbor who knows what you have and where you keep it.

Mass Arrests

When the news of the SNM attack on Burao reached Hargeisa, the government began rounding up men who it apparently feared would assist an SNM attack on Hargeisa. Detainees were taken to Birjeeh, the former military headquarters and now the center for the 26th sector of the army, to Malka Durduro, a military compound, to the central prison, to the headquarters of the NSS, to the headquarters of the military police, the headquarters of the military police, the headquarters of the *Gulwadayaal,* as well as to secret detention centers maintained by the various security branches. One of the first group to be arrested were Isaak military officers, even those who had resigned along time ago. They were sent to Mogadishu and detained.

Mohamed Ali Abdillahi, a former bank manager, interviewed by Africa Watch in Djibouti on August 3, 1989, told us:

Hundreds of men were arrested. They arrested anyone they feared could contribute money, experience, or military know-how to the opposition. In short, anyone they thought might provide leadership. They began by detaining all the people they had arrested in the past — which in any case was in itself a significant proportion of all Isaak men in northern cities. There was no escape. We thought of going to Mogadishu but then we heard on the BBC that Isaak men were being arrested there as well. There seemed nowhere to go.

Ahmed Mohamed Hawsi, "Kirih," one of 53 Isaak businessmen and elders arrested on May 28, was interviewed by Africa Watch in London on July 9, 1989. (Others included Jama Nur, Mohamed Aboker and Abdillahi Yusuf Mahdi, who owned a bakery.) Ahmed gave us the following account of his experiences:

> Immediately after our arrest, we were taken in buses towards Mandera prison near Berbera. During the bus ride, we were told that we were to be killed. There were 60 of us, 53 from Hargeisa and 7 men from Gebiley. At Mandera, eight of us were crammed into a tiny room. On June 1, the soldiers that had been sent to carry out our executions were killed by the SNM in an encounter unrelated to our arrest. Fortunately, they searched their pockets and found our death warrants. As a result they rushed to Mandera to free us. When we heard the first shots, we didn't know where they were coming from. We had no idea what our destiny would be.

> We were of course very happy when the SNM overpowered the soldiers and the guards. During the eight days in prison, we had not been fed, except for two isolated occasions, when Ethiopian prisoners of war who cooked the food and who had known many of us during our previous stays in the prison, sneaked us a bit of maize. We were all in bad shape. Ismail Gabas, who suffered from blood pressure problems, went into a coma after the second day because of the lack of food and medical attention.

Mawliid Nuh, an NSS officer, who was arrested in March 1988 described conditions in Hargeisa Central Prison after the mass arrests began. He told Africa Watch when we interviewed him in Djibouti August 11, 1989, that when the war broke out, to make room for the Isaaks arrested in large numbers, *all* non-Isaaks were released, including people sentenced to death or

135

life imprisonment for murder and drug-related offenses. Some were given arms and made guards over the Isaak detainees, while many others joined the military and subsequently participated in the war.

When the mass arrests began in Hargeisa, about 700 Isaaks from the armed forces were brought to the prison, which was already crammed. After four days, an additional 70 military personnel were brought — 40 from Gebiley and 30 from Hargeisa. The director of the prison argued that he could not accommodate any more people. That same evening, the 70 newly arrived detainees were executed by a firing squad at Malka Durduro. They included:

Inspector Hassan Abdillahi Maawel; Inspector Ali Mohamed Diriye; Inspector Mohamed Ali Abdillahi; Inspector Yusuf "Mig"; Inspector Abdillahi Muruq; Inspector Osman "Dooh" and Inspector "Turmeeg."

Up to now, the government still pretends that they are alive. At first, it claimed that they had been detained at Garoe. It continues to pay their salaries to their wives to keep up the fiction that they are alive.

In March, when I was released, there were still 664 prisoners mainly from the army.

At the time of the interview with Africa Watch, he said he had learned from former detainees who had just been released that about 200 of the 700 military personnel had been released.

Mawliid continued:

When the war was two days old, 12 men from Gebiley, were executed. They included:

Aden Abdillahi, an old man in his 80s;

Mohamed Abdi Kofi, about 25 years old.

Shab'an Ali Dualeh was arrested in Gebiley in March 1988 and transferred to Hargeisa Central Prison. He was working in the administrative office of the prison when the war broke out. He told Africa Watch when we interviewed him in Djibouti on August 10, 1989, that the prison authorities refused to release a group of 45 Isaak prisoners who were completing their sentences. Most had served three to five years for criminal offenses such as theft. According to the information he received from former prisoners who had been released shortly before this interview, they were still in detention.

The SNM attacked Hargeisa at 2:15 a.m. on May 31. For the first day or two, the military did not use their full force, apparently trying to work out a plan by which they could defeat the SNM. Then they counter-attacked with heavy weapons. Long-range artillery guns were situated on the hilltops near the Zoo, and also at the hill-tops behind the *Badhka*, an open ground used for public executions. From there, the city was shelled. Expatriate relief workers who were evacuated by the United Nations spoke to journalists on their arrival at Nairobi airport and provided details about government atrocities. Jean Metenier, a French hospital technician in Hargeisa, told reporters that at least two dozen people were executed by firing squad against the wall of his house and the corpses subsequently dumped on the streets to serve "as an example".* Apparently as the military realized that the Isaaks welcomed the SNM attack, they turned their fire-power against the local population. It appeared they were intent on punishing the civilians for their SNM sympathies and attempting to destroy the SNM by denying them a civilian base of support.

Jama Osman Samater, was a political detainee from 1982-1988. He was released in February 1988, but the war broke out soon thereafter.

> I had just come out from the mosque from Friday prayers when I heard the news of the SNM attack on Burao. It was lunchtime. At 2:30 a whistle blew, announcing a curfew. I went home. The next morning I learned that many businessmen and elders had been arrested. I saw soldiers herding people into cars. They were confiscating all vehicles, including taxis, because when the SNM attacked Burao, taxi drivers had helped the SNM. When they couldn't find the keys quickly enough, they punctured the tires and broke the windows. I understood immediately the gravity of the situation. The soldiers were looting food and medicines from the shops and loading them on to cars. The *Gulwadayaal* were assisting the soldiers.
>
> As a former political prisoner, I was in danger of being re-arrested. I had to disguise myself. I went into the back of

---

*   Peter Godwin, *The Sunday Times*, June 12, 1988.

our shop, shaved my head and dressed as a nomad. As I left, I saw two other men arrested. They were "Guun," and Abdillahi Khalif, "Ku Cadeeye," both elders. I don't know what happened to them.

I went towards my house. As I was about to board the bus, one of our shop assistants told me not to go home. Soldiers had just come to the shop looking for me and they must be on their way to the house. I went to hide at a neighbor's. That night, soldiers and NSS officers went to my house. They took all valuables. One of my little sons screamed "faqash" at them and they slapped him across the ears. We learned later that his eardrum burst. I stayed a second night at a neighbor's house. Then, a friend and I hid ourselves in a big rubbish bin on the outskirts of Hargeisa for an entire day. The next night, the SNM attacked Hargeisa and we came back to town. On our way back, we passed a house near a military checkpoint belonging to Yusuf Elmi Samatar and saw soldiers and a tank on the move. We learned that 18 civilians, who had fled the city center and taken shelter there, had been killed. They were robbed of everything and some of the women were raped.

Jama continued:

We stayed in Hargeisa until June 8. My wife, mother, six children, two sisters and their children gathered in one house. After a few days, the shelling started. It was relentless. They shelled homes, even when no one was in the house. The objective was to ensure that no one escaped alive and no house left to stand. Volleys of artillery were being fired from every direction. There was burning everywhere. In front of my sister's house, a wooden house was hit and eight people, mostly women and children, perished. The shock was so overwhelming that we soon lost any sense of fear.

I realized that my suffering in prison was nothing compared to this. In prison, my pain had affected just me. Here everyone was a victim. The shelling did not discriminate. There were even dead animals, dogs and goats, everywhere. The first dead bodies I saw were two or three traders of Asian origin who had lived in Somalia for generations. I went to hide in a mosque. I couldn't walk fast as there were so many dead bodies on the road.

I wanted to go to the shop. As I approached, I saw there were soldiers inside. From a distance, I could see that one of our shop assistants was on the floor and the other, naked, had a gun held against him. I left immediately. It was clear that the shop had been ransacked.

Dumbuluq, located on the south side of the dry river bed which divides Hargeisa into north and south, apparently suffered most. People did not evacuate as much from this area in the first few days. When they tried to leave, it was too late. They were surrounded by too many soldiers. The army knew that civilians had been helpful to the SNM in other parts of Hargeisa and they seemed intent on ensuring that the residents of Dumbuluq did not extend similar assistance. The SNM had not established a presence there.

Khadra Muhumed Abdi, interviewed by Africa Watch in London on June 2, 1989, gave a vivid description of the outbreak of war in Dumbuluq:

On the Friday, I came to our hotel (Oriental Hotel), unaware, at the time, of the SNM attack on Burao. I learned that businessmen and elders were being rounded up. As a former political prisoner, I was nervous. NSS officers came to look for me. I escaped through a back door and hid in a store next door. Later, I asked a young boy to fetch me a taxi and I went to hide in my aunt's house in Dumbuluq district. I was afraid to go home for fear that they would be waiting for me.

The morning after the SNM attack on Hargeisa, I could see our district, Radio Station area, burning. It seemed as if the whole city was on fire. The government was going around with loudspeakers saying that "Four lice-ridden bandits on a suicide mission entered the town and we have now driven them away." They insisted that everything was back to normal and urged people to return to their homes. Unfortunately, many people believed them and were killed.

It was clear that the war was going on whatever the government said. I could not run because of the disability in my leg. (She limps in one leg). My mother and my two children joined us on the third day of the fighting. A part of our house had collapsed and they tried to hide in the undamaged section. They left when it was no longer safe to stay there. A neighbor

139

gave them shelter but the children had no milk and food was scarce.

We stayed another twelve days in my aunt's house. Soldiers came and took everything we had. What they couldn't take with them, such as trunks, they destroyed. When he sensed our tension, one of them turned around and said to me, "If I hear one word out of you, I will make you carry the heads of your children after I have cut them off." Fortunately, I made the two boys (one was a year and 3 months and the other was two years and 3 months) wear dresses, so they thought they were girls. If they had recognized them as boys, they would have shot them at once. We knew of so many boys, including babies, who had been killed. A neighbor of my aunt's, known as "Cirro," had five sons and two nephews in the house. Because of their ages, he wouldn't let them out of the house. When they ran out of food, he went to buy it himself. When he came back, all seven boys were dead — their throats slit. In that same neighborhood, in a house belonging to Abdillahi Ibrahim Aden, soldiers heard them listening to the BBC. They killed four boys with bazookas.

The shelling wouldn't cease, so we hid in another house. We tried to escape between the compounds of the 24th and the 11th sector of the army. We went to the dry-river bed, about 100 of us, but were driven away by soldiers. Then we tried to escape through a place called Meegaga but turned back when we saw soldiers again. Everyone then just fled — escaping in whatever way they could. I couldn't walk fast, let alone run, because of my foot. One of my cousins and I got lost. We hid in a hut and were found by another cousin who had come to look for us. I couldn't go on. My leg hurt too much. My cousins found a donkey cart for me. We reached Qool'Aday after three days. We found thousands of other people there. I had no idea what had happened to my children and mother.

Yurub Yusuf Iggeh, a resident of Dumbuluq district, interviewed by Africa Watch in Cardiff on July 8, 1989, described the outbreak of war as follows:

As soon as I heard the attack on Hargeisa at 2:15 a.m., I jumped out of bed. I prayed both for our safety and our

140

success. When the military couldn't defeat the SNM, they turned on us. The soldiers were tense and nervous. They were shooting wildly, firing at everything. They jumped at the slightest sound. As soon as a door creaked, they would shoot, afraid there was an SNM fighter inside. We poured oil on all the doors and hinges so they wouldn't creak. Anyone who craned his neck out of his house was dead. In the Dumbuluq district, we were even too scared to stir pots for fear of making a noise and giving the soldiers who guarded every house an excuse to burst in. So even though we had food, we were afraid to cook it. As soon as they caught a glimpse of a man, they went beserk, broke down the door of every home that he could have gone into, beat the residents and accused them of complicity with the SNM. We were too scared to listen to the radio for fear of being shot. They didn't want us to know that the world was aware of our problems. Three men were killed and one woman wounded at a house that belonged to a neighbor called "Dagayase" when they were caught listening to the BBC. Soldiers arrived while we were being searched by another. They argued as to who should search us.

They were desperate for cars and went in search of garage owners to get the keys. They went to the house of Ali Farah, who managed a garage belonging to the Botaan family. He said he didn't know where the owners had left the keys. He was shot and wounded in the arm.

Later, when the air-raids started, we heard many accounts of the bombing of garages, especially in the Dumbuluq district, in an effort to cripple civilian transport that the military apparently feared would be used to assist the SNM.

Yurub continued:

Given the kind of weapons used, it's a miracle any of us have survived. So many live bullets came through our windows. The whole city seemed to be ablaze. At first, we all lived together in one room, then decided to separate so that maybe some of us could survive. My younger sisters couldn't stop vomiting. Even when the mortars didn't hit you, the brittle chips which fell from the roof and walls, because of the vibrations, wounded you. They cut deep into the skin.

141

After nine days, we fled, with nothing on our backs.

Hassan Ismail Omaar, interviewed by Africa Watch in Cardiff on July 8, 1989, gave a similar account:

> As soon as the SNM attacked Hargeisa, my first reaction was to cry out of joy. I thought, I hoped, that this would mean a taste of freedom for all of us. But there was little joy in store for any of us.
>
> From dawn to dusk, day in and day out, and intermittently during the night, every night, there was shelling, bombing, people being slaughtered by soldiers on the streets, in their homes, and in all the places they sought refuge. We saw corpses littering the streets, the bodies of people we knew and others, lying there, unattended. It makes you wonder if the people doing this believe in God. How could they?

The following account is the testimony of Samia Sheef, interviewed by Africa Watch in London on June 3, 1989, :

> The shooting started in Hargeisa at 2:15 a.m. I panicked, grabbed my four-month-old daughter and ran to a room in the house with no windows, in the hope that I would be safer there. We all crowded into that room. So intense was the fire power, that the town seemed aflame.
>
> Initially, I thought the fighting would last at most ten days. We had stored all we needed, so we were not worried. But there was no light, not even an oil lamp. The children were scared but we adults were happy. The old women in paricular were joyful. They too had been persecuted — beaten and humiliated by the soldiers — as "the stinking mothers and grandmothers" of the SNM.
>
> The first sign of civilian casualties that we saw were neighbors, hit in the shooting. The mother died. Her sister came to the house, grabbed the three children and closed the door on the dead woman. There was no time to think of burials. It was the lucky ones who managed to bury dead relatives inside their walled courtyards.
>
> The war continued all day, but morale was very high, as we thought our helplessness was coming to an end. That night, the shooting stopped. No one dared to make a sound — no

visiting, no light. The next day, shooting started at dawn. The soldiers came a bit further into town. Then tanks came into town. They aimed at homes. Their strategy was to squeeze between houses so to hide the body of the tank, with only the barrel of its gun showing. Many people were crushed to death, as the tanks sought to achieve this position of defense. No effort was made to avoid civilians, to warn them to get out of houses or to check if people were inside.

Then the shelling began. They shelled from different directions. When a lot of people gathered in one area, shelling became intense. That way, they could kill the greatest number of civilians. People fled their houses in terror, coming out covered in dust. You saw people frantically trying to grab things as their houses caved in. But they were in such a state of shock, shaking, unable to hold onto the bundles they had grabbed, that they dropped everything. You saw distraught people desperately trying to find their relatives.

She recalled one woman with a child strapped on her back, screaming that she couldn't find her child.

As she ran in and out of the rubble, a female relative tried to persuade her to get out before more of the house collapsed. She just kept shouting back that she couldn't leave her child behind, not realizing in her panic that she was carrying the child on her back.

Samia continued:

Things got worse very quickly. Obviously the soldiers were waiting for the evacuation of UN personnel and other expatriates. Once they left, everything was let loose. The soldiers began house-to-house searches, looking for men to kill. By then, any Isaak man who could grab a gun and join the SNM did. The men were either shot on the spot or stabbed. Some of them were taken out of their homes, and strangled in their undershirts, strapped to the gates of their house. In some homes, men were slaughtered in groups. Every Isaak woman who had a father, a husband, a brother, a son, or any man in the house became frenzied, thinking of where to hide them. I had Hassan in the house, my young brother-in-law. I didn't know what to do with him. I wanted to swallow him. They were

143

also raping the women. As we heard all this, we became sick. My young cousin, Kaltoon, went beserk at the stories of rape. She kept praying aloud to God to kill her first, before the soldiers arrived.

The artillery shelling started on the third day of the fighting. The noise was deafening — houses shook and your eyes filled with the dust falling from the houses. Neighbors' houses collapsed all around you. In shock, you waited in turn to die in your house. The shelling, from 6:00 a.m. to 6:00 p.m., was what really destroyed the towns and finished the people off. The decision to destroy the city was not accidental. Long before the war, both Gani and Morgan used to say in public, "If the SNM attacks us, do you think we will leave this town of yours as it is?" It was also meant to destroy any food left behind and to ensure that there was nothing between the soldiers and the SNM.

Many refugees told Africa Watch that government spies would tell the soldiers which houses had SNM sympathizers or where SNM fighters were hiding. The army would then cordon off the whole area and start shelling, row by row, until the area was destroyed.

According to Samia:

A relative of my mother, Haji Ali Nur, a father of 12 and a furniture shop owner, had three grown children killed by shelling. He had popped out to look for food. He came back to find that his house had been shelled. Two of his children had died instantaneously — Samira, about 21, a university student from Mogadishu who was visiting, and Abdiqani, about 17, a schoolboy. The third, a girl, Nasra, was dying as he arrived. Her thigh and leg had been blown off and she was bleeding profusely. He could do nothing for her. He couldn't get an ambulance or any medicine. He just held her and read the Koran over her. She died a half hour later. He had no time to bury them. He collected some stones and covered the three bodies and fled to save the other children. In his shock and grief, he forgot to take any money from the house. The family headed for Daloodoo near Hargeisa, where they had a farm. But the shelling started there too after their arrival, and killed many of their animals. They fled again and went to Geed-

144

Deble. They are now at Harta Sheikh camp. The mother has not been normal since the death of her three children.

During the nine days we remained in Hargeisa, the whole family lived in one room — cooking in there and sleeping. We didn't dare take the children even as far as the courtyard.

As the fighting became more savage and death was everywhere, we lost hope of survival if we stayed. There was no respite. More and more people were leaving. As one house fell, people sought shelter with neighbors. But soon there was nowhere to go. As the shelling intensified, we were forced to think of leaving, but we held back. Most of us had never lived in the countryside. We didn't know how we would cope there.

On the eighth day, part of our house was hit by mortars. The walls separated, windows fell apart — everything crumbled. Luckily no one was killed. After that, we knew we had to leave. We prepared small bundles of essentials, like milk and clothes for the children. But we didn't think of taking much, because even then, we thought we would only be away about ten days. We left behind our best clothes, so as not to ruin them in the countryside.

Before leaving, I crept out and went to check on my grandmother. But there was no way to reach her house, even through alleyways. There were soldiers everywhere. Terrified, I ran back, clinging to the walls. The fear was overwhelming. I felt as if I had died and come back.

That night we packed. We had to get ready in pitch dark. We didn't dare use a torch or a paraffin lamp. We left the house at 4:30 a.m. We whispered to call out to our neighbors who were leaving with us. People were departing from every house we passed. There were thousands of people on the road, moving about in eerie silence. As we passed our local bus stop, an old blind woman who begged in our area, was leaning against a door, crying out for help. To this day, I am haunted by the sound of her voice, her plea not to be left behind. But everyone strong enough to help her was already burdened by the old, the sick and children. I had three children. I could do nothing but, still, I felt so guilty. I still feel bad about it.

We started walking. Everyone was already weak from lack of food, sleep and fear. There were people ferrying elderly parents and grandparents in wheelbarrows, pushing them over rocky terrain. We headed towards the Radio Station area. So many houses and huts we passed had been burned by the shelling. Other homes were gutted by fire after they were hit by grenades. We came upon heaps of corpses everywhere, charred and bloated. One couldn't tell if they were human corpses or animal carcases, until one came closer. The sight had a terrible effect on all of us, especially the children.

We reached Biyaha Shinaha* at 8:30 a.m., exhausted. There were thousands and thousands of people. Many of them had already established tree shelters. I soon realized that because of the shock, I couldn't breast-feed the baby and I had left her bottle behind. Another mother and I used the same bottle.

We left Biyaha Shinaha. We kept going. We had no idea where to go. We walked to Annayo and arrived at night time, more dead than alive. We had to clear some bushes for a space to sleep. It was raining heavily. The little food — rice, sugar and salt — got soaked. It was cold and windy. We got help in lighting a fire. The children were in a terrible state and their cries were frightening. The baby had been screaming all the time we were on the road. I thought it was hunger. At Annayo, I realized one of her ear-drums must have burst.

The next day, we reached Udaan. Again, there were tens of thousands of people everywhere. Seven or eight families had to squeeze into each hut, as people scrambled to find shelter from the heat. Normally, there are many nomads living in Udaan, but they too had fled and taken their livestock. We were very worried about the rest of the family. We decided to leave Udaan and go somewhere else where we were more likely to get news of them. We returned to Annayo. We stayed for about two and a half months at Annayo.

---

*   Biyaha Shinaha is about 15 kilometers kilometers outside Hagreisa. Its name is literally the "Chinese waters" and refers to a project funded by the Chinese government for the development of water tanks.

The SNM line of defense was behind the Radio Station, which is why people first fled in that direction.

As the fighting intensified, many detainees held at various centers were shot. Africa Watch received many accounts of the killing of men killed inside the military compound at Malka Durduro, shot lined up. The victims would drop dead into a trench dug below for that purpose.

Hassan Muhumed Abdillahi, a former truck owner/driver interviewed by Africa Watch in Djibouti on August 13, 1989, arrested on May 29 in Borama and was taken on June 7 to *Qaybta*, the headquaters of the regional military commander. He described the killings there in the following terms:

> There were hundreds of soldiers and civilians detained there, mostly men, but there some women as well, accused of cooking food for the SNM fighters or giving them water. There were also a number of mentally sick people who had been rounded up. I was there for eight days. Every day, there were executions both of Isaak soldiers and civilians. A number of C.I.D. officers were also shot. The smallest number of people killed during any day was thirty, but usually it was much higher. In one day alone, eighty Isaak soldiers were shot, forty from Gebiley, thirty from Darar Weyne, a base near Nasa Hablood where the 26th sector of the army stored weapons, food and petrol, and ten from Boqol Jirreh, the headquarters of the anti-aircraft fighters. They were taken in a truck, their watches and money stolen and then they were shot by a firing squad along the banks of the dry river bed, in batches of ten. Their bodies were left there. Some of those killed Abdi Bilaal, a driver, Ahmed Warsame, a trader and Ali Mohamed, "Ali Dherre," a trader.

For those who did not flee in the first few days of the war, an additional worry was the fear of being shot by soldiers in their own homes. A large number of people were killed as soldiers stormed houses, looking for SNM fighters. Yelling, "Open up! Open up!" They would start shooting straight away if the occupants were slow in opening the door.

Abdirahman Mohamed Jama, interviewed by Africa Watch in Djibouti on August 3, 1989, described his experiences with the soldiers:

About 18 days after the war broke out, 20 heavily armed soldiers came to our house. There was a big group of us gathered there. They banged on the door. We became scared. One of the men, Osman Jalle, panicked and hid inside a cupboard. They searched under every bed and finally the cupboards too. They found Osman and shot him. The soldiers argued among themselves whether the rest of us should also be shot. They took us to the *HANGASH* center. They decided not to kill us. We requested an escort, to protect us from the other soldiers in the street. The soldier who accompanied us back said it had been foolish for so many unarmed Isaak men to be together in one place. We dispersed immediately. I stayed in Hargeisa until the SNM left. The group included Ahmed Farah Arbi, a businessman, Mohamed Haji Dualeh, a local employee of UNICEF, Ahmed Shambaniyeh, owner of a pharmacy, Shageeb Seerar, a businessman, Mohamed Ahmed Yassin, a businessman, and four of his younger brothers, Zeinab Hassan Ali and her two sisters, and Fawzia Qazaali.

Safia Ali Mataan and two of her daughters remained in Hargeisa until the end of September. She was interviewed by Africa Watch in London on August 17, 1989:

We finally left Hargeisa on September 26. We lived in the Sha'ab, a part of Hargeisa that remained in government hands because most of the residents were government employees. Soldiers came openly into houses to loot. People who had temporarily taken refuge in other houses would return to their homes and were too scared to say anything as soldiers helped themselves to everything in their houses. A lot of the people they stole from them, they shot.

Food became scarce and expensive. They continued to shoot wildly long after the SNM had withdrawn from the city. A neighbor, Safia Seef, was killed when a stray bullet hit her as she stood outside her house. After that, as the insecurity became too much, we felt we had to go. Two of my daughters, four other women and I left and went towards Haraf, just outside Hargeisa. We couldn't let any men accompany us, for fear that they'd be be killed.

148

Amaal Aideed Yassin is a soft-spoken 17-year-old former student at
Sheikh Bashir School. She was interviewed by Africa Watch in Cardiff on July
6, 1989:

> We remained in Hargeisa until October as my mother refused
> to leave my grandfather. Even after the SNM left in August,
> they kept up the artillery shelling and bombing, right up to our
> departure. Many old people and the disabled, who had
> remained behind, died from the shelling or were shot. The
> soldiers and the policemen would have shoot-outs among
> themselves as they argued over who had "liberated" Hargeisa
> and who had a "right" to the houses which had not collapsed.
> Many soldiers and policemen died as a result. When there was
> nothing more to loot, the soldiers fought among themselves
> over the booty. When there was nothing left to take from the
> houses, they dismantled the doors, the windows and the roofs,
> which they took to Borama, Galkayo, and other cities, to sell.
>
> Life was terrible for those left in Hargeisa. There were severe
> shortages of food. Fear prevented us from going out to look
> for provisions. Women were afraid of getting raped or killed,
> or both. There were hardly any men who remained. There was
> also the fear of getting hit by stray bullets and mortars. But
> when we couldn't bear our hunger any longer, we used to go
> to "Isha Borama" where soldiers sold the things they stole.

Like many other refugees, Amaal commented cynically on the
government's efforts to keep up the fiction of "normality."

> When some white people came to take videos of Hargeisa, the
> government brought the Ethiopian refugees living in the Har-
> geisa area and put them in tents next to the houses that had
> collapsed. They told the visitors that "These are the residents
> of Hargeisa. They have not fled." Throughout these months,
> loudspeakers on cars circulated in Hargeisa, telling us that
> "everything is normal. The people of Hargeisa are OK." Of
> course we in Hargeisa knew that these were lies, but this was
> for the benefit of outsiders.

The GAO team noted the extent to which residential districts were
targeted by the army.

Hargeisa....has suffered extensive damage from artillery and aerial shelling. The most extensive damage appeared to be in the residential aeas where the concentration of civilians was highest, in the marketplace, and in public buildings in the downtown are. The U.S.Embassy estimated that 70 percent of the city has been damaged or destroyed. Our rough visual inspection confirms this estimate.*

Berbera

Berbera, on the Red Sea coast, is, after Mogadishu, the country's principal port.

The SNM never launched an attack on Berbera, but civilians were not spared the arrests and killings suffered by the residents of Burao and Hargeisa. Confiscation of civilian property was widespread, especially goods at the port: cars, luggage, food. Several hundred cars were apparently taken to Mogadishu. Vehicles belonging to civilians were confiscated by force, and only military transport was allowed to function.

Mass Arrests

Mass arrests were carried out immediately after the SNM attack on Burao. As in Hargeisa, many Isaak elders and businessmen were arrested, apparently because the government feared that they would support an SNM attack on Berbera. From May 27 until June 1, detainees were transferred to Mogadishu by plane. The planes which brought soldiers from Mogadishu carried detainees on the return flight. Thereafter, came an order from Mogadishu to cease the transfer of detainees. After that the killings began. The *HANGASH*, which had a large compound in the center of town, arrested people at night.

Abdifatah Abdillahi Jirreh is an articulate and exceptionally well-informed thirteen year-old. He was interviewed by Africa Watch in Djibouti on August 6 and 9, 1989. He made the following comments about the arrests in Berbera:

---

*   GAO report at p. 6.

Several members of my immediate family were arrested. On June 4, my brother was arrested while trying to buy airline tickets for the Danes working in his company "Intercool Denmark," a company that made ice to cool fish. He was detained for four nights in the old airport built by the Russians. Seven cars belonging to the Danes were used as an excuse to keep coming back to us, accusing us of hiding the keys.

Then, soldiers came to our ice factory and demanded ice at gunpoint. Arrests and killings took place all the time.

One day in mid-August, Dahir Riyaaleh, head of the NSS, came to our ice plant and took my father away. They also arrested one of the watchmen, an old man, Farah Badeh Gheedi. They were detained in the police station, accused of talking about the prospects of the SNM coming to Berbera. They accused my father of having said that the SNM would definitely come to Berbera. They said the conversation took place at 5:30, which is not possible, because at that hour, every day, my father listened to the BBC news and no other conversation could take place when the BBC news was being broadcast. He was released after three days.

Jibril Mohamed Yey, a former employee of the government-owned cement factory, was arrested on July 21, 1988 and released in December. He was interviewed by Africa Watch in Djibouti on August 10, 1989.

The *HANGASH* came to my house at 6:15 p.m. on July 21. Eleven of us, all Isaaks, were arrested the same day, three elders and eight workers. While we were there, the military commander of Berbera, who had been particularly brutal and responsible for most of the killings, General Ahmed Warsame, was transferred to Hargeisa and replaced by a more humane man, General Yusuf Talan. We felt we had been given a reprieve from the deaths we were certain of. We hoped that maybe, just maybe, we would escape death. Luckily, by the time we were arrested, the intense campaign of killings had subsided a little. After seven days at the *HANGASH* center, we were transferred to prison. We were never charged; we were detained simply on the basis of a note hand-written by the deputy military commander of Berbera, Colonel Abdi Samad, telling the prison to keep us behind bars.

151

The three elders were: Ali Mohamed "Waraba," in his 60s; "Cutiye," a man of about 65, lame in one leg and Saleeban Abdi Omer;

The workers included:

Abdi Osman Warsame, a Customs clerk;

Mohamed Yusuf Kaiser, "Gacan," a Customs clerk;

Haybe Yusuf, a Customs clerk.

There were 310 Isaak prisoners, all arrested since the war and 15 non-Isaaks who had been sentenced before the war broke out. Some of the prisoners were people who had arrived in Berbera from abroad and arrested in their hotels. Most were released after paying bribes.

Every day more prisoners were brought in, mainly from nearby villages or from Sheikh. A separate group was 98 Isaak military and prison officers, serving in the Berbera and Mandera area and arrested in early June.

When the interview took place, in mid-August, according to his information, the 98 officers were still in prison.

They included:

Hussein Abdillahi, former head of "Mijas," a correctional center for young criminal offenders, near Bihin, between Berbera and Sheikh; Hussein Osman, a sub-lieutenant at Mandera prison; Ali Yare, a sub-lieutenant at Mandera prison; "Hareed", a sub-lieutenant at Mandera prison; Abdi Handule, a sub-lieutenant working at a military training camp near Mayd.

The prison could only accommodate 120, but at one point there were 485 prisoners. About eighty of us received food from relatives in Berbera. The other 400 got nothing. The people from the countryside suffered from malnutrition. They didn't know anyone in town to bring them food. They became extremely sick. Three nomads died of hunger while I was there. Some of us asked our relatives to bring them food but there were too many people to feed.

Four of us were released when our families petitioned a visiting high-ranking military officer, senior to the military commander of Berbera.

After my release, General Yusuf Talan, who had replaced the butcher, Warsame, called the Mobile Military Court from Burao and told them to sort out the detainees and to identify those who had actually committed offenses.

He released 40 people — the very sick and the very old. The rest were up for bargaining. Those who could raise at least 300,000 shillings were released first, then 200,000 and eventually for much less. Although the amnesty program came into effect in early 1989, they were not released because of that, but because money was involved in every case.

In May [1989] I learned that there were still about 60 people left in the prison.

Kaiser Ismail Adan was an employee of the Somali Shipping Agency in Berbera when the war broke out. He was arrested and transferred to Mogadishu. He provided the following testimony when Africa Watch interviewed him in Djibouti on August 10, 1989:

> I spent three nights at the *HANGASH* center in Mogadishu and was then taken to Barava, about 200 kilometers away, where we were detained for three months. We were allowed no family visits. People would visit us and bring food, money and clothes, but the guards confiscated everything. We had no way of letting our visitors know this. At the slightest hint of trouble, we were beaten with wet plastic hose pipes. There were only two toilets for 125 people. If you didn't come out of the toilet immediately, the guards would come with the hose pipes.

Among the 125 detained [all Isaaks] were:

> A group of Air Force pilots working at Hargeisa Airport when the war broke out. They included:
>
> > Hassan "Jacail"; Ali "Baba"; Yusuf "Afkalahaye" and "Sheekho."

153

Another group had been brought from Ballidoogle, the headquarters of the Air Force, near Baidoa — again, all Isaaks. They included:

Hussein Haji Nur; Ahmed "Iraq"; Ali "Engineer."

Another group of five was from the Somali Airlines. They included:

Abdi Rodol; Muhumed Haji Abdi, "Caamir"; Mohamed Ulujoog, flight engineer; and Mohamed Ismail, flight engineer.

A small group of soldiers based near Baidoa were transferred to fight in Hargeisa. Nineteen Isaaks were excluded and detained at Barava. All the other detainees were from Berbera.

After three months, all 125 detainees were transferred to Laanta Bur prison* and released on March 12, 1989, as part of the amnesty. At Laanta Bur, we were not allowed to see visitors, but we were allowed to receive the food and other provisions.

Killings and Arrests of Passengers on the Ship, "Emviyara"

Many refugees told Africa Watch about the fate of Isaak passengers on a ship called "Emviyara" that docked at the port of Berbera on June 21, 1988. The passengers had been imprisoned in Saudi Arabia before the war broke out and deported, accused of irregularities in their residence documents. They had apparently appealed to Saudi officials to rescind the order of deportation because of the war situation, but their request was unsuccessful. Out of about 400 passengers, 29 men identified themselves as Isaaks. There were many others, but they claimed to be from other clans. The commander of the - HANGASH, "Calas" and "Dakhare," his deputy, sorted out the passengers according to their clan. The Isaaks were taken to the HANGASH center and their money and belongings confiscated. They included Saeed Barre Weraar, Abdillahi "Waji," "Duhut," "Falan" and "Adiyare." Some were severely tortured. Saeed Barre Weerar has become paralyzed in both arms. Eight were

---

* Laanta Bur is a maximum security prison about 50 kilometers outside Mogadishu.

subsequently killed, including Abdirizak Ibrahim Mohamed. The other 21 were imprisoned in Berbera and later released.

Killings

By all accounts, Berbera suffered some of the worst abuses of the war, even though the SNM never attacked Berbera. Victims in Berbera were killed in an extremely brutal fashion: most had their throats slit, then were shot. According to many refugees who were in Berbera for several months after the war broke out, at least 500 people were killed, mainly in June, by having their throats slit. The killings took place at night, at a site about 10 kilometers from Berbera, near the airport. People were killed in batches of 30-40. The victims were overwhelmingly men of fighting age that the army feared would join the SNM. A few women were also killed.

Kaiser Ismail Adan provided the following testimony:

> The town received news of the slaughters from a survivor, Abdi Waal. Abdi Waal was among the first group of 21 who were taken to the site. He pretended to be dead and escaped with serious wounds. He was taken to the hospital by his family; soldiers then stole him from the hospital. No one knows his whereabouts.

> The overwhelming majority of the victims were seasonal laborers from Hargeisa, Burao and the nearby villages, hired for loading livestock for export and unloading goods at the port. It is difficult to identify them because they were temporary workers.

Africa Watch learned the identities of some of the victims: They include:

Ibrahim Qasim Elmi,"Gaagale", restaurant owner
Mohamed Ahmed, "Shabelo", taxi-driver
Saeed Abdillahi Dualeh, employee, cement factory
Ahmed Omer Mushteeg, port employee
Abdi Ali Arabloo, driver
Mohamed Ismail, watchman
Abdulla Nur Ali, soldier

155

Kayse Ga'an, Customs employee
Abdi Isse, electrician
Mohamed Aw Abdi, Customs employee
"Dumbush," Customs employee
Mohamed Dage Abdi, "Bakayle"
Abdi Mohamed Aden, "Suhaye"
Abdi Sugule Muse, "Kirih"
Haji Ibrahim, "Faras'Ade
Ibrahim Yassin Bolaleh
Ali Muse Elabe
Omer Elmi Egeh
Sulieman Abdi Omer
Mohamed Warsame Guled
and his two sons
Nico Muse Tur
Ismail Adan Wais
Awil Awale
Dahir Hassan Egal
Abdi Hashi Elmi

Some of the women killed included:

Habiba Warsame Kirih
Waris Hassan "Gaagaab"
Khadija Omer

Abdifatah Abdillahi Jirreh provided details about another group of people who were murdered:

> One night they arrested a group of men at our hotel, "Jirreh" hotel situated near the *HANGASH* compound, and took them to the hills outside the old airport built by the Russians and slaughtered them.

They were:

> Adan Mohamed, an employee of the Electricity Agency, and his two brothers; one brother, "Cirro" was an employee of Somali Airlines and the other was unemployed;

156

An employee of Arablo restaurant;

The brother of "British," a driver at Chevron;

Ali Babel, a driver for UNHCR.

Africa Watch also learned that eleven Isaak men, who included nomads, were arrested on the outskirts of Berbera and accused of aiding the SNM. Three senior officers, amongst them the Marine Commander of Berbera, Colonel Muse "Biqil" ordered that they be burnt alive. They were burned and buried in a spot about 10 kilometers east of Batalale, a tourist spot in Berbera.

Khadra Hassan Mohamed is sixteen years old. Her family are nomads who lived in Mandera, near Berbera. She told Africa Watch the following in an interview in Djibouti on August 2, 1989.

> Immediately the war broke out, soldiers came and took all the animals and money. They captured me, my sister, cousin, father and two other elders living in the same settlement. Luckily, my mother was in Hargeisa at the time. They took us in the direction of Adaadley, near Mandera prison. Shortly before we reached the army training camp outside Adaadley, they shot father and the other two men in front of us. Just like. The soldiers argued among themselves whether to shoot the rest of us; one of them loaded a gun and pointed it at us. Just before he fired, another soldier grabbed it from him and said, "Leave them, they're young girls". They dropped us in the middle of Berbera, which we did not know and where we knew no-one. Some people took pity on us and took us to their homes. After a month, my mother arrived in Mandera and somehow found out what had happened. She could not come to fetch us herself as she was wounded; she got injured in Hargeisa when a mortar hit the house she was staying in. As additional protection, she sent a woman married to a soldier to escort us back. This woman fetched us one by one, to avoid suspicion. As soon as we were altogether, we left for Ethiopia.

Between June and the end of September, a series of villages between Berbera and Hargeisa were raided by the army as well as armed Ethiopian refugees, and burnt, many villagers shot, women raped, livestock confiscated and elders arrested to be detained in Berbera. Some of the villages included Da'arbuduq, half-way between Hargeisa and Berbera; Dara-Godle, about 20

157

kilometers southwest of Berbera; Sheikh Abdal, near Mandera central prison; Dubato; Dalaw, located east of Mandera prison, in the Golis mountain range; and Lasa-Da'awo,

See Appendix One for a list of some of the people killed in Berbera.

Erigavo

Though the SNM did not attack Erigavo, and there was no armed conflict there for at least several months, the Isaaks there escaped neither killings nor arrests.

Fadumo Ali Farah, a 58-year-old woman, is the mother of 14 children. She had been in Erigavo for three months prior to the outbreak of war. Interviewed by Africa Watch in London on July 24, 1989, she reported:

> As soon as news of the war in Burao and Hargeisa reached Erigavo, the head of the police told the non-Isaaks to leave to avoid the conflict. The government confiscated the cars of the Isaaks to transport them to safety. The first three days, the government spent transporting the Darood and their goods.
>
> The Isaaks and non-Isaaks lived in different parts of town, so it was easy to isolate the communities and to target the Isaaks. Tanks were positioned to point at our section of town. There was always the threat that if we made the wrong move they would be used against us. The Isaaks also decided to leave, but they only had donkeys and camels left to transport them. The military were everywhere in town to ensure that we couldn't leave and to confiscate our provisions. They surrounded the city. All Isaak men who didn't manage to escape, young and old, were arrested, and women and children were told to return to their homes. The men were detained in the central prison.
>
> Everyone who could escape left for the mountains. But you had to be physically fit to climb those mountains. I remained behind. I was too old to think of climbing mountains. The rape of women and looting intensified as people sought to flee. Civilians had no value in their eyes.

158

Even if they hadn't been arrested, the men had no weapons to defend us. Some nomads who had gone to the coastal region of Mayd and Hiis were forcibly returned to Erigavo.

The only Isaak men left were the old men who couldn't run away. The non-Isaak men — including nomads who had never handled guns, even the local riffraff and thieves were armed. It was simply enough not to be Isaak. They were given instructions to defend Erigavo if the SNM came and in the meantime to kill any Isaaks who moved.

For the first month, there was mainly looting and rape. There were not the house-to-house killings as in Burao and Hargeisa because there was no SNM presence. The SNM had advised the Isaaks in Erigavo not to fight because they couldn't defend us and because they knew we had no weapons ourselves. The government was also anxious to avoid a conflict there in order to ensure that the coast was clear. So they sent a "reconciliation" committee. But no reconciliation was possible. Apart from the looting, rape and the intense hostility we had experienced, we knew of the horrors that Isaaks in Burao and Hargeisa had suffered.

After a month, about 35 Isaak policemen were taken to Galkayo as "hostages" in case the SNM mistreated Darood civilians. No one knows what happened to them.

Then Abdi Mohamed Sahardeed, "Abdi Dibo", was sent to Erigavo and he got the military out of town. He forbade the military to enter the town after 6:00 p.m., and insisted that only policemen could remain in town after that time. They came, of course, after 10:00 p.m., and then there would be shoot-outs between the army and police as they fought each other for the right to "guard" the town — an opportunity to loot. Still, we welcomed having the military at some distance.

Fadumo continued:

There were no aerial raids until after I left. But since then, because the SNM has entered the town, there has been aerial bombardment and artillery shelling.

I eventually left for Mogadishu. I had to use my Darood connections and pay a lot of money to find transport. There was no other way you could go by road. In Mogadishu, I learned of the death of my eldest son, Abdirahman Mohamed Saeed, 32, who had joined the SNM. I didn't dare cry for fear that I would be reported as an SNM sympathizer by neighbors. I have no news of my second son, Muse, 31, a teacher. He was newly married and he and his young wife had fled. I don't know if he is in this world or not. It would even be some sort of relief to know that he was dead.

In January 1989, Community Aid Abroad (CAA), an Australian aid agency which ran a primary health care program for the Sanaag region, based in Erigavo, withdrew its program after eight years in Somalia and published a report "to draw attention to recent events in Somalia which have resulted in civil war, a huge refugee problem, persecution of a large section of the population along tribal lines and widespread human rights violations." Deploring the "lack of basic freedom and human rights" in the country, the agency stated that it was leaving the region "due to a drastic decline in security and human rights." They said that their "staff have reported many violations of human rights for which they believe the Somali Government must take the main responsibility." In describing the government's reaction to the SNM offensive, the report observed:

> The government response to the attack has been particularly brutal and without regard to civilian casualties — in fact there is ample evidence that civilian casualties have been deliberately inflicted so as to destroy the support base of the SNM, which is mainly comprised of people from the Isaaq tribe. Following the SNM attacks on the major towns of Hargeisa and Burao, government forces bombed the towns — causing over 400,000 people to flee the atrocities across the border into Ethiopia, where they are now located in refugee camps, living in appalling conditions, with inadequate water, food, shelter and medical facilities.

> In Sanaag Region access to villages by CAA staff was denied by the military and project resources such as vehicles and drugs misappropriated by government officals. This, combined with poor security, made primary health work impossible and endangered the lives of staff, leading to a withdrawal by the agency. Project staff were frequently harassed by the

160

military even when attending medical emergencies and on one occasion shots were fired.

Whilst human rights have been deteriorating for some years in Somalia . . . we believe that the government must bear a particularly heavy responsibility for events over the last six months.

With regard to specific incidents and patterns of abuse in Erigavo, the report noted;

> The military occupation of Erigavo, has resulted in widespread suffering for the people of that area forcing many people to flee to the bush including most of the population of Erigavo. It is believed that the military gave the elders of the village money in payment for boys as young as twelve and thirteen years of age. Untrained and undisciplined these youths were armed with AK47s and sent to patrol the town, unsure and ignorant of how to use their newly acquired power."

> It is known that many people have fled from the town of Elafweyn following bombing attacks by the government forces. A "scorched earth" policy applied to the villages in the Elafweyn plains. These displaced people are hiding in the bush without adequate access to food and medical supplies.*

Peter Kieseker, a spokesman for the CAA, describing government policies in the region, commented: "Genocide is the only word for it".**

Shamis Farah who visited Erigavo in April 1989 described to Africa Watch in an interview in London on October 14, 1989, the war that continues to rage there. Visiting Erigavo a few months after publication of the CAA report, her testimony is consistent with the findings of the agency:

> I arrived in Erigavo on April 29, 1989. I had gone there to fetch my mother. On the way there, I was advised to hide the fact that I was Isaak. I learned the lineage of other clans by heart in order to save my skin.

---

* Community Aid Abroad, Agency Statement on Somalia, January 12, 1989.

** Alison Whyte, "Human crisis that has poisoned a nation," *The Independent*, February 13, 1989.

161

The situation in Erigavo was unbelievable. There were hardly any Isaak civilians left there, except for some old men and old women. There was one middle-aged woman, a mother with two daughters. One daughter was 17 years old and she was never allowed out of the house. The others had fled; I heard horrendous stories of killings and rape, even of very old women. They all lived in one part of town and heavily armed pro-government militias lived in another part of town. It was the militias that were really in control, but they were armed by and worked closely with the military. Even though by then, there was no fighting in town, bullets flew all night long, as the militias fired off their weapons. I was told that the SNM had attacked the town at the end of March and killed a lot of soldiers; the militias had fled; two days later, the militias returned and killed a lot of Isaak civilians. People were apparently shot even inside mosques. There are mass graves everywhere. I left Erigavo on 23 July.

The military became very suspicious of me and wanted to drive me out of town. While I was there, a mentally retarded Isaak man who remained in town, Dualeh "Wareer," advised me to leave. He was shot, his body strapped to an arm chair which was placed in front of our house, to intimidate me. My sister and I tried to bury him but shots were fired at us, which frightened us.

There were so many corpses everywhere; the stench was terrible.

There is absolutely no government or law in Erigavo. The biggest business is arms dealing. While I was there, 18 Hawiye soldiers deserted the army. They were young men — no more than 18-19. They told me they had been conscripted near Baidoa and Kismayo, taken to Dhananeh military camp in Mogadishu, given crash training, had their heads shaved and then sent out. They had no idea where they were, not the slightest sense of direction about the region. I heard again and again that the government told the Darood population that the Isaaks planned to take over the whole country — that they planned to destroy the Darood and that it was essential to prevent this.

162

See Appendix A for a list of some of the casualties.

El Afweyne and Kalsheikh

During July and November 1988, villages located in Sool, Sanaag and Toghdeer regions, suffered a series of attacks by government forces.

Africa Watch received the following written testimony from an eye-witness:

> ...during July 1988 [the] military has been assigned to stay permanently at El Afweyne secondary school for controlling the nomadic population. After that, they looted the property, they killed around 50 persons, in the first attack. So people ran away to the mountains. The commander ordered to chase them and to hunt them. The people went to the wells. . .the military found them and they killed them. The names of the area [are] as follows; Kaliyokal, Daburdalol, Durbarmumma, Kal Sheikh and other different places. In other various area around, 50 or 60 dead persons. People run away, far away... in high mountains. Food is prohibited...to shift from the towns. Just they are alive from meat (their animals). Diarrhea is everywhere.

> [The] military [are] using weapons like cannon [out of] American jeeps, heavy guns at the nomadic people . . . their livestock shot and the rest is looted, taken by the military, 3,000 camels and 10,000 sheep and goats. Small huts [were] fired at . . . his order is from the following two men; Lt. Mohamed Abdi Diriye of the Police and Lt. Coloned "Korton", in charge of the military.

> Kalsheikh is empty — no one is left. El Af Weyne as well, as well as the other areas — Good'Anood, El Ad, Bihin and Fadigab. These villages [and] all the material inside the houses is taken, and some [villages] are fired at.

> I have seen with my own eyes dead bodies at Kalsheikh. They collected them in a truck...41 dead bodies at Kalsheikh [At] El Af Weyne I have seen the planes bombing. The planes damaged so many houses. [After] that the military damaged beautiful houses by bazookas.

Jama Osman Sugule, interviewed by Africa Watch in Djibouti on August 9, 1989, provided the following details about the atrocities in these regions.

> Between July and the beginning of December, many villages located in various districts were burned between June and August 1988; Sinaro, Bohol, Fadigab, Garadag, Oog, Gawsaweyne, Godheeli, Kalsheikh, El Afweyne, Dararweyne, Bohol, Berde Analeh and Gureed. Many people were killed as a result.

See Appendix A for a list of some of the casualties.

Sheikh

As soon as the news of the SNM attack on Burao reached Sheikh, armed Ogadeni refugees and the army started to loot homes and to kill civilians. There were also widespread arrests of Isaak men; they were detained in the nearby military compound. The SNM did not attack Sheikh.

Asha Ibrahim Haji Hussein, a resident of Newport, went on holiday to Somalia in March 1988, for the first time in ten years. Her family is from *Dariiqaddah* quarter of Sheikh. There was special government hostility towards this district because many former high-ranking soldiers from the area had defected to the SNM.

When we interviewed her in Newport on July 7, 1989, she told Africa Watch the following:

> Before I left for Somalia, I had heard many stories about the hardship of life in Somalia. But I had not believed them.

> From the 27th, there was non-stop looting. Our homes were searched. The soldiers ripped chairs apart and destroyed everything, both in their desperate search for money and valuables, and out of spite. They even shot the clay water-pots, although they knew that there was only water in them.

> Abdillahi Muse Aw Jama, a nomad, came to Sheikh from the Berbera region, after he received news that ten members of his family had been killed. He was arrested and spent three days at the police station. Then he was shot. His body was put in front of the police station to serve as an example.

164

The army sought out women whose husbands or sons were known to have joined the SNM. Fadumo Ali Dinkaal, whose husband had owned a shop, had her husband and two sons in the SNM. She was arrested, her house ransacked, and then she was shot at the military compound.

Saeedo Haji Ahmed, stayed in Sheikh for three weeks after the war broke out. She provided this testimony when Africa Watch interviewed her in London on October 31, 1989.

The worst abuses were committed by the refugees from the camps between Sheikh and Berbera, such as Bihin Dole and Biyole. They arrived armed and did whatever they wanted. They did not even know how to carry their rifles. Their ignorance of the weapons they were given made them all the more dangerous. They were so eager to shoot. Shots rained everywehere. They raped many women and stole everything. The soldiers were for the most part, young men, hardly more than boys, brought form Mogadishu by plane. They also lorded it over us. They kept telling the refugees that "these are the filthy supporters of the qurmis". Many young men were shot in their homes or killed with a knife as they tried to escape, including Farah Yare, his brother-in-law and Osman Gaas.

Arabsiyo

Arabsiyo experienced the same pattern of atrocities as other northern towns.

Abdi Kahin Hadliyeh, a seaman interviewed by Africa Watch in Cardiff on July 6, 1989, recalled:

I was in Arabsiyo when the war broke out on May 27. Looting and searching private homes became an all-day affair; the soldiers took everything, even dismantling doors and windows. The hardship increased day by day. When the war spread to Hargeisa, people left Arabsiyo and went towards Ethiopia. The soldiers started killing people in their own homes. On June 6, they killed two old people in their houses — Fadumo Ahmed, about 70, and Ismail Hersi, about 70. On June 10, we fled towards Ethiopia.

165

Ismail Isse Heyeh, also a former seaman, interviewed by Africa Watch in Cardiff on July 7, 1989, had a similar tale to tell:

I owned a farm and some buildings in Arabsiyo. My wife, children and young siblings were there, so I went back every year.

When war broke out in Burao, soldiers broke into our house and tried to mistreat my 17-year-old daughter, Hodan. My 19-year-old son, Ahmed, and her mother tried to protect her. He was shot on the spot and they beat my wife with the butt of a gun. The noise alerted our neighbors; my daughter managed to escape in the confusion. She took her 4-year-old brother by the hand and just ran. She had no idea where she was going. She just went berserk with fear and ran. The next day, she reached Duriya, near Allay Baddey and met some former neighbors. They looked after her and her brother.

Everyone in the family then fled somewhere. When I went back in September 1988 I collected them from different places. My daughter Hodan has become mentally unstable from the shock of that experience. In Ethiopia, we were joined by my two sisters. They are both widows each with eight children. Their husbands were killed in Hargeisa. One was married to Hassan Darood, a former local government employee who was shot on the road while he was trying to escape, and the other was married to Bashe Abdillahi, a former soldier. He was shot in his house.

Mogadishu

Nor did Isaaks in Mogadishu escape arrest and abuse. There was a massive wave of arrests, of businessmen, of Somali Airlines staff, of army officers, employees of relief agencies and civil servants. Over three hundred detainees were held at the NSS headqarters, at *Godka*, an NSS prison, at a military camp at *Salaan Sharafta*, where military parades are held and at *Laanta Bur* prison, a maximum security prison about 50 kilometers from Mogadishu. Most of them were released only after their families paid exorbitant bribes. All small hotels were searched at night and guests sorted out into Isaaks and non-Isaaks; the Isaaks were then detained. All Isaak senior officials were forbidden from leaving the country, for fear that they would join the SNM. Abdi Rageh, a former military officer was forcibly taken out of an airline while en route to Frankfurt; Omer Mohamed Nimalleh, "Omer Yare", a businessman and a former colonel in the police, was arrested at the airport on his was to Kenya on a business trip. Among the detainees were:

Ismail Saeed Araleh; Mohamed Abdi Aden, "Iskeerse," businessman; Colonel Abdillahi Kahin, armed forces; Ismail Hashi Madar, lecturer at a military academy; Mohamed Hashi Madar, brother of above, accountant; Jama Abdi Farah, "Takroni," businessman; Ibrahim Elmi Bulaale, civil servant; Dahir Ahmed, "Burso," Catering Officer, Somali Airlines; Dahir Haji Mohamed, "Dahir Somali," businessman; Abdi Mohamed Rodol, chief pilot, Somali Airlines; Ahmed Robleh, pilot, Somali Airlines; Faiza Ahmed Mohamed, Stewardess, Somali Airlines; Ahmed Hussein Shakur, partially crippled, financial director, Somali Airlines; Haji Jama Mohamed Miyateen, businessman, in his 70s; Ali Ahmed Hassan, "Ali Jinnah," businessman; Ahmed Nur Jama, lecturer, Faculty of Agriculture, Somali National University; Abdi Rageh Jama, businessman; Abiib Mirreh, director of civil aviation; Abdi Jama Sed, geologist, State petroleum company; Hassan Hawadleh, general manager of Somali Petroleum Agency; Mohamed Ibrahim, "Sa'abo Yar", director at Mogadishu airport office; Haji Ibrahim Osman, "Basbas," businessman and former minister, in his 70s; Aden Nur Awale, businessman; Ali Ahmed Sahardeed, "Arab," manager director of the National Flour Factory; Mohamed Ali Isse, civil engineer and contractor; Mohamed Saleh Muse, 64, businessman.

Mohamoud Ahmed Isse, 23, was in Mogadishu at the time. He was interviewed by Africa Watch in Cardiff on July 6, 1989:

> I was a first year languages student at Gahayr College in Mogadishu. We were due to sit for our exams in June when the war broke out. About 50 Isaak students at our college were dismissed. They tried to conscript us. We were taken to Dhanane, a military camp. You would only be released if you paid money. No Isaaks could leave through the airport. If you gave Hargeisa, Burao or Berbera as your city of origin, your ticket and passport were confiscated and you were arrested. A friend of mine, Abdi Ismail, an engineering student at the University, was detained at Galshire prison. He was still there

when I left in August. On July 1, I learned that my mother had been killed in Burao. She was standing outside our house when she was hit by an artillery shelling. My father disappeared. With this and the lack of security in Mogadishu, I decided to leave and I went to Egypt.

Those who went in search of relatives in the north experienced their share of hardship.

Amina Mohamoud Hussein, a young mother of three, left Mogadishu when to look for her family in Burao. She was interviewed by Africa Watch in Newport on July 7, 1989:

On June 12, 1988, I left Mogadishu by car to go and look for my family. I knew I couldn't get to Burao but I was mad with worry. I forgot all about security and threw myself onto a truck going in the direction of Las Anod. As no Isaak trucks were allowed to leave Mogadishu, I went in a truck that belonged to a Darood. When we reached Jowhar, we were stopped and asked about our clan. I pretended I was Dulbahante [one of the Darood clans]. I prayed they wouldn't ask me any details. I talked in a southern accent to disguise I was Isaak. Luckily, I recognized an old schoolmate who is Dulbahante and I talked to her. When they asked me more details to prove my clan, she saved me. At Galkayo, we were stopped at another checkpoint. One of the civilian passengers told them he suspected I was Isaak. We disembarked and all the others were allowed to return to the truck. They started to question me. I stuck to my story about being Dulbahante. Otherwise, I knew how serious the consequences would be. They ordered the truck to leave without me. Luckily, my former classmate made a real stink. She insisted that I was Dulbahante but that my mother was Isaak. She told them that I had powerful Dulbahante uncles in the military and they would have to face their wrath if they mistreated me. They hesitated. The driver, who clearly believed my friend, put pressure on them and they finally let us go.

Two nights later, we reached Las Anod. There, I recognized lots of people I knew from Burao. I covered myself up to avoid recognition. I met another Isaak woman there whose children are Dulbahante. She coached me to use the clan of her children. I learned all the names by heart. There were trucks everywhere loaded with videos, furniture, carpets, crockery, which were apparently the "wares" from Hargeisa and Burao. On the journey, I met another woman who was also pretending to be Dulbahante. We had to go through all this if we were to save ourselves. By this time, it was not a matter of trying to trace my family's whereabouts. I had given up any hopes of that. I was trying, literally, to save my own skin. We redirected ourselves towards Ethiopia. The other Isaak woman and I walked and walked for five days.

Land Mines

An additional worry for those left behind in Hargeisa was the danger of land mines. According to many refugees who remained in Hargeisa for a few months after the evacuation of the SNM in August, the army mined and blew up many of the city's principal buildings, such as the Union Hotel and a private maternity clinic near the Sha'ab Girls School, in an attempt to clear the space between them and the SNM. Houses belonging to civilians, which were near important government offices were also blown up. Land mines were used to blast tall buildings that wouldn't collapse easily. Roads that the army thought the SNM would take were also mined. The Somali refugees we interviewed testified that many Ethiopian refugees living in the camps, who were encouraged to come into town, died when they stepped on land mines.

But land mines were not only used in Hargeisa.

Hassan Mohamed Abdillahi, a man in his early 50s is the victim of a land mine explosion near Tug Wajale in January 1989. He had both feet amputated in Borama. A resident of Hargeisa, he owned the truck he drove, which transported salt. He was interviewed by Africa Watch in Djibouti on August, 13, 1989:

> On May 27, when the war broke out in Burao, I was in Zeila, on my way to Borama. I was arrested in Borama on May 29, together with twelve other Isaak drivers. We were taken to Hargeisa. We were prisoners but at the same time, the army used us to drive our cars for their benefit, to transport armaments and food for soldiers.

The drivers were taken to different locations. Initially, I was taken to Giriyaad, a military barracks in the west of Hargeisa. We were detained there. We were given nothing to eat.

Apart from transporting armaments, the soldiers also used the trucks commercially for their own purposes. In December, I was taken to an agricultural project near Tug wajale and told to transport hay that the army planned to sell in Borama. Two officers asked me to take them to Dila, west of Tug wajale. A mine exploded just before we reached Dila, hitting my side of the truck. My legs were badly burned. I was taken to a hospital in Borama which had no medicine, not even gauze to wash the wound with. I had no family there either. The wound had to be washed with salt and water. I was unconscious on arrival because I had lost so much blood. Both my feet were immediately amputated — with no anaesthetic. After a month in the hospital in Borama, I made contact with relatives in Djibouti. They had connections with the NSS and got the OK for me to be discharged and I arrived in Djibouti on February 6 and was hospitalized immediately.

Some of the other truck drivers also became injured by mine explosions. Hassan Ali, for example, was injured when a mine exploded at Garbahaadley on the Somali/Ethiopian border.

He said that the mines are plastic so that they cannot be detected by metal detectors. All the mines he saw had been imported from Egypt, although he did not know if they had been manufactured in Egypt.

11. SEEKING SANCTUARY:
FLEEING TO THE COUNTRYSIDE

The mass exodus began after the fighting intensified in the towns. People fled in vehicles and on foot, ferrying the old and the sick in hand carts. Other dangers awaited them; the planes followed the exodus. Also mobile military units patrolled the exits of towns. Troops that intercepted the fleeing civilians killed, raped and extorted. In desperation, many hid in the bushes or sought cover of woodland areas to avoid the air raids and the soldiers.

The GAO team noted that:

The Issak refugees began evacuating the cities of Hargeisa and Burao by the end of the first week of fighting (early June), and it appears that the evacuation was completed by the end of the month....The refugees reported remaining in Hargeisa and Burao until the last possible moment and then fleeing in a panic with only those possessions they could carry on their backs. The refugees gathered by the thousands on the outskirts of the cities, assembling their families and relatives. A number of the refugees we interviewed indicated that, while gathering their families and deciding what course to follow, they were strafed by Somali military aircraft.*

Yusuf, interviewed by Africa Watch in Djibouti on August 9, 1989, described what happened as the fighting intensified:

People fled by the main roads in speed and panic, oblivious to danger. They were just too desperate. It was certain death if you remained and it was death if you left. If people met soldiers on their way, that was bad luck for them. As you ran, you came across small children weeping over dead parents. They were too small to run themselves or to understand what was happening.

---

*   GAO report at p.6

171

Mohamed Karshe Mohamed, a former seaman whose wife and children lived in Hargeisa, was interviewed by Africa Watch in Cardiff on July 6, 1989. He spoke of the fear that caused the flight:

> After nine days of fighting, we left our house. We had no money, no clothes, nothing. Fear kept us going. We just followed the crowds. We had no idea where we were going or what we should do because we were so disoriented. Everyone else was in a similar state of mind. Because of the planes you never lost the fear, so you just kept going.

The aerial attacks as people fled the towns caused a substantial number of the civilian casualties. Contrary to the laws of war which require that military action should be directed against military targets only, the aerial bombardment in Somalia targeted primarily civilians, according to the accounts we received. The planes hit residential homes, mosques, schools, public buildings, even centers for the wounded, such as the center at Geed-Debleh. The planes followed some people into Ethiopia.

Yusuf described the planes responsible for the air-raids:

> When people fled the town, they went after them in planes as they could not chase them all by foot. The planes used were British-made "Hunters," Chinese made Mig 19s, Russian Mig 17s and 21s. Three or four seaters made in Italy were used for surveillance. The surveillance planes would identify the long caravan-like rows of people. Then the planes would come and drop their bombs. They would fly very low because they knew that civilians did not have anti-aircraft guns. The Hunter made 9-12 rounds on each flight and the Russian-made Mig came back five or six times. Some days, the planes were non-stop, from 6:00 a.m.-6:00 p.m., hitting the same area again and again. They also killed the livestock so there was nothing to eat. They would even bomb the trees to deprive us of shelter. If there was a piece of clothing on a tree, that immediately became a target.

Hargeisa

A dry river bed, known as *Dihda*, divides the city of Hargeisa. Those who lived north of the *Dihda* fled north and northwest, while those who lived to the south fled southwest.

Fadumo (not her real name), commented:

We lived in Goljano, near Hargeisa General Hospital. On Monday night, May 31, at 2:00 a.m., we woke up to the sound of gun fire. Artillery shells directed at the Radio Station were passing overhead. We were at the bottom of the hill and therefore fortunate. On the fifth day, some government soldiers came in a tank and shelled areas of the neighborhood for showing sympathy to the SNM fighters. On the seventh day, a large SNM force arrived in our neighborhood. We decided to leave while they controlled the area. We packed mats, blankets and whatever dry food supplies we could carry. About 100 people departed with us. Shells landed everywhere. We kept going. We had no idea where to go; we headed towards Annayo to the west of Hargeisa, on the advice of a traveler who was returning from Annayo and was looking for some members of his family. Along the way, we got a lift. We arrived at Annayo after three days. I went around to the neighbors and begged for food. One family assigned part of an area to us. We built a waba, [a hut created under a tree with the trunk as the supporting structure and the branches overhead as the roof, reinforced with additional branches].

We stayed at Annayo for a month. We used to watch the planes fly by on bombing missions. We were running out of food supplies. We sent some of the youths to look for food wherever they could find it. On the 30th day a spotter arrived over our village. By then we knew the bomber always arrived after the spotter. Early the next morning, we all left the village and hid in the bush. As expected, the bomber came and bombed the village. This was the pattern. The village population and the newcomers sustained many casualties. The SNM had until then discouraged us from crossing the border. We finally decided to leave.

173

On July 30 at around 6:00 a.m. we left Annayo and arrived at Udaan at 3:00 p.m. The bomber arrived and we continued our travel. We arrived at Geed-Abeer area and camped there for a night, leaving early the next day. We took cover in the maize farms whenever we saw planes. We kept heading for the direction of Alley-Baddey, but had to cross the paved road near Arabsiyo under government control. We were lent a camel to carry our beddings to Dabeel-Weyne. Some of our group stayed there, while others continued to Harta Sheikh camp in Ethiopia and then on to Harshin — a nine-hour hike from Harta Sheikh.

Speaking emotionally, Jama Osman Samatar, interviewed by Africa Watch in London on June 1, 1989, recalled his family's flight from Hargeisa:

The aerial bombardment started on Tuesday, hitting everything. We decided to escape to the open countryside before our house collapsed. We left the next morning. Everyone was scrambling to get out. We had no idea where to go, but we had to escape the shelling and bombing.

We went towards Geed-Debleh, about ten kilometers from Hargeisa. We arrived there after a seven hour trek. One had the impression that the entire city was there. But then the shelling started there as well, even though the SNM was nowhere to be seen. Real pandemonium broke out. People were even more desperate there then they had been in Hargeisa. It made them feel they could never escape. Many people were killed, some by the bombs dropped by the planes, others by the machine-guns fired out of the airplanes, others by the shelling or because they were trampled on in the panic. Family members lost each other. Some parents became separated from their children. I lost my mother-in-law and learned much later that she eventually got to Djibouti.

We knew that the shelling was the work of the government alone because the SNM only had bazookas and AK 47s.

We went on to Annayo, walking at night and hiding during the day. We set-up a make-shift shelter. The next day, some of us stole back to Hargeisa to look for food. We had no idea how long we would have to live like this so we had to get provisions.

174

In Hargeisa, I saw that our shop had been completely destroyed.

On the way, we got attacked and my brother-in-law, Ali Qaudan was shot in the foot. We tied his foot up and transported him to Geed-Debleh. I also came upon other relatives and friends who were all in bad shape.

Every week or ten days we sneaked into Hargeisa at night and would leave at daybreak, before the shelling and the bombing started. One of those days, I saw the bodies of two brothers I knew — the Abbas brothers — their arms and legs had been blown off. The area near the Radio Station, which used to be a market, was covered with dead bodies and dead dogs.

After three weeks at Annayo, we left because there was no food left to collect from our houses in Hargeisa and nothing else to eat.

We started walking towards Ethiopia, at night of course. We walked for five nights under extremely difficult conditions. For small children and older women it was particularly difficult. Most of those five nights and days we had practically nothing to eat. We had saved a bit of sugar and mixed the sugar with water whenever we could get water. That was practically all we had to sustain us. Later, we picked corn we found growing in the fields and ate it raw. It was difficult to look for food at night. During the day, we did not dare go out. I have a problem with high blood pressure, which got worse and I became ill.

All day long, we hid in the bushes to escape the planes which were buzzing overhead, dropping bombs and strafing everything in sight. We saw many people, camels and cows killed as a result. There was also the danger of attacks by soldiers. The worst part was the road between Hargeisa and Arabsiyo because of the proximity of the soldiers. We knew that soldiers had killed many civilians and then robbed them.

The SNM had given us an escort of twenty men to lead us through the dangerous parts of the road where soldiers might be waiting. Once we had the SNM escort, the enemy was not soldiers but the planes. We were the lucky ones. There were thousands of people on the road and the SNM could not give escorts to every group.

Finally we crossed the border into Ethiopia at Dabeel-Weyne. We stayed two days at Dabeel Weyne but as there was nothing to eat there, we went on to Harta Sheikh camp in Ethiopia.

Ahmed Yunis Awaleh, a former seaman and a resident of Hargeisa, interviewed by Africa Watch in Cardiff on July 6, 1989, described the air-raids at Geed-Debleh:

The air-raids at Geed-Debleh, a center for the wounded, were intense. As the bombing continued, the number of wounded increased and the old ones were replaced by the latest casualties.

Hassan Ismail Omaar, interviewed by Africa Watch in Cardiff on July 8, 1989, recalled his attempts to find refuge:

Two weeks after fighting broke out in Hargeisa, conditions became unbearable and we fled to the north of the city and trekked to Annayo. We lived there under the shade of trees on river embankments.

When the planes came there too, we couldn't believe that further suffering was in store for us. There were several raids daily in Annayo and adjacent areas. The shortage of food was such a serious problem that in spite of the fear of the planes, people were forced to sneak back to Hargeisa to find something to eat. The shops they knew and their homes had mostly been destroyed or ransacked. Every time we went back, we would see additional dead bodies and more homes destroyed.

In late July, we decided to cross into Ethiopia. We tried to cross to the west of Hargeisa, at Abudleh. There was a contingency of the Somali army stationed there and if they got you, that was it. Five times we thought of crossing and were forced back when the soldiers fired at us. The army was stationed at various places to prevent people from crossing into Ethiopia. The people they were doing this against were unarmed civilians that had nothing with them except their barest possessions. They killed many and then robbed them. From the

176

distance, I witnessed the killing of many women and children, including an old man who was nearly blind.

His words, apparently incredible, even to his own ears, he repeated several times, "I saw all this with my own eyes!"

We finally crossed into Ethiopia and I left my family at Dabeel-Weyne. There were 11 of us: my wife, three children, my in-laws, siblings and myself.

He added:

As we tried to escape the bombs and guns that were aimed at us, I heard Radio Mogadishu announcing the results of an imaginary football match between Hargeisa and Burao. Hargeisa was already rubble by then and Burao had more or less crumbled. They would do anything to keep up the fiction of "normality." It was sickening to hear such nonsense.

According to Sahra Ahmed Arteh, interviewed by Africa Watch in London on June 17, 1989:

We stayed two months at Biyaha Shinaha, constantly moving around to avoid the bombing and the shelling from the guns placed at the top of the surrouding hills. Hunger became a real problem. We were afraid to look for food because of the planes. We couldn't cook either, for fear that the planes would spot us more easily. The planes bombed from 6:00 a.m. to 6:00 p.m., killing only civilians. There were no SNM fighters in the area and they knew that. Two of my cousins were killed by bombs at Biyaha Shinaha, Ahmed Ibrahim Jibreel, 25, and Gureh Mahdi Yusuf, 23; Gureh's brother is still missing.

Then soldiers surrounded Biyaha Shinaha and killed a lot of civilians. There were so many dead people there — rows and rows of dead people. No one dared to bury them because of the bombs during the day, and at night, you couldn't see anything. Finally, common graves were dug for them. It's difficult to remember all the dead. Our hearts fill with grief when we think of what that government has done to us. Just to hear its name mentioned brings back tormenting memories.

We fled again and went to Annayo, hoping to avoid the aerial bombing. We stayed there a week, constantly changing the trees under which we hid. But the bombs and shelling continued. Finally, we decided to cross the border into Ethiopia. We walked at night. Nomads living along the way gave us a bit of food, but they couldn't give much because there were thousands of people on the road. It took us four nights from Annayo to the Ethiopian border, walking under difficult conditions. The children had no shoes; we had no blankets and it was raining a lot. All this time I remained hopeful that we would be able to stay in our country. We saw bodies all along the way — of children, men and women killed by the soldiers.

A particular source of anguish for parents was separation from their children.

Sahra reported:

Families split. Many parents couldn't find their children. Two of my children, a boy of 12 and a boy of 13, had fled to my uncle's house the first day of the war. They were too scared to try to find us. I gave them up for dead. I found them with relatives after I crossed into Ethiopia.

Samia Sheef, interviewed by Africa Watch in London on June 3, 1989, told of the devastation caused by the bombing campaigns at Annayo:

We knew that the bombing had already started in Hargeisa and Gebiley. One day we heard loud speakers coming from an SNM car warning the people about the bombs. Suddenly, from the direction of the wind, we heard a piercing noise. There was panic. Some people instinctively threw themselves on the ground, while others ran in all directions, only to be chased by the planes. The first plane had obviously been sent to get a sense of the settlement. Then the second plane came to drop the bombs. They flew very low.

The first to be hit were two young girls. We became demented with fear. My children were not with me; they had been looking at a vehicle. I became terrified at the thought of my children being hit by the bombs. I started to inch towards them, but I couldn't move much because of fear of the bombs. There was smoke everywhere and people suffocated. Everyone started to choke. As the bombs dropped relentlessly, children started to wet themselves from fear. Many suffered diarrhoea immediately. Many adults and children couldn't stop vomiting. The noise was piercing. Children clung to you

178

and wouldn't let go no matter what you did to shake them off. It was as if they had lost their reason. In fact, when the bombing ceased for a while, people "came back," shaking themselves as if they had just been in a trance. Some pregnant women went into premature labor. Mohamed Guled's wife, only six months pregnant, lost the baby.

Annayo is a mountainous region and the bombs sent pieces of sharp broken stones flying in all directions which wounded the people they hit.

The planes were concentrated on areas where people were gathered or settled. They flew very low so the pilots could see us clearly and we could see them looking out of binoculars as they decided their next target. From where we were, you could get a glimpse of the men — and even tell how many were in the plane. They also targeted transport — to cripple the SNM — and also to make it impossible for the SNM to provide transport for the people. But, above all, they killed and wounded ordinary people. One family lost 6 children. The wounded became too numerous to count. Later, we saw buses with charred bodies inside. The smell was awful. For a while, there was no transport — no vehicles, no petrol, nothing.

Life became even more difficult. People couldn't carry on the efforts they'd been making to survive. If not every day, the bombers came every other day from 6:00 a.m. to 6:00 p.m.

Every day the air-raids became worse and worse. Sometimes they started at 5:00 a.m. which took us unawares. When there was a "surprise" attack, people in the same families fled in different directions. You didn't know who to follow. Everyone needed you. At daybreak, you saw people roaming around, looking for family members who had scattered when the planes attacked.

To escape, we hid in the mountains all day long. We did not cook in spite of constant hunger, for fear that the bombers would spot the smoke. We had to stop the children from making the slightest movement. Being cooped up all day was terrible. I soon wished that the bomber would kill both me and my children. We began to hate each other. I became depressed at not being able to feed them, so angry at having to deny them freedom, putting my hand over their mouth if they made a sound. Too small to understand why we had to do this, they hated the adults for controlling them so much.

After about 2-1/2 months, soldiers came to Annayo and started shelling. Cars, which they suspected belonged to the SNM or that might be useful to them, were the target. They started to move to within one hour of Annayo. In addition, the bombings became constant. They started to come in great numbers during the lunch hour, between 12:00 and 1:00, when normally, people were fetching water. Also between 3:00 and 4:00 p.m., when people settled down after lunch. It was civilians they were after. The SNM was not their target.

People would have been better prepared for the hardship if they could have transported food to the countryside. But that carried the serious risk of being caught as a "qurmis."

Samia continued:

Soon after we arrived at Annayo, we ran out of food and out of money. In any case, there was nothing to buy. I would spend hours begging people for a bit of milk for the baby, but everyone faced the same shortages. The only food available was either what the SNM gave people or what was brought back by family members who dared to steal back into Hargeisa. But soon, there was nothing for them to bring back, and nothing anywhere else. We decided to go to Ethiopia before we died of starvation. But we didn't have transportation which was very scarce. There was a fierce struggle over vehicles. When a truck finally agreed to take people, they would spend the entire day guarding it. Families with adult men were in a stronger position. They could fight for them. We only had two young boys. So much of their transport had been destroyed by the bombers that the SNM was reluctant to let all the vehicles they had left cross into Ethiopia. But we were so hungry by then and our fear of bombings so intense that we were even prepared to walk.

Finally, the SNM provided 40 vehicles when they realized how we felt. There was havoc as people scrambled for space. Once you got a place, you didn't care about comfort. Under normal circumstances, one wouldn't treat an object the way people

180

had to treat each other. They put goats on top of you, but, so long as you got a place, the rest was not important. People were hanging out from the sides of the vehicles. The vehicles had to be camouflaged to avoid the bombers.

All the trucks were in a terrible state, the roads are not paved and the terrain is rough. The brakes in our car failed and it would often slide back on the mountainous road, which was not only dangerous but slowed us down. In order not to attract attention, the headlights were turned off. It had to crawl so as to make the least noise. At dawn, the car dropped us at Udaan; we moved onto Gogol Wanaag the next day. Conditions there were miserable, especially the severe shortage of water. We had to fetch water in a roundabout way to avoid soldiers. We stayed six days. Food was scarce. Children and babies were extremely weak and sick by then. We divided food into tiny portions and fed the children at different times so as to give them the illusion of being fed regularly. But their hunger was obvious. It was painful to watch your children getting weaker and weaker from hunger.

The bombings continued, which made crossing the border the only thing that mattered. Also, hunger was making us less concerned about our safety. Some people became so desperate about the bombings that they took an enormous risk in walking. They couldn't make any noise. They kept a hand over every child's mouth and women put a breast in the mouths of babies to keep them quiet. Many didn't make it. Some groups were killed by soldiers as they tried to cross. The SNM escorted the bigger groups but the SNM could not escort everyone because of the size of the fleeing population.

Finally, we boarded the vehicles, by now several hours away from the border. Everyone said their final prayers. Families went in different trucks. En route, one of the vehicles was blown up by a land mine. Panic broke out. All the cars stopped and we disembarked. Luckily no one had been killed, but many people were wounded, several with broken limbs. Everyone was in a state of shock.

We continued. The mountainous road was treacherous. At times, we had to get off and walk. But many old people had difficulties — the cries of the old people were haunting — also the weak, and of course everyone was weak by that time. The worst affected were those with no relatives or with only one person accompanying. You heard so many people cry out for help but what could you do? Young men helped mothers with children, and did everything they could, but too many needed help. Many people were barefoot. Our feet were bleeding from the stones and the thorns which tore our clothes to shreds. Overweight people choked with the effort to keep up. No matter the hardship, only one thing was important — not to be left behind.

As we inched towards the border, soldiers opened fire and the SNM retaliated with their bazookas. We finally got to Allay-Baddey on the Somali side of the border. It was empty and abandoned. But we soon heard the sounds of the bombers. It was the same nightmare all over again — panic, fear, people fleeing in every direction, sand, dust and the heavy stones. The bombers were especially after the vehicles in order to cripple the whole caravan. The bombing continued. That's when I really despaired. We were so near to Ethiopia and refuge and still, death seemed just another air-raid away. We decided to stay the night anyway, whether we died or not, sleeping on cardboard boxes. We left the next day. Some of us went in the direction of Dabeel-Weyne and some of the others, including the vehicle that my two older children were in, went in the direction of Harshin. A few days later we received news that other relatives from Hargeisa were alive and in Ethiopia.

Amina Mohamed's husband, Farah Hussein, was a political detainee for six years until his release in February 1988. He left Somalia and obtained asylum in Norway. Amina worked for the UNHCR in Hargeisa. She lived in Ga'an-Libaah, near the Radio Station. In a written interview, she recounted her experiences of the outbreak of the war and her family's efforts to find sanctuary:

We awoke to the sound of gunfire at 2:15 a.m. It was centered at Boqol-Jirreh, near a military compound. At 10:00 a.m. there were reports of young men from Hargeisa families who were forming support groups and attaching themselves to SNM units. There was a mood of both anxiety and exhilaration. Government soldiers in commandeered taxis and private cars were driving around shooting at anyone who showed pro-SNM sympathies. The SNM units were on foot. We stayed indoors all day. Night was relatively quiet. The next morning at around 5:00 a.m. the fighting resumed. Government mobile radio units were telling people to stay indoors and threatening that anyone on the streets would be shot.

On Thursday, artillery shells started falling on our neighborhood. Many houses were destroyed, burying residents alive. We decided to leave on the sixth day of the fighting. My father stayed behind to see whether the fighting would die down. My mother and I, together with all the children and relatives in the neighborhood, carrying what little food supplies and bedding we could, escaped along the Berbera Road. We were heading towards Darar-Weyne where our family had a farm and a reservoir. There was a major military camp near Darar-Weyne and two refugee camps, Saba'ad and Adhi-Adays. We stayed at Darar-Weyne for about eleven days. We moved when armed refugee militias started attacking local farmers. Saba'ad refugee hospital was being used to treat wounded government soldiers. We relocated at Tug-Eel. On June 27 we were attacked by planes. Eleven people were killed, including a family of five, mother, three children and an uncle. My father rejoined us. We kept moving because of the planes. We started at 5:00 a.m. for Annayo, a staging area for cross-border escape. My uncle rented a donkey to transport my grandmother.

We left Annayo. Eight of us were transported on a truck owned by relatives. We aborted our first attempt to cross the border. On the second night we met two young men who were family friends and neighbors. They offered to escort us across the border. We were joined by a nomadic convoy moving across the border. We were attacked by government soldiers with machine guns and explosives. It was a nightmare. The crowd dispersed. Some returned to SNM-held areas. We walked all night with uncle and I half dragging mother. Our group arrived at Lafta-Faraweyne. We were missing two boys, one of my brothers and a cousin. Two days later, we were told by travelers that the boys arrived at Allay-Baddey. They were directed to our location. The truck carrying my grandmother and our supplies broke down and was attacked by government

183

troops, but grandmother arrived on the other trucks. Father's group was picked up by trucks coming to Aay-Daroosh. The entire family reunited at Qudha'a.

Amaal Jama, interviewed by Africa Watch in London on July 19, 1989, discussed her experiences of the air-raids:

When we left Hargeisa, we went to Geed-Debleh. But we couldn't bear the bombers. There was no time to bury the people killed by the planes because the plane would come back again and again. The dead just had to be thrown into mass graves, even with their shoes on, contrary to our religion. The others were left wherever the bomb hit them. Among the people killed by the bombing was Dr. Joseph, manager of the medicinal store at the General Hospital, his wife and 12 of his 13 children — only a small daughter survived.

I went back to Hargeisa three times in search of food and had to step over dead bodies turned into skeletons. The government finally burned some of the bodies when the stench became too much.

We continued on to Annayo. We didn't dare cook food, because once the planes saw the smoke, the bombing would follow.

My six-year-old sister is still terrified of the sound of airplanes, even here in England.

Safia Abdillahi Muhumed, interviewed by Africa Watch in Djibouti on August 2, 1989, provided the following testimony:

I had given birth to a little girl only ten days before the SNM attacked Hargeisa. On June 2, an armored tank hit our house. The next day, we left as we were afraid that the house would collapse on us. We went to Biyaha Shinaaha. After two days there, an armored tank came and everyone fled somewhere. We stayed in the area as I couldn't walk great distances. For a month and twenty days, we survived on what food relatives managed to sneak back from Hargeisa. Then the infantry came and started shooting, even though the SNM was not in the vicinity. We headed for Annayo. Previously, we had seen the planes flying overhead, but this was our first direct experience of the bombing. Two people, Saada Ahmed Jama, a cousin of mine and Hussein Osman Abdi, were killed, and seven people, including me, were wounded the first day. My right leg was injured.

I was rushed to Geed-Debleh, for treatment. But after one night, the planes came there too. On the first occasion, twenty-four people died on the spot. The wounded were also hit and sustained new injuries. After each raid, the number of wounded people increased. In the evening, I was transferred to a place just outside Geed-Debleh where I spent twenty-five days. Then my children and I, the baby and a boy just under two, managed to cross the border and to arrive at Harshin. After two days at Harshin, I was taken to a clinic at "Geneva" refugee camp. Five days later, alot of other wounded people and I were taken in a UNHCR car to go to Adari. Between Jigjiga and Adari, we had an accident and my mother who was looking after me, was herself wounded. My mother and I both spent five months in hospital at Adari, then arrived in Djibouti. In that time, my children were with their paternal grandmother. My little girl died of dysentry in Ocotber at Harta Sheihk camp. I also learned that my father, who was old and refused to leave Hargeisa, was killed, stabbed in our house shorlty after the SNM left Hargeisa, in August.

Mohamed Hassan Isse Awaleh, ten years old, provided these impressions of the war;

Mukhtar, another boy, and I saw the airplanes at Annayo. We were collecting firewood from the banks of the stream. There was a crowd of adults and children washing clothes. We ran to take cover under a tree. Two girls joined us. The bombs fell near us and the two girls were killed. I then ran to the other side and hid under another tree. There was a man hiding under it. He recognized me from the waab, [tree shelter] and he took me back to the village, That was not the only time I saw the planes. Another time, one of the village boys was killed as we ran.

There were so many people I knew fleeing the war. I saw the grade five teacher in our school, Abdikarim. Thursday, May 26, the day before the SNM attack on Burao was the last day of school. We had just received our results. I came in second

185

place. I saw the boy who was in first place at Annayo. His name was Hamza Ahmed Mohamed. He told me his father was arrested by government soliers between Hargeisa and Burao and killed. Hamza's father was visiting Burao when the war started there. He was trying to return on foot to Hargeisa when the group he was traveling with were intercepted by soldiers.

Burao

Muse Saleh Ali, "Geldoon," interviewed by Africa Watch in Cardiff on July 6, 1989, recalled the fear and confusion in Burao:

The fighting was so intense, people just ran. There was so much gunfire, we couldn't decide which direction to take. People dropped dead in front of you and you just jumped over the corpses. Some people even left their children behind and many families became separated. I was one of the people that God spared. I remained 11 days in town. I left on the 12th day. We knew the route, so we chose back roads to avoid the soldiers. We had to climb so many hills. Food was scarce and sometimes there would be no water for a day or two. I finally joined my family in the countryside. Later, I went to Addis and came back to England on December 24.

Mona Ahmed Yusuf, "Qulumbe"'s testimony of leaving Burao, taken by Africa Watch in London on July 2, 1989, is grim:

At first, people didn't want to go too far so they could come back for food. We went to a place called Looya, about two hours away by car. After we had been there for three days, the military came to a nearby place called Wadhan where there was a stream. Sixty people, most of them nomads, were massacred. We left to escape the soldiers and went to Kala Ha. After one night there, three male relatives who had gone to fetch water at a reservoir were captured. We learned later that they were killed.

We kept moving. The next day, we encountered soldiers. Luckily it was raining heavily and there was no bridge so they couldn't cross. They just shot at us; no one died. After that, we became really desperate. We found a relative who gave us a car and we went to Haji Salah, a village on the Somali side of the border, five and a half hours away. The rest of our family

186

who had been left in Burao joined us there. They had escaped in different cars. After security, food was the greatest worry. Food from Burao and Hargeisa had stopped two weeks after the war broke out. People survived on food from Ethiopia, available at exorbitant prices.

At Haji Salah, I got malaria and jaundice. There were no medicines. I was given traditional treatment by nomads living in the area. I became weaker and weaker. Finally I was taken to Dire Dawa, Ethiopia and then came to London on May 19, 1989 via Djibouti.

Many people who had taken refuge at Haji Salah and in the surrounding villages died of malaria and jaundice, including several family members — my uncle, Muse Yusuf, his son, Omer Muse Yusuf, another uncle, Abdillahi Kahin Ibrahim, his wife and his brother, Ali Kahin Ibrahim, and his son, Bashir Abdillahi Kahin.

Women caught by the soldiers faced a substantial risk of being raped.

Ahmed Saeed Elmi, interviewed by Africa Watch in London on June 14, 1989, reported:

In June I saw two young women in their twenties who had tried to flee Burao and then got lost in the countryside. They decided to return to Burao and got captured by the military on the road. They were gang-raped by the soldiers. When I met them, they looked as if they were dead — dragging their feet.

We heard many accounts of massacres, in which civilians — men, women and children — were killed.

Massacre at Wadhan

We received numerous independent accounts of a massacre at Wadhan, about 20 kilometers outside Burao, where some 60 people were killed. The victims were all people who had sought to escape the air-raids, including some residents of Burao but mainly nomads from neighboring villages.

Yassin Karshe Mohamed, interviewed by Africa Watch in Cardiff on July 7, 1989, described the massacre at Wadhan:

187

Soldiers surrounded the settlement. No one escaped. Among the victims are:

Gurrey Doylaweh, a very wealthy trader;

Abdillahi Ghelle, a trader;

Warsame Ghelle, a trader, brother of above;

Adan "Timer," a businessman;

"Dolayare," a businessman;

Hashi Shire Diriye, a nomad who had come to Burao to buy necessities and was returning to his family;

Ismail Suleiman Yusuf, a trader in Burao;

Yusuf-Roon Abdillahi, an elder from Hargeisa;

Ali Abdi Dheeg, 26, trader; and

Khader Ahmed Abdi, 26, trader;

Berbera

Many fleeing Berbera died from thirst, in the scorching summer heat of Berbera where the temperature reaches about 43.C (110o F) in May-August. Unfamiliar with the outskirts of Berbera, people often got lost and were unable to find drinking water or shelter. According to all the refugees from Berbera we interviewed, the worst civilian casualties were inflicted by Ogaden and Oromo refugees armed by the government, especially in the villages between Sheikh and Berbera, from the camps at Bihin and Biyole.

Jibril Mohamed Yey, interviewed by Africa Watch in Djibouti on August 10, 1989, described the problems faced by those fleeing Berbera:

They attacked the people fleeing without discrimination. Most of those fleeing were Isaaks because the non-Isaaks had already been evacuated by the government during the first few days of the war. Soldiers formed a circle around the city to prevent people from leaving. Anyone who got caught was finished. There was a shoot on sight order — after they robbed the victim. There was no effort to capture people and return them to Berbera, just shoot.

Sheikh

Asha Ibrahim Haji Hussein, commented:

As we climbed the mountains, we would see from the distance
something that looked like shrubs and gratefully, we would
think of shelter. As we got closer, we saw that it was dead
bodies — so many dead bodies you could not believe your eyes
even at close range.

Attacks by Soldiers

When the military realized that people were fleeing, soldiers were
positioned along the roads to force them back. Once in the countryside, after
air-raids and land mines, the worst fear was an encounter with soldiers, who
executed men, raped women and stole from all. Some threatened to look at
women's private parts to see what they might be hiding. However cautious, it
was not possible to avoid them, because the soldiers were usually sheltered in
ravines that could not be readily detected. When the soldiers started shooting,
people scattered; dropping the bundles they were carrying; families became
separated, often losing children.

The GAO reported that:

Breaking into smaller groups of 300 to 500 the refugees began
a 10 -to 40-day trek to Ethiopia. Shortly after they reached the
outskirts of the cities, the refugee columns were stopped by
the Somali army, which had formed a ring around the cities.
Refugees reported that at military checkpoints and ambushes,
they were robbed and men suspected of being SNM members
were summarily executed.*

Khadra Muhumed Abdi, interviewed by Africa Watch in London on
June 2, 1989, survived to recall an encounter with soldiers:

When we were at Gumburaha Banka a group of soldiers came,
led by Koore Jaan, in charge of the army at Sallahlay, an officer
notorious for his anti-Isaak attitude, particularly towards the
nomads. Two jeeps, two tanks and two army trucks, full of
armed soldiers arrived while we were cooking. We became

---

* GAO report at p. 6.

paralyzed with fear. We were about 45-50 in the group, seven of them men. Four of them had left a short while before to look for kat. They immediately ordered the other three to lie flat on their stomachs.

They took everything from everyone. They threatened us. Luckily the three men in our group were not armed. They said they had orders to shoot us on the spot but they were sparing us as the men were not armed. The other four men were not that far away and could see the arrival of the soldiers and hear the sound of their vehicles. They hid deep in a nearby well. The soldiers then went to a nearby village, Goodbrear, and captured 20 men. I don't know if they were killed or what.

From the shock of the incident, a pregnant woman in our group went into early labor and she lost a lot of blood. Some nomads nearby gave us fresh camel milk which they said would stop the bleeding. It seemed to work.

After that we packed up again. We left at day break the next day, including the woman who had just given birth. We walked all day and stopped at Gumar. Then the planes came; the bombs fell like heavy raindrops all around us. The pilots saw some linen a family had put out to dry. They mistook this for tents and dropped many bombs, killing one man and 20 cows.

The aerial bombardment continued to target civilians, even after they crossed the border into Ethiopia, making it clear that there was no place they could regard as a secure refuge.

Khadra continued:

The bombers beat us very badly. The children got very sick from the fear and shock. The ones that dropped the bombs would be preceded by a smaller plane, the spotter, which scouted out targets. The air raids killed thousands of people, hit either by the bombs or the machine-guns they fired out of the planes. The bombs usually rained from 6:00 a.m. to 6:00p.m. We tried to take cover in the bush. We fled to Laanta Taloog but the planes were there too. There were so many corpses there. While I was there, I witnessed the bombers kill in one day 23 people and in another day 51 — mainly children because they wouldn't hide or sit still. I also heard that it killed 150 people there but I did not witness that with my own eyes.

190

The next day, we reached Udaan on the Ethiopian side of the border. We arrived exhausted. You thought nothing of abandoning your own child; no-one could bear any more hardship and responsibility. And then the planes came again. That's when we really despaired. It killed one of the women in our group, who left a little girl behind. Two Ethiopian men were wounded.

We fled again. We arrived in Harshin after trekking for 31 days. It was our first day of peace, in spite of other problems. I finally located my mother and two children in Ethiopia.

Safia Ali Mataan, interviewed by Africa Watch in London on August 17, 1989, recounted a similar experience:

We left Hargesia at the end of September because of the lack of food and the danger of stray bullets.

When we reached Haraf, a group of 15-20 soldiers fired in our direction. That was a real point of danger. We completely lost hope. They stopped and searched our belongings. They took our jewelry. They threatened to kill us unless we gave them a large sum of money which we did not have. They kept us for over three hours while they kept going off for consultations. One soldier, who we found out was half-Isaak, took pity on us and threatened to kill the others if they didn't let us go. We were released but some of them came after us and took our money and a watch.

We changed our route and walked in the darkness. As it was raining heavily and night came, two of our companions fell into a ditch. They spent the night in the ditch. That was safer. The next morning we continued.

Amaal Aideed Yassin, interviewed by Africa Watch in Cardiff on July 6, 1989, remained in Hargeisa for several months and finally left because of the insecurity:

In October, a group of us, all women and children left. Some soldiers stopped us at Sheikh Omer, just outside Hargeisa. They took everything we had. They kept two women behind — a woman about 50 and a woman of about 25.

I don't know what they did to them or if they are still alive. What saved us is that there were no men in our group. They would have been killed and they would have endangered us as well. On our fourth attempt, we crossed into Ethiopia.

Ahmed Haji Hussein Omer Hashi, who fled Hargeisa, and was interviewed by Africa Watch in Djibouti on August 5, 1989, owed his lucky escape to his Ogaden relatives:

We escaped death because we fled with my Ogaden uncles and we pretended to be Ogaden ourselves. At Isha Oboshe, we ran into the army. We told them we were Ogadeni refugees trying to return to Ethiopia.

We received numerous accounts of women who gave birth under these difficult conditions, in the absence of any medical facilities and without sufficient food, either for the mother or for the baby. Fear prevented most of the new mothers from being able to breast-feed their babies.

In the course of a number of interviews conducted by Africa Watch in London with their parents, small children became hysterical at the sound of airplanes landing at or taking off from Heathrow airport. Apparently traumatized by their experience of air-raids, it has so far proven difficult to calm their apprehensions that the planes would follow them to England.

12. ABUSES BY THE SOMALI NATIONAL MOVEMENT (SNM)

Under the Geneva Conventions the conflict in Somalia is not an international conflict. The body of international standards applicable to the conduct of the SNM is Common Article III, which is applicable to all the parties to such non-international conflict. This Article which is the basic statement of humanitarian law that applies to internal military conflicts forbids torture and execution of prisoners, attacks on non-combatants and indiscriminate attacks upon civilians. As a human rights organization concerned about violations wherever they occur, we hold rebel organizations accountable for respecting the basic humanitarian law standards set forth in Article III. Application of Common Article III standards does not involve any comment by Africa Watch about the legitimacy of any party to the conflict. Also, each side's duty to respect the requirements of Common Article III is independent. That is, the abuses by the other side relieve neither party of their own duty to respect the requirements of international humanitarian law, or the laws of war.

Prior to the Outbreak of the War

Africa Watch learned of a number of incidents in which the SNM shot Isaak civilians on the basis that they were apparently government spies.

Abdisalaan (not his real name), interviewed by Africa Watch in Djibouti on August 4, 1989, reported that:

> I was visiting Geed-Debleh in 1987 when I learned that the SNM had recently killed two men, nomads, who had informed government forces that they had spotted SNM fighters in the vicinity.

> In January 1987, the SNM kidnapped a group of doctors and nurses working with the French medical organization, Medecins Sans Frontieres. I think there were either 11 or 13 in the group. They were released after about a week.

193

The War Breaks Out

Execution of Government Officials

When the SNM attacked Burao on May 27, 1988, a number of high-ranking government officials, were shot. At 7:00 a.m., the SNM attacked the city and at 5:00 p.m. they had retreated to their base. Then government soldiers entered the town. In the period they occupied the town, the SNM was followed by huge crowds consisting of townspeople, Isaaks who welcomed the attack. The SNM questioned the local residents about the attitudes and actions of the most senior government officials. Those who were identified as particularly abusive towards civilians were "condemned" to death. A number of them were shot on the spot in their homes or on the street. They included "Ed'eed," the local military commander; Abdiqani, the head of the NSS; Captain "Falso," the police commander; Ina Afrah, the deputy police commander; and "Inda Dilo," head of a special force dealing with control of the kat trade and the head of the main prison. The SNM did not have the opportunity to execute government officials in Hargeisa *hors de combat*, in light of the fact that a full four days elapsed between the attack on Burao and Hargeisa.

According to Ahmed Saeed Elmi, a resident of Burao:

There were some soldiers who were known not to be hard on civilians and the civilians told this to the SNM. They were not killed. But the others, who had killed, raped and stolen from the public were reported to the SNM and killed.

Abuses Against Civilians

In Burao, the SNM also arrested some civilians, mainly Darood but also some Isaaks, mainly businessmen, who were seen as collaborators and unpopular with the public and who the public insisted must be shot. The SNM arranged their transport and took them to their different villages and homes. Africa Watch learned of an incident where the SNM was transporting a group of non-Isaaks, when they ran into a group of Isaak nomads who had taken up arms on behalf of the SNM. They refused to let the convoy pass and shot the Darood passengers.

194

After the first few days of the war in both Hargeisa and Burao, when the government started to arm Darood civilians to fight against Isaaks, there were a number of incidents where young men who had joined the SNM when the war broke out killed a number of non-Isaak civilians who were themselves unarmed. The government provided transport for non-Isaaks, but clearly they could not evacuate every single non-Isaak and thousands of them fled the bombing and shelling along with the Isaaks. A number of refugees interviewed by Africa Watch recalled the killing of Hassan Abole, a teacher at Hargeisa Technical Institute, and another teacher, of Koranic studies in Hargeisa, both shot while fleeing. However, we have not received any information to indicate that the SNM as an organization had a policy of deliberately targeting civilians, on the basis that they were non-Isaaks, though there were incidents in which a particular group of SNM fighters shot Darood civilians who were not armed. Isaak refugees we interviewed expressed anger at the stiff warnings they received from the SNM not to take revenge against civilian non-combatants who were not involved in the war. When non-Isaak civilians were armed, the SNM regarded them as an integral part of the government's fighting forces, and as such, legitimate targets of attack.

According to the refugees interviewed by Africa Watch, the SNM has also shot a number of Isaak civilians who were suspected of being government spies. As soon as the SNM entered Hargeisa, In a Nur Yey, a businessman, was shot on the basis that his spying activities had led to the imprisonment of SNM fighters. Another businessman, Muse Hurre, was later also shot as someone who had collaborated with the government.

Abdisalaan also told Africa Watch:

In November 1988, when the SNM attacked a military compound at the village of Habaas Weyne, near Geed-Debleh, a number of Isaak women, married to the soldiers, were killed as government spies.

Abuses Against Ethiopian Refugees

One of the principal aims of the SNM was to ensure that refugees from the Ogaden left northern Somalia and returned to Ethiopia.* To this end, they told the refugees at a number of the main camps, in particular Las Dhurr and Agabar, to leave. Most of them left. However, the situation immediately became entangled with the decision of the Somali government to arm and to enlist in the war, either willingly or by forced conscription, the Ogadeni refugees. The SNM regarded anyone who took up arms as their military adversaries, whether they were government soldiers, pro-government armed civilians or armed refugees.

An article in the *Atlanta Journal and Constitution* made the following comments about the conscription of refugees after the war broke out:

> According to a foreign aid official who was in the north after the fighting broke out, the Siad government was so eager to arm the Ogaden refugees that it enlisted workers of the civilian National Relief Commission — which administers the Ogaden refugee camps — to help distribute weapons....Now all the camps are heavily armed, an experienced Western aid official said....
>
> Some of the camps' adult males are thought to have headed for the bush to avoid being drafted by the government....Many others are said to have accepted weapons form the government and left their camps in search of Isaaq....Recent travelers in the north add that many Ogaden from the U.N. refugee camps — and fair numbers of another pro-government group, the Oromo — have been seen carrying American-made M-16 rifles.**

In some of the towns, the government relied almost exclusively on armed refugees to conduct the war against Isaak civilians. According to the testimonies Africa Watch received from residents of Sheikh, it was principally

---

* See Background chapter for information about the political tensions caused by the presence of Ogadeni refugees in northern Somalia.

** Colin Campbell in *The Atlanta Journal and Constitution*, October 6, 1988.

the refugees who killed civilians and looted the town, as well as attacking the villages between Sheikh and Berbera and confiscating the livestock of the nomadic population living in the area. Again, the residents of Berbera we interviewed emphasized the role played by the Ogadeni refugees in the abuses committed against the urban population fleeing Berbera, and especially against the nomads who lived in the adjoining villages.

In a report issued in August 1989 by the U.S. Department of State, entitled "Why Somalis Flee," the author, Robert Gersony, makes clear from the interviews he conducted that refugee conscripts were either incorporated into the army or organized into associated paramilitary militia units. These units participated in armed raids against the villages and the nomads in the surrounding areas of their camps. They have been responsible for repeated lootings and numerous civilian casualties. In some instances, some of these communities retaliated against the refugees, and casualties resulted on both sides.

In retaliation for the attacks against Isaak civilians, the SNM has launched a series of attacks against the Ogadeni refugees, such as Saba'ad, near Hargeisa and the camps near Berbera, such as Bihin Dule and Biyole, where the casualties included number of women and children.

The GAO report stated that:

During our visit to Somalia in early March 1989, 11 Ogadeni refugees(5 men, 3 women, 3 children) were killed and 16 were wounded during an SNM attack on a truck carrying Ogadeni refugees. We were told that incidents of this type were characteristic of an emerging SNM pattern of terrorizing the Ogadeni refugees to force their removal from traditional Isaak territory.

In his report, Gersony accused the SNM of dozens of systematic attacks against refugee camps and concluded that at least "four hundred or more" unarmed refugees, including women and children, had been killed by the SNM.*

He added that there may have been "a few" instances of SNM attacks provoked by refugees. He also argues that the refugees were armed by the Somali government *only after* repeated attacks by the SNM, for their own

---

*   "Why Somalis Flee", Robert Gersony at p.63.

self-protection. We do not dispute Gersony's contention that the SNM has killed as many as four hundred Ogadeni refugees. We condemn killings by the SNM of unarmed refugees and indiscriminate attacks by the SNM in which non-combatants were killed by the SNM other than in crossfire with combatants. We do take issue, however, with Gersony's contention that the refugees were armed only after the SNM attacked some of the camps. International journalists and human rights organizations reported the arming and the conscription of Ogadeni refugees *long* before the war broke out.

In November 1987, Agence France Presse reported a May 1987 raid at the Bihin Camp near Berbera where 200-300 refugees were seized, as well as a raid which apparently occurred on the same day at Biyoley Camp, a distance of 50 kilometers. While forcibly recruiting hundreds of male refugees at the Bihin Camp, it was reported that the military also seized auxiliary health workers and even patients with tuberculosis.*

According to a report in *The Economist* in early 1988:

The UNHCR has officially protested, without response, about the recent press-ganging of up to 7,000 Ethiopian refugees into the Somali army, many of them taken by force inside refugee camps in direct defiance of international law....If the Somali authorities bother to explain, they say the conscripts are ethnic Somalis, liable to military service and "morally obliged" to fight against Ethiopia.**

Africa Watch also learned that on several occasions, the SNM has diverted material sent for the benefit of the Ethiopian refugees. The vehicles, while bearing the insignia of the UNHCR, were escorted by military convoys.

The Somali government's long standing policy of conscripting refugees is in breach of a number of international obligations to which Somalia is a party, namely the 1951 Convention Relating to the Status of Refugees, the 1967 Protocol Relating to the Status of Refugees and the 1969 OAU Convention Governing the Specific Aspects of Refugee Problems in Africa. Again, the

---

*   Eric Sauve, "Somali Army Pressganging Refugees", AFP, October 1987.

**   "Profit in Poverty," *The Economist*, January 9, 1988.

violations committed by either party to the conflict provide no justification for violations committed by the opposing party. Each party has an independent duty to comply with international humanitarian law.

13. LIFE IN THE CAMPS

For most of the refugees, security meant escape to the harsh conditions of refugee camps in Ethiopia. The misery of the camps has come to symbolize further the enormity of the loss inflicted by the war.

Most were taken first to "Geneva," a refugee camp about 30 kilometers from Harshin. They were then settled in two principal camps, Harta Sheikh and Harta Sheikh B. Smaller camps were also set up in the east; they are Camp Aboker, Rabasso and Daror. Some refugees had to wait as long as two months to obtain ration cards. There was such a shortage of coal that people had to walk three hours to fetch it. Malaria, jaundice, meningitis and diarrhoea have taken a heavy toll. The severe shortage of water, and the absence of sanitary facilities have created a public health disaster.

Jama Osman Samatar, interviewed by Africa Watch in London on June I, 1989, described the situation he encountered when he crossed into Ethiopia:

> Life at Harta Sheikh was hard. It was dusty and as we had no tents during the first week, we had to sleep out in the open. There was no water either. Luckily it was raining heavily and we got some muddy water from the puddles left by the rain fall. We ate raw corn. Finally we got cards and became entitled to UNHCR rations.

Yassin Karshe Mohamed who stayed in the camps from August 1988 to February 1989, was interviewed by Africa Watch in Cardiff on July 7, 1989. He echoed the views expressed by many others when he described his reactions to the camps:

> No one who hasn't seen them with his own eyes can imagine life in the camps or believe what he hears. The lack of medical attention is chronic. There were many Somali doctors and nurses among the refugees, but the Ethiopian authorities refused to let them attend the sick. Everywhere you went, there were burial posts. There was no central cemetery. People just buried their relatives wherever they found an

empty plot. The food was inadequate and of very poor quality — at first a bit of flour and later dry wheat. Small children who could not eat this died like flies and continue to suffer a very high rate of mortality. Many people also died from the shortage of water. My wife gave birth to a little girl after the war broke out; and there was no way to get any milk for the baby as my wife could I used to see Ethiopian refugees in Somalia but they had food and shelter. There were so many international agencies looking after them. That made it hard to understand why the world chose to close its eyes against Somali refugees in Ethiopia. Why are they getting so little attention?

A Somali living abroad who visited the camps in search of relatives described them to Africa Watch in an interview in London:

The Harta Sheikh refugee camp (also known as Dul'ad), is a teeming tent city with more 250,000 people. The camp is in the middle of a desolate desert with no permanent settlements prior to the influx of the Somali refugees. Its name literally means "barren top." Apart from the few water catchments which get filled during the rainy season, there are no other sources of water. A limited amount of water is trucked down from Jiggiga, about 50 kilometers away by the few aid agencies there. The temperature is hot during day and hovers around freezing point at night, during the dry season. The residents have little or no protection. Clouds of dust cover the camp engulfing all those in it. There are no latrines and the open space between the tents are used, posing severe health hazards, especially when it rains. The rain wash the dirt to the water catchments, the only reliable source of water. The place looks like hell on earth.

There are tight controls everywhere. In addition to controls on movement of refugees, attempts by the refugees to help themselves are constrained. Despite the presence of a number of doctors and a relatively large number of nurses among the refugees, high death rates especially among the children and old were left unaddressed and the medical practitioners were among the refugees not allowed to attend to their own by the Ethiopian authorities. Cloth to cover corpses for burial are given out by the Ethiopian authorities only after the

202

corpses are produced. It turns out that slogans condemning the Somali government were written on white sheets on the 19th anniversary of Siad Barre's rule in October 1988, and Ethiopian authorities, mindful of their new friendship with the Somali government, wanted to control the supply of burial sheets. The corpses have to be transported by donkey or on the backs of relatives miles outside the camps.

Despite the severe shortage of water, a large number of water tankers brought by their owners when they left Hargeisa could not be used. The distance within the camp is vast, covering some 5 kilometers, with the water catchments and UNHCR offices at one end. Thus, transporting food and water on foot is difficult. A large number of buses and trucks have been brought from Hargeisa by their owners as they fled but the authorities won't allow them to be used, even for transportation within the camps.

The system of emergency food distribution is cumbersome, degrading and leak-prone. Some families hadn't got any food allotments for weeks. When they got something at last, it was only flour. Sugar, oil and other desirable commodities donated by the international community could only be obtained at the "black market" that has developed within the camps and supplied by siphoned off rations. Somali refugees weren't allowed to participate in the distribution system. The UNHCR was instructed to employ only Ethiopian nationals.

Mona Ahmed Yusuf, "Qulumbe," interviewed by Africa Watch in London on July 2, 1989, also told of the difficulties of life in the camps.

Because of the lack of medicine, both in the settlements within Somalia and in the camps in Ethiopia, some families sent a member, usually a woman, to Mogadishu to buy medicines. If a man was stopped, they would look for the mark of a gun strap or boot marks. Else, he would be stripped and forced to do exercises, to test if he was fit enough to have been an SNM fighter or a former soldier who had defected. The woman would have to disguise the fact that she was Isaak and to learn by heart another lineage in case she was questioned on the way. If she was caught on her return journey with medicines, they knew it was for wounded people and so arrest was certain and execution a real possibility. In September 1988, Ruqiya Jama was arrested in Garoe for this. She was sentenced to death. She is still under a sentence of death. The problem was made worse by the fact that Ethiopian regulations made it impossible to buy medicines and take them across the border into Somalia for the wounded there.

Security was an additional problem. The Somali government was determined to ensure the expulsion of Somali refugees from Ethiopia. By jeopardizing the security in the camps, apparently it hoped to persuade the Ethiopian government to regard the refugees as a liability, and to facilitate their expulsion. The government seems to have sent spies into the camps, to inform on those who ventured to nearby villages. Refugees report that several men were killed as a result. Subsequently, guards were provided during the nights.

Hassan Muhumed Abdillahi, a truck owner/driver was arrested by the army on May 27 and his truck and services commandeered by the military until he was injured in a landmine explosion on January 7, 1989. Africa Watch interviewed him in Djibouti on August 13, 1989.

After the SNM told the Ethiopian refugees at Las Durre and Agabar camps to go back to Ethiopia, many of them were intercepted by government forces and armed and trained in Borama, in preparation for attacking the Somali refugees in Ethiopia. The government's strategy was to pretend that they were ordinary Ethiopian refugees returning home from Somalia. The Ethiopian authorities arrested alot of them and they returned to Hargeisa. During November and December, I saw alot of them in Tug Wajale on their way back from Ethiopia. The government's aim was firstly, to attack the refugees; secondly, to encourage the expulsion of the refugees by the Ethiopian government by encouraging it to see the refugees as a security liablity.

Despairing of camp life, Mohamed Karshe Mohamed, like many other refugees, found it better to leave the camps and to look for relatives in the countryside in Somalia. One of the worst problems encountered in Ethiopia was tagfi, a bug that punctures the skin, sucks blood and leaves marks all over the skin. Interviewed by Africa Watch in Cardiff om July 6, he told us:

The tagfi was terrible. When you woke up, your shirt was all
bloody from the bites. Life there was intolerable. Because of
that, it was better to take your family and look for relatives in
the countryside. At least that way you avoid the tagfi and you
might find milk for the children.

Mohamed Ismail Kahin, a resident from Hargeisa, interviewed by
Africa Watch in Cardiff on July 6, 1989, said:

The camps were terrible. Food was scarce and of very poor
quality. The camps were overpopulated, dusty and lacked
adequate water. There was lice everywhere. Anyone who
could, left. But of course only a small percentage could afford
to leave.

Though conditions have improved slightly over when the refugees first
arrived in Ethiopia, Africa Watch's most recent information indicates the
continued prevalence of the deprivations described in these testimonies.
Malaria, jaundice and diarrhoea continue to be leading causes of death; medical
facilities are grossly inadequate; and there are no sanitation facilities. Food is
inadequate, unless supplemented by what the refugees themselves buy in the
markets that have been created in the camps. However, not all refugees have
sufficient cash to buy both food and medicine. New waves of refugees continue
to arrive, many fleeing the growing insecurity in Mogadishu, as well as other
regions in the country. Additional resources apparently have not been provided
to meet the needs of these refugees.

Apart from the refugees who crossed the border into Ethiopia, at least
another three hundred thousand people, who were either unable to undertake
the difficult journey to Ethiopia or unwilling are displaced within the country,
scattered all over the northern region. They are in an extremely vulnerable
position, for they do not have access to international assistance or to urban
centers for food and are prey to the insecurity that is prevalent throughout the
region.

14. UNITED STATES ROLE

The United States has been Somalia's most important source of economic aid since 1978, when the U.S.S.R. switched its support from Somalia to Ethiopia in the Somali-Ethiopian war. Since the outbreak of the war in the north of Somalia in May 1988, the U.S. has followed an ambiguous course. Although the Administration has undertaken thorough investigations of human rights violations and made its findings public, it has refrained from following those investigations by publicly condemning the Siad Barre regime for the abuses it documents. It has continued to request aid for the Somali government while admitting that the same government it seeks to assist has murdered thousands and driven out hundreds of thousands of its own citizens and destroyed their homes and cities.

The ambivalence of the U.S. Administration appears to be based on a concern that, no matter how bad the Siad Barre regime is, it may be preferable to entrust that government with the protection of U.S. interests than a government of uncertain identity and character that might replace it. U.S. interests include a naval and military facility for the U.S. Central Command at the port of Berbera, on the Gulf of Aden, that is used for surveillance of the Gulf and the Indian Ocean. The U.S. also has naval, miilitary and electronic facilities elsewhere in the country. The ten-year old Berbera agreement is due to be renegotiated early this year, and it is unclear at this writing whether the U.S. will be willing to pay the price for using the port facilities, namely economic and military aid for Siad Barre's crumbling regime. In the past, successive U.S. Administrations have based their policies towards Somalia on the illusion of stability provided by the Barre regime, despite evidence of Siad Barre's sharp policy swings. The regime has gone from a hard-line doctrinaire "scientific socialism," to frantic efforts to be a loyal supporter of the West, to its current attempts to rebuild ties with the U.S.S.R., Cuba and Libya in an effort to obtain arms.

By late 1989, the Bush Administration appeared to be reevaluating its policy towards Somalia. Largely as a result pressure from Congress, the U.S. Administration took steps to limit assistance to the government (see below). Another factor in the Administration's reassessment is the erosion of the confidence of U.S. military analysts in the capabilities of the Somali army since the summer of 1989 when intense fighting broke out between government forces and Ogadeni soldiers who deserted the army. Despite brutal reprisals against Ogadeni and Hawiye civilians, government forces have been unable to retake portions of the south held by the Ogadenis. This poor showing apparently prompted the U.S. military to cancel the "Brightstar" exercises in Somalia this year. These exercises are high-visibility U.S. military maneuvers conducted with a number of countries and their cancellation is a blow to Siad Barre's image as a close U.S. ally.

If indeed the Administration is distancing itself publicly from Siad Barre, it will signal a significant change in policy. Up to now, the Administration's refusal to take a strong stand against the Somali government has met with tragic results. In June 1988, for example, U.S. military assistance consisting of automatic rifles and ammunition valued at about $1.4 million was shipped to the Somali army under the Foreign Sales program. It arrived on June 28, 1988 and was used to arm Ethiopian refugees living in UNHCR-sponsored camps within Somalia. The shipment arrived at precisely the moment when government forces were waging indiscriminate warfare against unarmed civilians throughout the north. It was during this period that hundreds of thousands of northern Somalis were fleeing into Ethiopia to escape government terror. In fact, the shipment had been authorized in November 1986, but was delayed repeatedly. Its arrival in Somalia at such a critical time during the war sent a signal, even if unintentional, that the U.S. supported the government's war against civilians.

Despite its assurances at a congressional hearing in July 1988 that Somalia was on the road to recovery, a month later the Reagan Administration was sufficiently concerned about the situation to send a State Department delegation led by Kenneth Bleakley, then Deputy Assistant Secretary of State for Refugee Assistance, to Somalia and Ethiopia to investigate the situation of refugees and displaced persons. The delegation met with the displaced both in Somalia and Ethiopia, who told them of the government bombing campaigns. Secretary Bleakley told Africa Watch that he cabled his findings to U.S. Ambassador to Somalia T. Frank Crigler, who delivered the cable to President Barre. When Congress requested a copy of this cable in September 1988, however, the cable had been reclassified. Secretary Bleakley and other State Department officials assured Congress that they protested abuses vigorously and urged greater access to the north for the U.S. and international agencies, but they issued no public statement to this effect, citing the "sensitive" nature of the discussions.

After the ill-fated June 1988 arms shipment, the U.S. limited military assistance to Somalia to "nonlethal" items, including spare parts for previously supplied weapons. The U.S. also provided $1.9 million in disaster assistance to help the victims of the war; included in this assistance was a program for training Somali soldiers to keep their jeeps and other light vehicles running. The assistance also included $350,000 for food for the displaced, and $1 million for a field hospital, but it is unlikely that the victims of the war ever benefitted. According to a Congressional General Accounting Office (GAO) report released in May 1989 (see below), the hospital was set up in Berbera because it was considered a secure area to which supplies and patients could be quickly transported. According to other sources, however, the U.S. Embassy originally urged that the hospital be set up in Burao or Borama, because it feared that the Somali government would use a hospital in Berbera, where it was fully in control, to treat only its own soldiers.* The GAO report indicates that these fears may have been warranted: "During our visit to the hospital, we noted that the hospital was providing assistance to military personnel, Ogadeni refugees and local townspeople." Apparently Isaaks were not among those receiving treatment.

U.S. support also included staples such as wheat and sugar for the displaced and for the Ogadeni refugees which were distributed through the

---

* Colin Campbell, "Libya, Mercenaries Aiding U.S.-Supported Somalia," *The Atlanta Journal and Constitution,* October 6, 1988.

Somali government. According to the GAO report: "Detailed information about displaced persons who are to receive this assistance, such as location and estimated population, was unavailable."

Close consultations between the Administration and Somalia's military leaders continued well into 1989. An American team helped the government to repair and maintain the military's communications network in the war zone in the north to boost the government's military capacity. In early October 1988, the Deputy Commander of the U.S. Central Command, Army Major-General William Riley, was in Mogadishu for talks with the Somali army.* In March 1989, the Central Command's new commander paid an introductory visit to Somalia. According to a news bulletin by the U.S. Information Service in Mogadishu, in a dinner speech introducing the commander, U.S. Ambassador to Somalia T. Frank Crigler toasted "the health of our distinguished visitor and his companions, as well as the strong ties of military cooperation between the United States and Somalia that his visit represents."

U.S. economic aid for 1988 totaled about $30 million. During the year, the U.S. Agency for International Development (USAID) withheld $15 million of these funds on the grounds of Somalia's failure to comply with certain economic reforms, without mentioning human rights concerns. In July 1988, during the height of the conflict, the Reagan Administration notified Congress of its intention to "reprogram" an additional $21 million of economic aid for Somalia and of its desire to release the suspended $15 million. The Administration insisted that its requests for aid had nothing to do with the war. The timing of the request was, to say the least, unfortunate, and despite its insistence to the contrary, as with the June arms shipment, gave the distinct impression that the U.S. condoned the conduct of the war.

In January 1989, the State Department not only failed to condemn flagrant human rights abuses, but instead rebuked Africa Watch for calling for an investigation of the problem. Numerous credible reports by the U.S. and international media in 1988 and 1989 reported that Somalia had received shipments of chemical weapons from Libya. One story, which was aired on

---

* *Ibid.*

January 12, 1989 on NBC News, reported that the Reagan Administration had information eight months earlier that Libyan President Qadafy gave Somalia chemical weapons. The State Department denied the account, but NBC stood by its story when questioned by a Congressional office. When Africa Watch raised concerns about the possible use of chemical weapons against the Isaaks with Assistant Secretary of State Chester Crocker, he rebuked our organization for making such a suggestion and indicated that the State Department was satisfied with the Somali government's categorical denials, stating that "prudence and fairness warrant a heavy burden of proof with respect to charges against willful use of weapons of mass destruction by a government against its own people." In view of the Somali government's campaign of destruction in the north, it is difficult to justify Mr. Crocker's confidence in the Somali government on this issue.

Britain did not share the U.S.'s confidence in the Somali government and in December 1988, suspended $9 million in foreign aid. In January 1989, Community Aid Abroad, a prestigious Australian relief agency, announced that it was withdrawing its health care program from Somalia "due to the drastic decline in security and human rights."(For details see Chapter 10.)

The UNHCR halted assistance when the war broke out, but resumed food deliveries by the end of June 1988. However, after protesting to the Somali government about arming the Ogadeni refugees living in the UNHCR camps, the UNHCR halted deliveries of food assistance, and in February reached an agreement with Somalia whereby food deliveries would be resumed for three months and the refugees would be disarmed. However, the UNHCR announced in May 1989, as the war intensified, that it was phasing out its operations in Somalia which it planned to end at the end of 1989. A dispute between the UNHCR and the Somali government over the number of people in the camps has complicated hopes of a resumption of supplies. The UNHCR chief representative in Mogadishu left on August 2, 1989, after being ordered to go

211

two months earlier. Somalia claims that there are 840,000 people in the camps, which the UNHCR believes is greatly exaggerated.*

A positive aspect of U.S. policy towards Somalia has been the high level of interest demonstrated by the U.S. Congress, and its extensive efforts to pressure the Administration to change its policy towards the Siad Barre regime. In July 1988 House Foreign Affairs Committee held a hearing on human rights in Somalia and by September 1988 Congress had decided to withhold $9 million of the $21 million reprogramming request and $7 million from some $15 million in aid suspended from fiscal year 1988. On September 29, 1988, U.S. Representative Sam Gejdenson and 34 Members of Congress sent a letter to then Secretary of State George Shultz requesting: (1) a special State Department report reassessing U.S. policy towards Somalia; (2) a suspension of assistance until this assessment was completed and the ICRC and other relief agencies were allowed back in; (3) assurances that the Somali government was taking steps towards internal reconciliation.

Largely in response to Congressional concerns, the Somali government began a public relations campaign in an effort to improve its image. In August 1988, President Siad Barre appointed a 13-member committee to investigate and find a solution to the problems in the north. The committee included only one Isaak, who was a member of the ruling party. The committee's December 1988 report did not offer a serious discussion of the causes of the conflict, but instead stressed the need for greater amounts of foreign aid to rebuild the north.

To further shore up support, a delegation led by Somali Prime Minister Ali Samatar visited the U.S. on a "diplomatic damage control mission"** in January 1989, accompanied by a lobbyist from Black, Manafort, Stone and Kelly (BMS&K) Public Affairs Company, a public relations firm well known for its strong political connections. The delegation met with members of the Foreign Affairs Committee, including Congressman Sam Gejdenson. The *New African*

---

*   Andrew McEwen, "Refugees face starvation as fighting intensifies," *The Times* (London), August 17, 1989.

**   "Somalia Fights Charges of Human Rights Abuses," Mary Battiata, *Washington Post*, January 25, 1989.

reported in November 1989, that BMS&K advised Mr. Samatar that although Congress was effectively blocking U.S. aid, other institutions, including the World Bank, might offer a friendlier reception. The strategy seemed to work because in June, 1989, the Bank approved a $70 million "quick disbursing cash loan" out of its agricultural sector adjustment program and the African Development Bank supplied an additional $25 million. According to Congressional staff, human rights conditions in Somalia were ignored in the Administration's and World Bank's deliberations on lending to Somalia. Economic considerations appear to have been ignored as well: the loan was based on the dubious premise that Somalia's moribund economy would revive with an increase in agricultural exports. Such a proposition is particularly unlikely in view of the fact that about 90% of Somali exports are accounted for by livestock and 90-95% of all livestock exports are sent throught the port of Berbera, which has come to a standstill since the war broke out. The rural economy of the north was destroyed by the army's counterinsurgency campaign, in which herds were slaughtered, water-reservoirs blown up and food storage facilities destroyed. The flight of nearly a million Isaaks from the area further assures that little economic progress can be expected.

When a hearing was held by the House Banking Subcommittee on International Development Institutions and Finance on June 20, 1989, before the loans were approved, the Administration refused to send a witness. The hearing was called to examine human rights and U.S. policy in the multilateral financial institutions toward China and Somalia. The Bush Administration's failure even to appear at the hearing, after having been invited by the Subcommittee Chairman Representative Walter Fauntroy, underscores the Administration's disinclination to embarrass the Siad Barre regime.

Section 701 of the International Financial Institutions Act requires that U.S. representatives to the multilateral development banks (such as the World Bank and the African Development Bank) oppose loans to governments engaged in "gross violations of international recognized human rights." The Reagan and Bush Administrations ignored the application of this law to Somalia. Indeed, far from opposing loans to Siad Barre, the executive branch has actually promoted Somalia's cause within the banks.

Chairman Fauntroy was sharply critical of the Administration's failure to appear before the Committee, and of its policy in the banks. On September 29, 1989 Chairman Fauntroy, along with 46 other Members of the House of Representatives wrote a letter to Secretary Baker, urging him to reexamine U.S. policy with respect to support for loans to Somalia in the World Bank and African Development Bank.

In March 1989, the Somali government announced a three-step package of "reforms" in an effort to appease the international community:

1. Release of about 300 out of an estimated 1,000 political prisoners;

2. An "amnesty" for Somalis living abroad; and

3. The formation of a three-person committee, composed of government officials, to deal with such problems in the north as rehabilitating the destruction "caused by the bandits," restoring security, revitalizing livestock export, and opening a dialogue with intellectuals, elders and religious leaders.

Aside from the welcome release of political prisoners, the package was meaningless. Regarding the second point, granting an "amnesty" to Somalis who fled their country implies that they committed a crime, instead of recognizing them for what they are — innocent victims of the government. As for the reconciliation committee, once again it did not include opposition voices, nor did it acknowledge wrongdoing by the government.* The U.S. Administration did not point out these shortcomings.

As recently as July 1989 the Administration requested Congress to grant $20 million in economic support funds to Somalia. Once again, its timing was most unfortunate, as it occurred within a week of a government massacre of some 450 civilians in southern Somalia as they departed a mosque.

When members of Congress blocked the additional aid and criticized the Administration for the poor timing, State Department officials offered the unpersuasive argument that the request had long been pending, and the

---

*   For details, see Chapter 15.

214

notification to Congress just days after the July massacre was simply an unfortunate coincidence.

The Assistant Secretary of State for Human Rights and Humanitarian Affairs, Richard Schifter, took a different tack, and actually defended the aid request in a letter to *The New York Times* on September 2, 1989 which was a response to an op-ed on Somalia written by Holly Burkhalter, of the staff of Human Rights Watch, that appeared in the *Times* on August 13. Secretary Schifter took offence at Ms. Burkhalter's suggestion that the aid infusion represented an attempt by the Bush Administration to shore up the faltering Barre regime, and defended the aid on the grounds that "The Administration's request to obligate $21 million in economic support funds for Somalia was directly tied to our support for economic reforms in that country. These reforms, worked out with the International Monetary Fund and the World Bank, are designed to transfer economic decision-making power from the Government to the people and the marketplace – to support the very people who are suffering both from poverty and from human rights abuses."

Secretary Schifter's defense of the aid request is even less plausible than Ambassador Crigler's excuse that the timing was an unfortunate coincidence. The $21 million was balance-of-payments support to the government, not project-oriented development assistance, as the Secretary's letter appears to suggest. Moreover, there is little likelihood that the people "suffering from human rights abuses" will be affected by an infusion of budgetary support to the government responsible for those abuses: fully a million Somali civilians – largely Isaaks – have been displaced either within or outside the country by the military's abusive counterinsurgency techniques. They are certainly not going to benefit from market-oriented reforms imposed by the International Monetary Fund and subsidized by the U.S. government, when trade has become impossible.

Although his public support for aid to Somalia outweighed his human rights message, Secretary Schifter's letter was nonetheless a welcome departure from the State Department's refusal to criticize publicly the Siad Barre government – even when the Department's own investigations revealed extensive atrocities. Prior to his letter, we are aware of no occasion in which a high-ranking

215

Administration official condemned the Siad Barre government for its abuses. Secretary Schifter's willingness is encouraging. However, that letter does not in itself constitute the solid condemnation of Siad Barre's government that would reflect a decision to champion human rights. The Administration, and thereby, the United States, remains identified with Siad Barre by its many acts of friendship and support.

Congress continued its efforts to restrict U.S. aid throughout 1989 and placed aid to Somalia on a "reprogramming basis," which requires advance notification from the executive branch before aid is disbursed. After Congress requested a hold on the $2.5 million available for Somalia in military aid for fiscal year 1989, the Administration, in order not to lose the amount completely, reprogrammed it to other countries. The Administration had already suspended shipment of arms and ammunition by July 1988, but continued to provide "non-lethal" military assistance left over from previous years. In July 1989, Congress also prevented the Administration from providing $21 million in economic aid which had been suspended from fiscal year 1988. In September 1989, the Administration had announced its intention to reprogram the $21 million to other countries in Africa. This welcome decision, which may well have been in response to congressional criticism, represents a new direction for the Bush Administration, one which will go much further in promoting human rights in Somalia than its previous position of support.

The Congress also contributed significantly to the investigation of human rights abuses. Representatives Dante Fascell, Howard Wolpe and Sam Gejdenson, requested an investigation by the General Accounting Office, a Congressional watchdog. A team from the National Security and International Affairs Division of the GAO visited Somalia and Ethiopia from late February to mid-March 1989. They met with government officials and other Somalis, and interviewed the staffs of the UNHCR, the World Food Program, the National Refugee Commission and private voluntary organizations. They also visited Mogadishu and the military facilities at Berbera and toured Hargeisa to assess the damage. In Ethiopia, they interviewed 60 Isaak refugees at all five refugee camps along the Ethiopian-Somali border, talked with UNHCR and government staff members, refugee committee officials and relief workers.

216

On May 16, 1989, the GAO published a 16-page report entitled "Somali: Observations Regarding the Northern Conflict and Resulting Conditions." The findings corroborate those of Africa Watch and other human rights organizations. They include the following:

1. Harassment by the army — looting, jailing, beating and rape — date back to 1982.

2. The Somali military used artillery and aerial bombardment in heavily populated areas in order to retake Burao and Hargeisa, although there were no SNM combatants there.

3. Somali military aircraft bombed and strafed those fleeing the northern cities.

4. Hargeisa was all but destroyed and remains a "ghost town." Extensive looting has occurred and the residents are now made up of dependents of the military, Ogadeni refugees and squatters.

5. Isaak refugees in Ethiopia indicated that they would be willing to endure the harsh conditions of the camps for an indefinite period, rather than return to Somalia.

In August 1989, the State Department released its own report from the Bureau for Refugee Programs, which Congress had requested. It was written by consultant Robert Gersony who spent nearly three months visiting 31 different locations in Ethiopia, Somalia and Kenya and conducted private interviews with more than 300 randomly selected displaced Somalis and Ethiopian refugees, as well as government officials and staff members of international organizations. Entitled "Why Somalis Flee," the report provides a devastating chronicle of the murder, torture and destruction surrounding the war.

Included among the findings are the following:

1. In response to the SNM's May 1988 intensification of the civil conflict in northern Somalia, the Somali Armed Forces appear to have engaged in a widespread, systematic and extremely violent assault on the unarmed civilian Issak population of northern Somalia in places where and at times when neither resistance to these actions nor danger to the Somali Armed Forces was present.

217

2. The Somali Armed Forces conducted what appears to be a systematic pattern of attacks against unarmed, civilian Issak villagers, water points and grazing areas of northern Somalia, killing many of their residents and forcing the survivors to flee for safety to remote areas within Somalia or to other countries.

3. Simultaneously, the Somali Armed Forces engaged in a pattern of roundups, summary executions and massacres of many hundreds, if not more, unarmed civilian Issaks....

4. In an additional pattern of systematic, organized and sustained Somali Armed Forces actions in Berbera, which has not been the object of an SNM attack or the scene of conflict, at least five hundred, and perhaps many more, Isaak men were systematically rounded up and murdered, mainly by having their throats cut, and then buried in mass graves, during the four months following the intensification of the conflict, apparently solely because they were Isaaks....

Mr. Gersony makes what he considers a conservative estimate that at least 5,000 unarmed civilians were murdered by the Somali Armed Forces between May 1988 and March 1989. Africa Watch believes the actual figure is much higher, between 50,000-60,000, when the victims of artillery shelling, aerial bombardment and war related diseases are included. Despite our disagreement with Mr. Gersony's estimates, Africa Watch welcomes the publication of the report.

* * *

The Somali government desperately needs U.S. aid to maintain what little grasp it has left on the country. If the aid is not provided, Siad Barre will be forced either to relinquish power or to take meaningful steps towards reconciliation and peace. Even with the aid, it is unlikely that Siad Barre can hang on much longer. The U.S. would be wise to cut its ties to him now, if it hopes to remain an influential force in the country in the future.

Yassin Karshe Mohamed expressed the feelings of the Somali people in an interview with Africa Watch in Cardiff on July 7, 1989.

We couldn't believe the news that the American government had sent armaments to the Somali army. What we need is people to help relieve us of our problems, not to add to our

218

difficulties. We have always thought of Americans as people who know the meaning of human rights and humanity. We can only assume that they don't know what kind of regime their government is supporting. They must know. You must tell them. We are all confident that once they know, they will not tolerate that their government is increasing our hardship. We have suffered enough already. I am sure they don't know this. If they do, it's difficult to understand that so little is being said or done about it.

Africa Watch urges the U.S. Administration to end its support for the Siad Barre regime and thereby to attempt to regain the confidence of the Somali people themselves. Before any more innocent people are murdered and bombed, we hope that the U.S. government will speak out on their behalf, openly and forcefully, and will distance itself from the government many have come to regard as their worst enemy.

15. PROSPECTS FOR THE FUTURE

The testimony provided to Africa Watch indicates that the joy of escape for Somali refugees is tempered by grief and anxiety. Painful memories of their own traumatic experiences, anguish about family members left behind and anxiety about the future — their own and that of their country, leave little room to enjoy the relief of flight from danger. However precious the haven of refuge abroad, the news about the death of relatives, friends and neighbors remind the refugees of the continuing ravages of the war.

After years of insecurity, they are now uprooted and dislocated, physically and psychologically. Families are strained to the breaking point by responsibility for those left behind in the camps, in Djibouti and in Somalia, and by adjustment to new foreign environments.

In the absence of meaningful reforms the refugees we interviewed expressed no confidence that they would return home and live free from fear, under the rule of law. The government's policies before the war and its conduct of the war have convinced these refugees that it is unwilling to create conditions to safeguard their lives or protect their rights.

The government has made no efforts to encourage refugees to return home in spite of the time that has lapsed since war broke out in the north. On the contrary, it has implemented the same repressive policies in the central and southern regions of the country. The conflicts that now rage in several other regions do not give grounds for optimism about resolving the conflict in the north.

Refugees interviewed by Africa Watch, as well as those interviewed by the team from the General Accounting Office, stated in categorical terms that they would not return as long as the current government remained in power. "The refugees exhibited alarm when questioned about returning home; fear remains the single largest factor in their decision to stay....When asked if government assurances of safety and gestures of goodwill (such as cross-border

food or water deliveries) would convince the Isaak population that it is safe to return, the universal response was incredulity. The refugees emphasized that President Siad Barre could not be trusted and that any cosmetic steps at rapprochement were meaningless in light of the trauma they had endured*.....
It is not likely that the Issak refugees will return until they are confident it is safe to do so. Most of those we interviewed indicated that the military would have to be removed from northern Somalia before the area would be secure."**

A Somali resident abroad who visited the camps remarked that:

> An old woman in a tattered tent...raises her hands to heaven and thanks God that she is living as a free woman.One would think that such expressions may be for public consumption and reflective of SNM pressure to put on a bold face for propaganda purposes. But individuals kept expressing the same views in the privacy of their own tents and with great consistency. There seemed to be no public posturing.

How could they think of going back? The policies that forced them to flee are still being carried out; and the politicians and military officers responsible for those policies and practices retain their positions. Africa Watch knows of no case in which an official of the Somali government has been disciplined or punished for human rights abuses.

One student who did go back, Yunis (not his real name), left the camps for Mogadishu. He was subsequently interviewed by Africa Watch in Djibouti on August 3, 1989, and described the fear he felt upon his return to Somalia:

> As soon as I crossed the border and saw government soldiers, the old feelings of insecurity came back. With all its deprivations, life in the camps was better than this. My nervousness at the sight of the soldiers made me realize why everyone preferred life in the camps; there were no soldiers to be frightened of.

---

*   GAO report at p. 11.

**   GAO report at p. 2.

Like the others Africa Watch interviewed, Sahra Ahmed Arteh was adamant in her view that no-one could think of going back, when we interviewed her in London on June 17, 1989.

No matter what the world gives Barre and what he does, we will never go back while he is there. How can we go back? Our hearts will not let us. The shock of it all, the heartbreak, the climbing of so many hills, the endless walking, all because of the fear that the military would put their hands on us. After all this, you can't just turn around and put your life in the hands of the people who did this to you. When you see your people suffer so much, when you have seen so much bloodshed, it is difficult to trust again. The most important thing to remember in thinking about the future, is to think about the past, clearly, beyond the war. It's not as if before the war, we were alive in any real sense. We never knew, especially if we had men or grown boys in the house, whether we would survive the next day.

Hassan Ismail Omaar, interviewed by Africa Watch in Cardiff on July 8, 1989, expressed similar views:

How can people go back when the military commanders and political leaders who gave the orders to kill unarmed civilians and to bomb their cities are still there. There is no place like home and we want to go home. But first the system has to go and we must get new leaders.

Yusuf Ahmed Ismail, interviewed by Africa Watch in Cardiff on July 6, 1989, told us:

There is no question of going back while Siad Barre is there. What have we got to go back to? If our homes have not been destroyed, they are occupied by refugees. If somebody tries to go back to take possession of their house, most likely they will be killed. You can be sure they will not get any protection from the military. They will be even more eager to kill us than the Ethiopian refugees armed by the government. We have nothing left at home. We don't have much materially here either, but we have the most important thing in life — we have peace. Until we can say the same about Somalia, we can't afford to think of going back.

Khadra Muhumed Abdi, interviewed by Africa Watch in London on
June 2, 1989, said:

> What have we got to go back to? Siad Barre had left us nothing
> — no country, no wealth and so many of our menfolk killed.
> He has encouraged the military to kill our children in front of
> us and taken women out of their homes to be gang-raped by
> his soldiers. He has destroyed the whole of Somalia. There is
> grief in every Somali home, because tens of thousands of
> soldiers have also died. They too have families who are griev-
> ing, including many Marehans. Every clan in Somalia forced
> to take part in this war has lost out. This is not a free govern-
> ment that gave anyone a choice. The government went into the
> countryside to whip up the Darood against the Isaaks. They
> also tricked people living in remote areas to encourage them
> to participate in the war. They went into the interior and told
> people that the SNM wanted to take everything away from
> them and to rule the nation by force. He told them to come to
> the cities where Somalis were dying of a mysterious illness, by
> which we assume he meant AIDS. He said nothing of the war.
> Many were conscripted. So the entire public are victims.
>
> Before people talk about the future, it is necessary to under-
> stand what brought this situation about. It is not only a ques-
> tion of what the solution is, but firstly understanding how and
> why all this happened. A part of the solution must lie in the
> answer to that question. We all have homes, cities to which we
> are deeply attached to. Today the lucky ones are refugees in
> Britain, Canada and Holland and the majority are in camps in
> Ethiopia, or waiting in Dire Dawa and Djibouti to get out or
> are trapped inside Somalia. We are here because this govern-
> ment left us nothing. Prosperous city dwellers, civil servants,
> businessmen, the experienced, the educated and our youth, all
> those who should be at home building our futures are all
> refugees. The world must understand that we are not refugees
> because we wanted to live elsewhere. We have been driven
> out.

Despite the passage of time since the war in the north broke out and
the growing international recognition of the seriousness of the situation, the

government has pursued similar policies in other parts of the country where it faces an armed insurgency.

The government has publicized a number of initiatives that it claims are genuine efforts towards peace in the north. To that end, it has sought international assistance for the displaced in the region. This has been largely an exercise in public relations and an effort to obtain funds to pursue the war.

Abdillahi Sheikh Ali worked in the Ministry of the Interior from September 1987-July 1989 and was part of two official delegations that visited the north to assess the damage and to submit recommendations for international assistance. Interviewed in London on October 23, 1989, he described to Africa Watch the reality behind the government's approach towards peace and reconciliation.

According to Abdillahi, the first commission established by the Ministry of the Interior was a Technical Team, which visited the north in January 1989 to examine the need for relief assistance. The delegation consisted of eleven officials representing eight ministries; no Isaaks were included. They spent twelve days in Hargeisa and eight in Burao.

> There were no refugees in the camps we visited in Hargeisa
> — only armed militias. In the Sha'ab area [which had been
> inhabited primarily by government employees], soldiers
> guarded the homes of the Marehan military officers, stacked
> with "bililiqo" [the local name given to the goods of the Isaaks
> who fled]. Their houses were piled with beds, carpets, videos,
> cupboards and a wide range of other goods. The "bililiqo" was
> taken to various cities for commercial sale and for the personal
> use of the soldiers. We discovered that military officers made
> arrangements to have the wares transported by soldiers in
> exchange for granting them leave. There was no sense of a
> government anywhere in the north.

> We did not see any refugees who had returned, either in
> January or in March. There were very few Isaaks, especially
> in Hargeisa. We were told to make a rough estimate of the
> population in Hargeisa. We calculated 15,000, but in our
> report, we were told to state 40,000. We estimated the popula
> tion in Burao at 12,000, but we were told to change that to
> 30,000.

On our return to Mogadishu, the delegation informed the Ministry of the Interior that there was no security in the north and no trust in the government.

As part its "reform" program announced in January 1989, the government established a committee to "establish the origins of the trouble in the north, evaluate the damage and seek solutions." If it conducted any investigations, its findings have never been made public. Abdillahi made the following comments about the committee:

On March 6, the president appointed a three-man Reconciliation Committee, composed of government officials, to look into the conflict in the north. But this was not a sincere effort. As a group, the committee never went to the north. One of the members, Farah Wa'ais [member of the Central Committee of the Party], visited Berbera in July, but didn't go to Burao, Hargeisa or anywhere else.

The Committee, and other members of the government were primarily interested in encouraging Western governments and donor agencies to allocate money for "rehabilitation," which they hoped would release substantial funds that could be siphoned off. To persuade donors that the money would indeed be used for rebuilding the northern cities damaged in the fighting, the UNDP was given assurances that all assistance from the donor community would be imported through Berbera. The government hoped to strengthen its own position. For that, they needed hard currency to reward pro-government militias and to buy arms.

Ever since the war broke out, most of the international assistance [food, blankets and beds] was resold to Marehan businessmen. In fact, they obtained the goods before they paid for them, so it was really given to them. They resold it in turn to wholesalers and eventually the merchandise appeared in the shops. Even some of the medicine sent to the Ministry of Health was resold.

The United Nations High Commisssion for Refugees took the unprecedented move in January 1989 of announcing a gradual withdrawal of aid to Somalia on account of the arming of Ethiopian refugees and the inability of the agency to monitor and supervise the distribution of the assistance intended

226

for the refugees. *The New York Times* reported that "United Nations officials say the Somali Government has been using much of the food aid it has received to feed refugees drafted to fight in an offensive launched last year against the Somali National Movement...."*

In response to Somalia's appeals for assistance, a United Nations team arrived in March 1989 to assess the country's needs. Four members of the Technical Team that visited the north in January accompanied them. The government had requested aid for what it claimed were 600,000 people displaced by the war, a figure that was inflated in order to encourage a massive infusion of foreign assistance. Abdillahi accompanied them during the visit:

> We were almost always in an airplane. The most we spent in any one city was a day and a night in Berbera, Borama, Erigavo and Garoe. We did not spend the night in either Burao or Hargeisa. It was considered too dangerous.

> In Erigavo and Las Anod, the local government managed to collect neighbors into a house and then argued that of the 15 or so people gathered there, "Normally five people reside here — the rest are displaced relatives." We were briefed about these "arrangements" ahead of time and were told to ensure that the local government was well prepared in advance.

The GAO report noted that:

> A rebuilding program without resettlement controls could result in former residents being replaced by people in the area who have been friendly to the government during the conflict and could hinder the return of former residents.**

The single most important initiative has been an amnesty under which about three hundred political prisoners have been released, a measure that the government hoped would deflect international pressure to alleviate human rights abuses. Those who benefitted from the amnesty include most of the prominent political prisoners who were the subject of international appeals,

---

*   "U.N. Withholds Aid in Somalia Dispute," *The New York Times*, January 28, 1989.

**   GAO report at p. 10.

such as the fourteen members of the Hargeisa group at Labaatan Jirow prison, Suleiman Nuh Ali, an architect and civil engineer, Abdi ismail Yunis, former director of Planning of the Somali National University and Safia Hashi Madar, an employee of a relief agency. Africa Watch has welcomed the release of these prisoners, who were arrested and detained without a shred of evidence to substantiate the charges against them, denied a fair trial, tortured, subjected to psychological initimidation and imprisoned for years under degrading conditions.

Nevertheless, it is important to remember that only a percentage of prisoners and detainees have been released. It has always been impossible to estimate the number of political prisoners in Somalia because the names and numbers of detainees are not published and many people are held in secret detention centers. Hundreds, perhaps thousands of people continue to be held completely outside the framework of the law. The hundreds of Isaak members of the armed forces arrested when the war began are still detained; Africa Watch has not received a reply from the government in response to its appeals for their release.

On August 30, 1989, the government announced plans to allow the creation of a multiparty system and said that parliamentary elections would be held at the end of 1990. It added two conditions that severely limit the possibilities. firstly, all those who have participated in or supported armed conflict against the state will not be allowed to form a party. Secondly, no party based on tribalism or regionalism will be allowed to exist. These conditions make it impossible for any of the existing opposition movements to participate in the forthcoming elections. The government is well aware of the fact that political parties have always been organized on a regional basis in Somalia. Its own policies of deliberately manipulating the clan system and exacerbating differences has reinforced the organization of opposition groups along regional lines. It is therefore not surprising that no opposition group has taken this announcement seriously.

On August 30, 1989, the government announced plans to allow the creation of a multiparty system and said that parliamentary elections would be held at the end of 1990. It added two conditions that severely limit the possibilities. Firstly, all those who have participated in or supported armed conflict against the state will not be allowed to form a party. Secondly, no party based on tribalism or regionalism will be allowed to exist. These conditions make it impossible for any of the existing opposition movements to participate in the forthcoming elections. The government is well aware of the fact that political parties have always been organized on a regional basis in Somalia. Its own policies of deliberately manipulating the clan system and exacerbating differences has reinforced the tendency to organize opposition groups along regional lines. It is therefore not surprising that opposition groups have not taken this announcement seriously.

In addition, the government did not give any indications that opposition groups would be able to make any contributions to the decisions or debates about the creation of the new system. President Barre will choose how many constituencies there will be, how the polling will be organized, who will supervise it and what role the courts will play with respect to the elections. It is extremely unlikely that groups who have taken up armed struggle against the government will agree to abandon their struggle for the sake of participating in a new parliamentary system on the government's terms.

In a manner that highlights its enduring hostility to civilians, the government announced an "amnesty" to Somalis abroad who agreed to return home. Prime Minister Samatar stated during a visit to London in January 1989 that Somalis abroad, which presumably includes the refugees in Ethiopia, are free to return "irrespective of their past crimes and activities". A statement making it clear that the potential beneficiaries were SNM fighters would at least have the merit of clarity. An offer to amnesty civilians who have been driven out of their homes by government violence is at best, a cynical gesture and underlines the government's continuing inability to draw a distinction between civilian non-combatants and the members of an armed guerrilla movement.

APPENDIX ONE

People Killed in the War

Name	Age/occupation	Cause of death
BERBERA		
Hussein Ali Abdalle (Dumush)	ex-port employee	shot
Ibrahim Qasim Elmi "Gaagale" elder		" "
Osman Abdi Deriye		" "
Ina Ahmed Warsame		" "
Ismail Yusuf		" "
Hassan Mohamed		stabbed
Mohamoud Abdi		" "
Abdillahi (Ina subhaanle)		" "
Hawa Elmi Dualeh	nine months pregnant	" "
"Badhyaune"	merchant	" "
Mohamed Ahmed Diriiye		" "
Bashe Farah		" "
Qoofal Geesood		" "
Saeed Abdillahi		" "
Abdillahi Yusuf	owner of a truck	" "
Abdi Fagaase		" "
Mahamud Mohamed Ahmed		died in prison
Mahdi Hassan Ahmed		
Idris Osman Abdi		
Yusuf Ali Abdi		
Elmi Araleh Farah		stabbed

Name	Age/occupation	Cause of death

BERBERA (Cont.)

Mohamed Elmi Araleh,
  son of above, child · · · · · · stabbed

Suleiman Elmi Hassan · · · · · · " "

Ali Haji Osman Dirrir · · · · 8

and his son, Mohamed · · · · · · " "

Aboker Hassan Diiriye

Nuur Hassan Farah

Elmi Isman Guleid

Yusuf Isman Guleid

Ali Abdillahi Bille

Ina Artan Hersi

Ina Hussein Hersi (Gaagaab)

Yusuf Diiriye Awale

Ina Bile Jama Khayre

Fadumo Artan Hersi

Mohamed Osman Abdi

Ahmed Ibrahim Mohamed

Abdillahi Haji Muse

Ilma Aw Nuur (two brothers)

Ina Jama Bihi

Ina omer Dhegaweyne

Aw osman Yusuf (100 years old)

Hassan Mohamed (80 years old)

Aden Mohamed, · · · · · an employee of the
Electricity Agency,
and his two brother;
one brother,"Cirro"
was an employee of
Somali Airlines and
the other was unemployed.

232

Name	Age/occupation	Cause of death
BERBERA (Cont.)		
The brother of		
"British"	a driver at Chevron	
Ali Babel	a driver at UNHCR	
Ibrahim Qaasin Elmi	owner of a restaurant	
Gaas Ibrahim Ahmed		shot
Ahmed Omer Mushteeg		" "
Digaale Husein		" "
HARGEISA		
Isse Hersi Dirrir		shot
Hodan Elmi Daad	3	artillery shelling
Ambaro Saeed Alin	75	" "
Ahmed Hassan Wabi	26	aerial bombardment
Omer Hassan Wabi	brother of above	artillery shelling
Abshir Yussuf Adan	30	" "
Samira H. Ali Nur	21, student	
Nasra	19, sister of above	" "
Abdiqani	17, brother of above	" "
Mohamed Yare	restaraunt owner	shot
Mohamed Haji Askar	businessman	" "
Mohamed Iid	businessman and his son	shot in their home
Mohamed Omaar		aerial bombardment
Sahra Dahir	housewife	" "
Abdirasaaq Dahir	brother of above	shot in front of the central jail
Abdilahi Dahir	" ", 30, captain of Hargeisa football team	artillery shelling

Name	Age/occupation	Cause of death
HARGEISA (cont.)		
Mohamed Jama Yey		
Mohamed Jama Dagaal		artillery
Sahra Omer Haji		shot
Yusuf Jama		shot during a raid on his home
ndlie Yare	cart truck owner	aerial bombardment
Hussein Warsame Mohamed and his seven children	engineer	artillery shelling
Ibrahim Aw Osman his wife and two children	shopkeeper mid-20s,	aerial bombardment
Nuh Mohamed Robleh	trader	cause unknown
Mohamed Dirisa his daughter	pharmacy owner	artillery shelling
Mohamed Muse	hotel cashier	aerial bombardment
Haji Tuyub	hotel owner	
Hussein Darrod	owner of a trus	shot on the road
Bashe Abdil!ahi	former soldier	shot in his home
Dr. Joseph	manager of medicinal store room at Hargeisa General Hospital	aerial bombardment
his seven children		" "
Ambaro Hassan		shot in her home
Deeq Fagaseh		shot
Ahmed Abdillahi Abdi	23	" "
Dhagi Cadami		" "
Bashir Omer Doodi		" "

Name	Age/occupation	Cause of death
HARGEISA (cont.)		
Mohamed Ali Afweyne	graduate unemployed at the time	shot in his home
Hassan Farah Afey	resident in Saudi Arabia, on holiday	shot
Amina Abdi Ghelle	housewife, in her forties	cause unknown
and her three children;		
Mohamed Mohamoud Guled	8	
Ahmed Mohamoud Guled	6	
Fadumo Mohamoud Guled	5	
Haji Abdullahi Nur Hersi	in his eighties	" "
Mawleed Aideed	13, schoolboy	shot
Daughter of Hassan Horre		shot outside her home
Muse Diriye		cause unknown
Ismail Saeed	a salesman, in his twenties	
his mother and		
his sister-in-law,		
Habiba		shot
Ali Abdi Farah	restaurant owner	artillery shelling
Abdillahi Farah Ahmed	shopowner	" "
Said Mohamed Nur	child	" "
Abdillahi Mohamed Osman	15, student	" "
Asha Mohamed Warsame	16, student	shot
Khadija Hussein Farah	widow	" "
Anab Mohamed Robleh		
daughter of the above		" "
Shamis Shirdoon		" "
Fawziya Shirdoon		" "

Name	Age/occupation	Cause of death
HARGEISA (cont.)		
Safiya Shirdoon		shot
Hussein Dahir Egeh	2	artillery shelling
Said Haji Dahir	32	" "
Ali Haji Dahir	28	" "
Sahra Ahmed Wayd	8	" "
Abdi Ali Nur	18	" "
Mustafe Abdi Hassan (Shine)	22	" "
Mohammed Abdillahi Samawi	60	" "
Mohamed Hassan Muse	35	" "
Abdi Ali Abdillahi (Shaxari)	20	shot
Hassan Mohamed Husein	30	artillery shelling
Osman Jalle	25	" "
Sahra Aw.Abdi Hanana Side	35	" "
Keyd Ibrahim Abdi	32	" "
Fawzia Ali Abdi	35	
and her son	1	land mine
A/risaq Abdi Abdillah	6	" "
Mohamed Dubad	35	artillery shelling
Mohamed Nur Osman Ali	60	" "
Ibrahim Farah Haruuri	32	" "
Ahmed Hashi Hussein	33	shot, July 88
Shawa Diria Madar	50	artillery shelling, June 88
Marian Hure Farah	45	shot
Ahmed Mohamed Hirsi	55	shot, Aug. 88
Hassan Hashi	45	shot
Eid Ali Shaba'a	27	artillery shelling, June 88

236

Name	Age/occupation	Cause of death
HARGEISA (cont.)		
Ahmed Abadir Meygaage	32	shot, July 88
Adan Bulbul	70	artillery shelling, June 88
Yusuf Ahmed Hussin	NSS	shot
Areef Galib Ali	businessman	artillery shelling
Abdi Suleman Farah		stabbed
Ismail Jama Arteh		" "
Geedi Dualeh Hersi		" "
Yussuf Hassan Waays	resident Saudi Arabia	shot
Adan Ahmed Handule	"Gocey" driver	shot
Abdi Muse Jama		artillery shelling in the same house
Hassan Issa Yusuf		" "
Amine saeed Mohamed		" "
Mohamed Ismail Mohamed	student	" "
Hassan Ibrahim Ali		" "
Mohamed Ibrahim Ali		" "
Abdillahi Mohamed Jama		" "
Safia Isse Yusuf		
		" "
Halwo Shabeed (mother)		artillery shelling
Ardo Ahmed Adan		" "
Ismail Hussein Gurey		shot
Adan Elmi Dheere		
Hassan Adan Elmi, son of above		
Ardo Adan Gudaal		missing
Mohamed Haji Askar		shot
Haji Husein Bilacurdayni		" "
Mohamed Hasan Abdi		aerial bombardment
Ahmed Abdi Mohamed		artillery shelling

Name	Age/occupation	Cause of death
HARGEISA (cont.)		
Abdi Hasan Begsi		artillery shelling
Seed Ahmed Abdi		" "
Abdi Ahmed Abdi		" "
Ismail Adan Nur		" "
Mohamed Elmi Mohamed		" "
Ahmed Dahir Malin		" "
Mohamed Malin Husein		" "
Ahmed Malin Abdi		
Yusuf Husein Arab		
Hasan Malin Abdi		
Osman Husein Ali		
Dhegjar Mahdi		
Abdi Hussein Guleed		
Abdillahi Abdi Hussein		
Nasir Muse Dirye		
Mohamed Abdullahi Hassan Rakuub		
Ahmed Mohamed Hayder		
Mohamed Geedi Dirye		
Asha Jama Ali		
Halimo Elmi		
Hussein Abdillahi Ismail		
Abdi Abiib Osman		
Marian Hashi		aerial bombardment
Kinsi Ali Omer		" "
Abdi Ismail Abiib		" "
Mohamud Dhagoole		" "
Abdi Omer Osman		" "
Abshir Dhair Omer		
Ahmed Abdi Farah		shot
Abdillahi Abdi		

Name	Age/occupation	Cause of death
HARGEISA (cont.)		
Mohamed Fiidar, "Dool"		stabbed
Ibado Hassan Gulaid		shot
Mohamed Abdillahi		
Ali Farah Gelle		" "
Haji Salan and		
4 of his children		artillery shelling
Hassan Ibrahim Jama		shot
Osob Abdi Seed		
Hodan Abdullahi Saeed		
Saeed Mohamed Egeh		
Layla Mohamed Goth		aerial bombardment
Ayaan Mohamed Good	14, student	" "
Idil Mohamed Good	5	" "
		Biya Chine
Mohamed Nuur "Sumuni"	owner of "Bada Cagaha Ghelli" hotel in Berbera. On holiday in Hargeisa; their house was hit by mortar	shot
Saiida Aar	60's	artillery shelling
Ibaado Mohamed	employee of Hargeisa section of the national Women's Democratic Organization	" "
Mohamed Dheere	accountant Somali Airlines	" "

Name	Age/occupation	Cause of death
HARGEISA (cont.)		
Nuh Ismai Sheikh Ibrahim	17, student, Omer Bin Khadaab School	cause unknown
Said Sulub Alin	14, student	shot
Mohamed Muse	cashier	
Bar Hargeisa		" "
Son of Osman Qorsheel		shot in his home as soldiers attempted to rob his home.
Ali Haji Adan	ex-police officer, mentally unbalanced	shot
Sheikh Ali	headmaster, New Hargeisa School	artillery shelling
Adan "Duuryo"	garage-owner	shot in his home when he refused to hand over a tape-recorder to soldiers
Ismail Hariir	technician at OXFAM	shot
Khadija Yusuf Egeh		" "
Ahmed Guud Adde Harbi		artillery shelling
Ahmed Hashi Shide	employee, Somali Airlines	artillery shelling
Ahmed Hashi Ali	nomad	" "
Abdillahi Dahir	Captain, Hargeisa football team	shot
Abdi "Finger"	businessman	artillery shelling
Ali Saddeh	" "	shot in his home
Abdirahman Yey	" "	aerial bombardment

Name	Age/occupation	Cause of death
HARGEISA (cont.)		
Mohamoud "Mahfud"	volley-ball player in Buroa	artillery shelling
Mohamoud Nur	elderly	shot in his store
Kinsi Adam	woman in her 70s	shot in her home
Mohamed Farah Nageeye	farmer	shot
Hassan Ahmed Janbiir	Action Aid employee	" "
Fadumo Abdi	60	" "
Abdi Yulyul H. Baruud	mentally unbalaced	" "
Jama Isse Daboole		" "
Abnid Aideed		artillery shelling
Muse Diriye Ahmed	60	" "
Hussein Hassan Wabi, "Food"		
Yusuf Ahmed Hassan	NSS	shot
Areef Qalib Ali	businessman	artillery shelling
Abdi Suleiman Farah		stabbed
Ismail Jama Arteh		" "
Geedi Dualeh Hersi		" "
Yusuf Hassan Ways		shot
Adan Ahmed Handule (Gocay)	driver	" "
Abdi Muse Jama		artillery shelling
Amina Saeed Mohamed		" "
Hassan Isse Yusuf		" "
Mohamed Ismail Mohamed	student	" "
Hassan Ibrahim Ali		" "
Abdillahi Mohamed Jama		" "
Safiya Isse Yusuf		" "
Halwo Shabeed	mother	" "
Ardo Ahmed Adan		" "

Name	Age/occupation	Cause of death
HARGEISA (cont.)		
Hajiyo Ardo		artillery shelling
Mulikhiye Yusuf		missing
Adan Hassan Mohamed		shot
Bowdo Husein Adan		
Adan Hebaan		bazooka
Ismail Hussein Gurey		shot
Adan Elmi Dheere		
and his son Hassan		missing
Ardo Adan Gudaal		artillery shelling
Abdi Ahmed "Ilkaase"	56	
Koos Ali Jama	31	
Mohamed Ali Hussein	33	shot
Marian Bile		
and daugther Faiza		land mine
Urdooh Mohamed Bulbul	27	" "
Rashid Mohamed Bulbul	24	" "
Mohamoud Mohamed Yusuf	24	" "
Nasir Mohamed Abdi	20	" "
Asha Hussein	70	" "
Abdirahman Hassan		
Hussein	21	" "
Mohamed Hassan Hussein	16	" "
Aideed Abdi Dheere	20	" "
Mohamed Abdi Dheere	28	" "
Shamis Haji Booqah	40	" "
Adar Didar	65	artillery
Rashid Hassan Baruud	21	aerial bombardment
Farduus Bare Ware	21	" "
Mohamoud Hussein		
Balurdein	25	artillery shelling

242

Abdi Shire Shariif	26	shot
Mohamed Mohamoud Dahir	20	land mine
Anab Ismail and		
her two sons, Awil and Iro	19 and 20, respectively	
Eid Ali Shabel	20	artillery shelling
Ali Sheikh Abdi	55	" "
Ismail Haybe	25	shot
Dahir Ibrahim Roble	50	" "
Hassan Ibrahim	45	" "
Abdi Dubad, "Alafdoon"	65	artillery shelling
Mohamed Haybe	25	aerial bombardment
Mohamed Jama	20	" "
Shugri Elmi	40	" "
Omar Ibrahim	55	artillery shelling
Amina Said Mohamed	60	shot
Asha Dhuxul Mohamed		" "
Faisal Said Ahmed	4	artillery shelling
Fadumo Ali Mohamed	70	" "
Mohamed Ahmed Aw Hassan	2	aerial bombardment
Hussein Yussuf Robleh	child	artillery shelling
Abshir Yussuf Adan	30	" "
Ali Abdi Farah	restaurant owner	" "
Abdillahi Farah Ahmed	shopowner	" "
Jama Farah Abdi	restaurant owner	" "
Yusuf Abdi Jama		" "
Sahra Mohamed Abdi	housewife	" "
Fadumo Ali Warsame	" "	" "
Ismail Hariir	employee, OXFAM	shot
Ismail Mattan		aerial bombarment
Bihi Yusuf		
Diirqadhaadh		land mine
Abu Raas		artillery shelling

Name	Age/occupation	Cause of death
HARGEISA (cont.)		
Mohamed Muse		shot
Ina Hasan Qeir		aerial bombardment
Adan Bul-Bul Mohamed	60	artillery shelling
Safia Seef	50	shot
Abdi Ali Nur	18	" "
Mohamed Hassan Muse	35	" "
Khadiji Abdillahi	70	artillery shelling
Hassan Mohamed Hussein	30	shot
Osman Jaale	foot-ball player 25	" "
Sahra Aw Abdi,		
Hanan Side,	35	" "
Kayd Ibrahim Abdi	32	" "
Fawzia Ali Abdi	35 and her son, 1	land mine
A/Risaq Abdi Abdillahi "Huriye"	6	" "
Mohamed Dubad	35	artillery shelling
Mohamed Nur Omar Ali	60	" "
Abdillahi Muhumed	65	shot
Ahmed Ibrahim Jibril	25	aerial bombardment
Gureh Mahdi Yusuf	23	" "
Raho Abdi Farah		shot
Yusuf Meygaag Samater Advisor to the Hargeisa Academy of Arts & Science	70	aerial bombardment
Mariam Meygaag Samater	65	" "
Daaniye Ali Good	15	" "

Name	Age/occupation	Cause of death
BURAO		
Mohamed Hussein Ibrahim	student	shot
Mohfud Mohamoud	26, student	" "
Ahmed Saeed Hersi	29, student	" "
Mohamed Ahmed Magan	25, civil servant	" "
Abdalla Osman Abdi	29, student	" "
Anab Kabade Abdi	56, shopowner	" "
Osman Haji Abdillahi	in his forties	artillery shelling
Abdillahi Ghelle	a trader	shot
Warsame Ghelle	brother of above, trader	" "
Yusuf Mohamed Dodi and his son, Ismail Yusuf,	contractor 20	artillery shelling
Ahmed Ali Suleiman	businessman	shot in the street
Yusuf Sheikh Osman Nur	a former member of parliament in the civilian government	shot
"Alamsay"	elder	" "
Mohamoud Warsame	a nomad in his 70s	" "
Fadumo Haji Nur and her husband, Raabi		killed in the fighting in June 1989 at Billadiig
Bille Mohamed Haji Hassan		

Name	Age/occupation	Cause of death
BURAO (cont.)		
Mohamed, brother of above		shot
Yusuf Omer Mohamed	23, student	" "
Deeqa Haji Abdi		artillery shelling
Amina Haji Abdi		" "
Dhool Salah		" "
Faduma Ali Warsame		" "
Amina Haybe Kahin	Sheikh	shot
Haybe Kahin	" "	
Khader Abdi Husein		" "
Kinsi Abdi Hussei	28	kidnapped while fleeing; presumed dead
Negaad Abdi Hussein,	23, sister of above	" "
Saade Abdi Hussein	19	" "
Samsam	12 and Ibaado, 7	
Ibaado		
Mohamed Abdi Jiir		killed by a tank
Abdi Guhaad Jama		killed by bebey
Jama Maxamoud Dirir, "Abdi Wadaad"		missing
Waris Hassan Jama	32	
Waris's children, all killed on the same day:		
Faisa Ahmed Mohamed	9	
Abdillahi Ahmed Mohamed	11	
Mohamed Ahmed Mohamed	10	
Mustapha Ahmed Mohamed	7	missing
Abdillahi Qaydeeed Egal	37	

Name	Age/occupation	Cause of death
BURAO (cont.)		
Five of his children		
abducted by the army		missing
Bashir Ali Dalmar	26, taxi driver	aerial bombardment
Abdi Qunle	27, trader	" "
Ashe Ahmed Gaas	70s	artillery shelling
Mohamed Ahmed Yusuf		stabbed
Farah Awad, 80s		
and his son		shot
Kawiyad Farah Awad		" "
His wife, and son Kawiyad		shot in their homes;
Osman Mohamed Yusuf		
"Mohamed Yare"	former seaman	shot
Ali Ahmed Hoolhool		" "
Aw Adan Nooh		" "
Sahra Ahmed Yare		" "
Ahmed Abdi	taxi driver	" "
Aw Yusuf Noor Duale	businessman	" "
Asha Elmi Yusuf	housewife	aerial bombarment
Mustafe Yusuf Sh Osman		shot
Abdi Ali Bedel (Toor)	taxi driver	" "
Hasan Jama Hayd	businessman	" "
Jamaal Hasan Ali	student	" "
Sh Ahmed Herow	religious man	" "
Bashiir Abdillahi Kahin,	employee, Somali	
	Airlines	" "
Ahmed Ali Waraabe	businessman	" "
Anab Hasan Ali,		
"Jiqyare"		shot
Ubah Saeed Adan		

247

Name	Age/occupation	Cause of death
BURAO (cont.)		
Farah Saeed Adan, brother of above	students	shot
Dubad Dhegole and his two sons, Mohamed and Jamaal		" "
Fadumo Mohamoud Ahmed	child	" "
Dhegakamaqal Abdillahi Guleid,	businessman	artillery shelling
Mohamed Abdi Ali	student	
Khadar Hasan Sh Osman		
Mahamoud Ahmed Ali		
Amina Ahmed Abdi	child	
Mohamoud Jirde Abdillahi	driver	
Hassan Aideed Elmi	businessman	
Abdi Ibrahim Ismail	driver	
Ahmed Hersi		
Jamaal Tarabi Abdillahi		
Tusmo Hayd Noor		
Ahmed Jama Hassan	student	
Fadumo Mohamoud Ahmed	child	
Amina Mahad Ahmed	student	
Ahmed Husein Qasbaaye	" "	
Adar Ibrahim Ali	housewife	
Hasan Osman Noor	businessman	
Fosiya Yusuf Ali	housewife	
Mawliid Aideed Hugur	student	
Saluugla Artan Ahmed	housewife	
Abdillahi Kahin	businessman	
Mohamed Abdillahi Husein	" "	
Khadar Sulub	student	

Name	Age/occupation	Cause of death
BURAO (cont.)		
Mohamed Sahal Husein	student	
Mariam Mhoamed	30, May 30, 1988	artillery shelling
Amin Ahmed Yonis		shot
Fadumo Yonis		" "
Asha Mohamed		" "
Fadumo Haji Abdi		artillery shelling
Khadija Haji Abdi		" "
Deeq Malin Said		aerial bombardment
Asha Khalif		shot
Usur Abdi Geele		" "
Amina Ahmed Yonis		artillery shelling
Fadumo Mohamed		aerial bombardment
Asha Ismail		shot
Khadiji Jama Mohamed		aerial bombardment
Khadija Aw Jibril		" "
Farah Ali Warsame		shot
Jama Haji Abdi Warsame		" "
Yusuf Haji Abei Warsame		" "
Faduma Ali Warsame		" "
Mohamed Ibrahim Ali		" "
Jama Ibrahim Ali		" "
Basra Ibrahim Ali		" "
Amina Ali Warsame		" "
Husein Warsame		" "
Hassan Baashe		" "
Ibrahim Yusuf		" "
Ina Ahmed Yey		" "
Hassan Husein	80	lack of medical care
Siraad Salaan	65	" "

Name	Age/occupation	Cause of death
BURAO (cont.)		
Marian Suleiman	60	lack of medical care
Ali Warsame		" "
Jama Noor	businessman	artillery shelling
Ismail Geedi	" "	" "
Adan Mohamed Abdi	" "	" "
Bile Mohamed	" "	" "
Omer Ahmed	" "	" "
Mohamed Duale	" "	" "
Osman Ahmed	driver	" "
Mohamed Jama	businessman	" "
Said Mohamed	" "	" "
Mohamed Arrale	" "	aerial bombardment
Abdi Mohamed	" "	" "
H. Husein Noor	" "	" "
Hassan Ismail	" "	" "
Ismail H. Ahmed	" "	artillery shelling
Said Dalmash	" "	" "
Abdillahi Ibrahim	" "	" "
Osman Abdillahi	" "	" "
Jama Abdalle	teacher	" "
Jama Ali Dahir	" "	" "
Ismail Geedi	businessman	aerial bombardment
Ali Handule	" "	" "
Duale Mohamed	" "	artillery shelling
Hassan Ismail	" "	aerial bombardment
Abdillahi Ibrahim	" "	artillery shelling
Mohamed Dirir	" "	aerial bombardment
Abdilkadir Yusuf	" "	" "
Jamal Dubad	student	" "
Adan Abdi Farah	mechanic	artillery shelling

Name	Age/occupation	Cause of death
BURAO (cont.)		
Mohamed Abdi Farah	carpenter	artillery shelling
Mohamed Abdi Saleeban	" "	" "
Saleeban Gaade	businesssman	" "
Ali Abdalle	chemist	" "
Abdalle Saeed Kharbuud	60, businessman	" "
Adan Hassan Kharbuud	businessman	" "
Oonadhe Haariye	" "	aerial bombardment
Anabuushe Yusuf	" "	" "
Mohamed Ali Kaadi	student	artillery shelling
Mohamed Bidhiidh		
Abdillahi	" "	" "
Mohamed Hassan	" "	" "
Ismail Afgaab	" "	" "
Rashiid Firirig	" "	" "
Shooqi Ahmed	" "	" "
Ibrahim Muse	unemployed	aerial bombardment
Farah Hassan	petty trader	" "
Ali Adan Ayaanle	store keeper	artillery shelling
Abdi Arab	businessman	" "
Mahdi Jama	student	" "
Abdi Abdillahi(Caydhaf)	customs officer	" "
Amina Awil	student	" "
Ayaan Awil Nur	" "	" "
Kaltuun Abdiwahaab	" "	aerial bombardment
Ifrah Abdi Adan	" "	" "
Shukri Umer	" "	" "
Dahabo Farah		artillery shelling
Nasiim Saleeban	4	" "
Safiya Ahmed Allale	student	" "
Khadija Abdi	" "	" "

251

Name	Age/occupation	Cause of death
BURAO (cont.)		
Zeynab Ali		aerial bombardment
Zeynab Ahmed		" "
Halimo Ahmed		artillery shelling
Hiis Husein		aerial bombardment
Sureer Duale		" "
Asha Koos		artillery shelling
Awo Mohamoud		" "
Kamar Hassan		" "
Indhadeeq Ismail		" "
Tooh Yar		" "
Abdikariim Hasan		aerial bombardment
Abdi Ali		" "
Mohamoud Yusuf		artillery shelling
Amina Jama Elmi		" "
Mohamedd Awil		" "
Amina Yasiin Ali		
Jama Botaan Aden	70	shot
Fadumo Mohamed Jama		
three of her children		" "
Jama Hersi Gaani	60	" "
Jama Bile	60	" "
Haybe Obsiiye Dhunkaal	taxi driver	" "
Hassan Obsiiye Dhunkaal		" "
Hurre Hersi Gani	businessman	" "
Mohamed dhegode Abaar	student	" "
Mohamed ahmed Arab	businessman	" "
Dalqaf Hersi Gani	" "	" "
Mohamed Adan Botaan	" "	" "
Mohamoud Adan Botaan	" "	" "
Abdi Arab Jama	diabled	" "

252

Name	Age/occupation	Cause of death
BURAO (cont.)		
Mohamoud Hassan Mohamed	student	shot
Ina Qasiim Qodah	businessman	" "
Ibrahim Farah Abaas	taxidriver	" "
Nimo abdi Yusuf	student	" "
Abdi Bile Duale	businessman	" "
Farah Raygal Duale	" "	" "
Suleiman Abdi Yusuf	student	" "
Saeed Abdi Yusuf	" "	" "
Ali dirir Hersi	businessman	" "
Suleiman Husein Yusuf	student	" "
Mohamed Mohamoud Adan	unemployed	" "
Yusuf Mohamoud Aden	" "	" "
Saeed Husein Yusuf	" "	" "
Mukhtaar Ibrahim Yusuf	" "	" "
Ismail Hussein Yusuf	" "	" "
Mohamed Mohamoud Aden	student	" "
Nuur Mohamed Aden	" "	" "
Marian Dubad Warsame	housewife	" "
Asha Mohamed		" "
Fozia		" "
Sureer Ali	60	" "
Raabi Duale Afhakame	70	stabbed
Abdillahi Jama Moallin	lawyer	shot
Fathiya Yasiin Fayog	student	" "
Khadija Aw Jibriil		stabbed
Khadija Aboker Duale		shot
Aideed Adan		stabbed
Faras Aideed Aden	businessman	shot
Ismail Haji Adan	" "	" "
Mohamed Ali Dahir	teacher	" "

253

Name	Age/occupation	Cause of death
BURAO (cont.)		
Asha Khalaf	housewife	stabbed
Kayd Mohamed Mohamoud	businessman	shot
Ina Keenadiid Aboker	" "	" "
Jama Omer Ahmed		" "
SHEIKH		
Ibrahim Mohamed Fooley		
Saleeban Abdi Dukus		
Ali Ahmed Fijaan		
ERIGAVO		
Mohamoud SalaH	shopkeeper	shot in his home
Mohamed Abdi, "Shaami"	" "	" "
Abdirahman Sheikh Saeed	trader	" "
Ahmed Matan	shopkeeper	" "
Ahmed Hasan (Ahmed Hayd)		
Isse Dheere		
Ahmed Mohamed Saleh		
Abdi Duale Arab	student, Mog University	
Saeed Ahmed		shot
Aboker Girgale	farmer	" "
Yusuf Dakharre	" "	" "
Qule	" "	" "
Abdi Hasan Omer, "Shifle"		" "
Kaltuun Mohamoud		" "
GEBILEY		
Jirre Abdi Hassan	farmer	shot

Name	Age/occupation	Cause of death
GEBILEY (cont.)		
Aw Abdi Hassan	72	
Khadija Awale	housewife	aerial bombardment
Amina Aw Mohamed	" "	
two of her children and		
her mother		" "
Lul Barud	businesswoman	
and her son		artillery shelling

KALABAYDH

Hassan Dahir
Rashid Ibrahim
Hufane Taynaan
Aw Muse Adan
Hassan Ahmed
Ismail Ahmed
Maka Ali
Abdi Yonis
Mohamed Husien Mohamed
Ali Sahal
Omar Mohamoud Ibrahim
Omar Madoobe
Abdi Goohe Careeye

EL AFWEYN

Name	Age/occupation	Cause of death
Abdillahi Abdi,	60, ex-police	
"Sawahili"	sergent	shot
Salaah Dhunkaal		
Saleeban Dhunkaal		
Adan Jama Abdi		

Name	Age/occupation	Cause of death

EL AFWEYN (cont.)

Abdi Mohamed Saleh
Khiif Yusuf Duale
Mohamed Hasan Deria
Abdi Omer
Mohamed Garaasi
Ali Ibrahim Deria
Awil Ahmed
Said Ahmed Hasan
Faisal Aboker Hasan Dhunkaal
Abyan Dhegoole
Gaariye Jama Farah
Atwi Abdi Deria
Dhega Adde
Shiine Hasan Husein
Faisal Bulaale Gabaydhe
Ina Mohamed Bulaale
Ina Abdi Gaas
Ina Hayir Duale
Salah Mohamoud Dube
Khaliif mohamoud Dube
Muse Ibrahim Dube
Warsame Ibrahim Dube
Abdi Ibrahim Dube
Ina Shire Duale Walhad
Ina Husein GWY
Ina Farah Abdi Deria
Ina Ahmed Shakuur
Anis Ali Aw Barre

Name	Age/occupation	Cause of death

People who have died of war related diseases while fleeing or in the camps:

Name	Age/occupation	Cause of death
Mohamed Hashi Ali		
Dool Wayab	businessman	malaria
Ismial Rusheeye	" "	" "
Mohamed Yare		" "
Ahmed Langadhe	shopkeeper	" "
Ibrahim "Sanqadyare"	court-clerk	" "
Osman "Askari"	poet	" "
Aw Yusuf Dimbiil	owner of a shop	jaundice
Mohamed Warsame		
a nomad from Darar Weyne		" "
Mohamed Omer Hashi		a diabetic and also had kidney problems
Dahabo Salah Ahmed		
Guled Karshe Mohamed		
Hussein Warsame Mohamed	father of six	
Mohamed Jama Yey		shot and wounded in Hargeisa; died of complications due to being a diabetic
Zeinab gsman Abdi		gave birth on the road and died for lack of medical attention as a result of complications
Fadumo Ahmed Yusuf	nurse	died of loss of blood at Dire Dawa in mid-1989
Kayse Omer Ileeye	businessman	malaria
Ifrah Abdullahi Farah		
Jirreh	13, student	" "

257

Name	Age/occupation	Cause of death

People who have died of war related diseases while fleeing or in the camps:

Name	Age/occupation	Cause of death
Aw Abdi Hassan	75	
Omer Abdillahi Dualeh		malaria
Mukhtaar Ibrahim Yusuf		" "
Ismail Hussein Yus		" "

The following is a list of those who were shot to death:

Date	No.	Name	Village	District
August	1	Rageh Ali Hurin	God-Hely	Ainabo
1988	2	Qormadobe Hashi Dheh	"	"
	3	Abdi Dabasr	"	"
	4	Farah Noor Ali	Gumaye	Lasanod
	5	Saleh Dirir Ali	"	"
	6	Jama Abdi Dualeh	"	"
	7	Ismail Yusuf Buhsin	Bohol	Hudun
	8	Mohamed Deria Midgan	"	"
	9	Saeed Adib Abdi	"	"
	10	Saleh Farah Fayako	"	"
	11	Suleban Ibrahim H. Ogleh	"	"
	12	Mohamed Bare Ali	Sinaro	"
	13	Musa Adib Abdi	"	"
	14	Abdilahi Abdi Jibril	Kalsheikh	Elafweyn
	15	Saleh Dunkal Hersi	"	"
	16	Suleban Ounkal Hersi	"	"
	17	Mohamed Grase Hohamed	"	"
	18	Awed Ahmed Hassan	"	"
	19	Aden Jama Abdi	"	"

258

Date	No.	Name	Village	District
August 1988	20	Yusuf Ahmed Hassan	Kalsheikh	El Afweyn
	21	Hassan Deria Awaweh	"	"
	22	Mohamed Hassan Deria	"	"
	23	Elmi Abdi Deria	"	"
	24	Ali Farah Abdi	"	"
	25	Son of Ibrahim Deria	"	"
	26	Son of Mohamed Saleh Dunkal	"	"
	27	Son of Awil Ahmed	"	"
	28	Son of Hayir Digaleh	"	"
	29	Son of Hassan Sheikh Jama	"	"
	30	Ibrahim Hassan Yusuf	"	"
	31	Mohamed Shireh Mireh	"	"
	32	Saeed Mohamed Abduleh	"	"
	33	Shireh Ali Hurin	"	"
	34	Missa Abokor Hassan	"	"
	35	Khalif Dube	"	"
	36	Saeed Khalif Dube	"	"
	37	Mohamed Ibrahim Dube	"	"
	38	Hassan Ibrahim Dube	"	"
	39	Basheh Hassan Hussien	"	"
	40	Son of Ali Aw Bareh	"	"
	41	Saleh Mohamed Ahmed	"	"
	42	Son of Bulaleh Gabayo	"	"
	43	Son of Mireh Robleh	"	"
	44	Ali Abdi Ibrahim	"	"
July 1988	45	Son of Khaireh Mohamed	El Afweyn	El Afweyn
	46	Son of Osman Mohamed	"	"
	47	Barood Jama Ali	"	"
	48	Son of Gisreye Aden	"	"
	49	Son of Gurey Abdi Seed	"	"

259

Date	No.	Name	Village	District
July 1988	50	Son of Warsame Jama Arraleh	Kalsheikh	El Afwein
	51	Son of Yusuf Abdi Boobeh	"	"
September 1988	52	Guray Ali Farah	Berde Analeh	"
	53	Awil Nahar Abdi	Geed Hamary	"
	54	Osman Aden Sehiye	Fadhigab	"
	55	Noor Shalqaneh	Garag	"
	56	Fardaleh Saleh Mohamed	"	"
	57	Suleban Ahmed Disaleh	"	"
	58	Suleban Mohamed Osman		
	59	Ahmed Hassan Gooh		
	60	Ahmed Ashoor Ateyeh		
	61	Sheikh Ibrahim Dualeh		
	62	Son of Jama Abdijleh Qorsheel	El Afwein	El Afwein
	63	Son of Jama Abdijleh Qorsheel	"	"
	64	Ali Liban Omer	"	"
	65	Son of Mohamoud Saleh	"	"
	66	Sheikh Hussein Hassan (blinded)	"	"
	67	Son of Sh. Hussien Hassan	"	"
	68	Abdi Noor Ali	"	"
	69	Essa Ismail Ashoor	"	"
	70	Son of Ahmed Jama	"	"
	71	Son of Aden Omer	"	"
	72	Jama Aden Deri	"	"
	73	Ahmed Saleh Yaloyalo	"	"
October 1988	74	Abdi Yusuf Deria	Dararweyn	Hudun
	75	Ibrahim Jama Dirir	"	"
	76	Son of Shireh Ali Farah	"	"

Date	No.	Name	Village	District
October	77	Ahmed Aden Ardaleh	Dararweyn	Hudun
1988	78	Son of Haji Mohamoud Dubad	"	"
	79	Mohamed Dualeh Ali	"	"
	80	Arab Sheikh Dahir Dualeh	"	"
	81	Mohamed Heerad Elmi	"	"
	82	Omer Jama Drisrieh	"	"
	83	Abdilahi Noor Dhashane	"	"
	84	Mohamed Saleh Noor Dhashane	"	"
	85	Saeed Jama Omer Falag	"	"
	86	Omer Ismail Ganeh	"	"
	87	Sijleban Awed Ali	"	"
	88	Hussien Salad Dorgeh	"	"
	89	Deeq Abdi Aden	"	"
	90	Ibrahim Gole Inarsame	"	"
	91	Jirde Saleh Farah	"	"
	92	Mohamed Farah Noor Faranug	"	"
	93	Abdi Fure Dirir	"	"
	94	Hawo Abdi Lahi Farah	"	"
	95	Awed Ali Hisrin	God-Hely	Ainabo
	96	Mohamed Elmi Bidar	"	"
	97	Ali Dijaleh Mire	"	"
	98	Mohamed Gooh Sugule Qaash	"	"
	99	Aden Abi Kanee	"	"
July	100	Abdilahi Inarsame Sayn	Bohol	Hudun
1989	101	Dahir Ali Muse	"	"
	102	Idiris Aden Godor	"	"
	103	Son of Bare Heerad	"	"
	104	Son of Bare Heerad	"	"
August	105	Saleh Mohamoud	Kal-Sheikh	El Afwein
1988	106	Warsame Mohamed Duale	"	"

Date	No.	Name	Village	District
August	107	Muse Mohamed Gabayre	Kal-Sheikh	El Afwein
1988	108	Mohamed Dualeh Mire	"	"
	109	Saeed Jama Dualeh	"	"
October	110	Jama Madar Abdi	Danano	Ainabo
1988	111	Ismail Hersi Ahmed	"	"
	112	Aden Haji Muse	"	"
	113	Ahmed Haji Muse	"	"
	114	Hadiyo Barkad Digaley, 100 year old woman	"	"
	115	Dooli Abokor Geedi	"	"
July 16	116	Saleban Guled Awale	Balideg	Bohodleh
1989	117	Ahmed Sugal Hersi	Balialanleh	"
	118	Mohamoud Ahmed Hussen	Oodinleh	"
	119	Ibrahim Mohamed Dualeh	Talabur	"
	120	Abdi Jama Abdi	"	"
	121	Yusuf Amay Noor	"	"
	122	Hassan Abdi Mohamed	"	"
	123	Abdi Hakim Kondas	"	"
	124	Abdi Arab Jama	"	"
	125	Rabi Dualeh Afhakame	"	"
	126	Ahmed Jama Saleban	"	"
	127	Abdi Ibrahim Ismail	"	"
	128	Jama Omer Aden (Indagod)	"	"
	129	Ahmed Aden Dabay	"	"
	130	Jama Kaireh Kabade	"	"
	131	Jama Baqarde	"	"
	132	Son of Amir	"	"
	133	Son of Hassan Ahmed Dabarlow	"	"
	134	Aideed Abdilahi Heery	"	"
	135	Hussein Haibeh Mohamoud	"	"

Date	No.	Name	Village	District
August	136	Omer Ali Awed*	Bali Mirow	Leh Burao
1988	137	His son, 13 years old	"	"
	138	Hadur Ahmed Ways, with his two sons and a flock of goats		

---

*   30 camels taken.

Appendix Two

Members of the Hargeisa Group

The twenty defendants who received prison sentences are:

Life Imprisonment

Mohamed Barud Ali	Geologist/Chemist
Ahmed Mohamed Yusuf, "Jabane"	Teacher

Thirty Years

Mohamed H. Mohamoud Omar Hashi	Economist
Abdirahman Abdillahi Haji Adan	Civil Servant

Twenty-Five Years

Mohamed Ali Ibrahim	Head of Self-Help Scheme

Twenty Years

Adan Yusuf Aboker	Medical Doctor
Ahmed Hussein Abby	Banker
Hussein Mohamed Dualeh, "Berbarawi"	Teacher
Dr. Mohamed Sh. Hassan Tani	Medical Doctor
Abdillahi Ali Yusuf, "Olad"	Veterinarian
Osman Abdi Meygag	Medical Doctor
Adan Warsame Saeed	Economist
Yusuf Abdillahi Kahin	Farmer and Businessman
Bashe Abdi Yusuf	Businessman

Eight Years

Ahmed Muhumed Madar	Biologist
Mohamed Abdi Jiir	Teacher
Mohamed Ma'alin Osman	Teacher

Three Years

Ali Egeh Farah	Civil Engineer
Omer Issa Awaleh	Civil Servant
Mohamed Ali Sulub	Medical Doctor

Twenty-nine detainees were brought to trial altogether; the other nine defendants were released for lack of evidence.

Appendix Three

Some of the People Killed in Hargeisa on November 17, 1984

Twenty-six Isaaks, nine civilians and seventeen SNM fighters were captured in Boqol Jirreh, a section of Hargeisa neighboring a military command. Twenty-four of them were accused of association with the SNM and the ohter two, Abdillahi Abdi Good and Ismail Sh. Ibrahim, both businessmen, were accused of assisting them.

Among the twenty-six were:

Ibrahim Sh Ibrahim

Yusuf Abdi Saleebaan, student

Mahdi Haji Ishal

Abdi Warsame Saeed

Daud Dahir

Ahmed Kossaar Farah Jirreh

Najiib Sh Ibrahim

Mohamed Abdillahi

Ismail Ahmed Ibrahim

Mohamed Dimbil

Mohamed Abdi Farseed

Abdillahi Abdi Good

Ismail Sheikh Ibrahim

The other victims were mostly nomads.

Appendix Four

The Massacre in Burao on December 20, 1984

The identities of the 43 victims:

Isse Ibrahim Ismail
Saeed Mohamed Ismail, "Madoobe"
Omer Sheikh Yusuf
Abdi Jama Hassan, "Sanweyne"
Awil Saalah Giir
Abdillahi Salah Giir, brother of above
Ibrahim Mohamed Handulleh
Ahmed Yusuf Mirreh
Mohamed Yusuf Ismail, "Umaas"
Abdi Mohamed Ali, "Dhegjar"
Diiriye Osman Yusuf, "Labalugood"
Ismail Salah Diiriye
Mohamed Samatar Ahmed
Suleiman Hirad Adan
Ali Abdi Hussein
Mohamed Mohamoud Abdi
Ahmed Ismail Mohamed
Ali Omer Diiriye
Muse Hassan Ibrahim
Abdillahi Mohamed Farah, "Taakuliye"
Adan Ali Ibrahim, "Qurmiye"
Abdi Mohamed Yusuf
Abdillahi Hassan Nur
Abdi Hassan Jama
Jama Abdillahi Saeed
Abdi Ali Ahmed

Saeed Osman Ghelle
Adan Nur Ismail, "Odaaq"
Aboker Abdillahi Robleh
Yassin Ahmed Warasame, "Soonaan"
Ahmed Hassan Ismail, "Yumbud"
Ahmed Abdi Hassan, "Leila"
Nur Doolah

A number of the victims were residents of Sheikh, arrested there and transferred to Burao shortly before they were executed. They were:

Abdirahman Mohamed Siraad
Abdirahman Mohamed Ali
Yassin Abdi Bisad
Qasim Qodah
Major Mohamed Ali
"Qorane"

Appendix Five

List of the twenty-five people killed in Gebiley and Tug-Wajale in March 1988.

Sh. Issa Yusuf Good
Mohamed Abdi Hawsi, "Jawan"
Mohamed Abdi Koffil
Dagal Dinbil
Muhumed Sahal
Kalinle Ashur Rageh
Muhumed Gurey Mihile
Hussein Amir Farah
Mawlid Hussein Amir, son of above
Ali Hussein Amir, brother of above
Haybe Gurey Hassan
Siad Isaak Haji
Aden Ali Ibrahim
Abdillahi Jama Aqli
Haji Hassan Abrar
Barre Muhumed
Suleiman Diriye Hersi
Mohamed Ali Samatar
Saeed Hassan Deqsi
Ardaale Warsame Farah
Aw Ali Sahal Tani
Abdi Sahal Tani, brother of above
Abdi Mohamed Sahal, nephew of above
Shamah Elmi Fahiye
Daud Qawrah

RECENT PUBLICATIONS

AFRICA WATCH REPORTS

News from Africa Watch, A frequent newsletter designed to provide up-to-the-minute information on human rights in Africa
Angola
Violations of the Laws of War by Both Sides, April 1989, 148 pages
South Africa
No Neutral Ground — South Africa's Confrontation with the Activist Churches, August 1989, 145 pages
The Persecution of Human Rights Monitors in South Africa, June 1988, 38 pages
Zimbabwe
A Break With the Past? Human Rights and Political Unity, October 1989, 109 pages

HUMAN RIGHTS WATCH REPORTS

Human Rights Watch Newsletter, designed to provide information on human rights developments worldwide. Published quarterly.
Forced Out: The Agony of the Refugee in Our Time, April 1989, 191 pages, 189 black and white photographs
Critique of the Department of State's Country Reports on Human Rights Practices for 1988 (Human Rights Watch/Lawyers Committee for Human Rights), July 1989, 216 pages
The Persecution of Human Rights Monitors, December 1989, 344 pages
The Bush Administration's Record on Human Rights for 1988, January 1989, 381 pages
Annual Report of 1988, April 1989, 101 pages, Free